Also by Dave Barry and Ridley Pearson

Peter and the Starcatchers
Peter and the Shadow Thieves
Peter and the Secret of Rundoon
Peter and the Sword of Mercy
Escape from the Carnivale
Cave of the Dark Wind
Blood Tide

Also by Ridley Pearson

The Kingdom Keepers—Disney After Dark
Kingdom Keepers II—Disney at Dawn
Kingdom Keepers III—Disney in Shadow
Steel Trapp—The Challenge
Steel Trapp—The Academy

SCIENCE Fair

Dave BARRY   Ridley PEARSON

Disney · HYPERION BOOKS
New York

Copyright © 2008 Dave Barry and Page One, Inc.
All rights reserved. Published by Disney · Hyperion, an imprint of Disney Book Group. No part of this book may be reproduced or transmitted in any form or by any means, electronic or mechanical, including photocopying, recording, or by any information storage and retrieval system, without written permission from the publisher. For information address Disney · Hyperion, 114 Fifth Avenue, New York, New York 10011-5690.
Printed in the United States of America
First Disney · Hyperion paperback edition, 2011
10 9 8 7 6 5 4 3 2 1
J689-1817-1-10073
Library of Congress Cataloging-in-Publication Data on file.
ISBN 978-1-4231-3140-3

We dedicate this book to the students.
Also, the teachers.
Also, while we're at it, the frog.

CHAPTER ONE

FIVE LARGE, HAIRY MEN were gathered for a top secret meeting in a bunker under the presidential palace in the city of Krpsht. Krpsht (pronounced "Krpsht") was the capital of the Republic of Krpshtskan, a poor, mountainous nation with few vowels and a population of four million, including goats.

The five were very powerful men, at least for Krpshtskan. The oldest and largest and hairiest man, known as Grdankl the Strong, was the president, a position he had won in a national election contest against nobody. His campaign slogan had been "Vote for Grdankl, or Die." The other four men were Krpshtskan's first, second, third, and fourth vice presidents, who also happened to be the president's brothers. Their

job was to agree with the president at all times.

These five men were looking over the shoulder of a very thin and very nervous young man seated at a computer. The young man's name was Vrsk, and he held the lofty title of Krpshtskan minister of technology. Vrsk had been appointed to this post because he was the only person in Krpshtskan who could work the official government computer, which was the only working computer in Krpshtskan.

At the moment the screen was dark.

"Why is it taking so long?" barked Grdankl the Strong, speaking in the Krpsht language, which has been compared to the sound of a duck burping. The first, second, third, and fourth vice presidents nodded vigorously and frowned to indicate that they, too, thought it was taking too long.

"It's booting up," said Vrsk. "It takes a while. It's Windows 98. I tried to upgrade to Vista, but the processor—"

"No more talking!" said Grdankl the Strong, who did not like to hear people say things that he did not understand. "Turn it on!"

Vrsk turned back to the computer screen, relieved to see that it was now flickering to life. His relief turned to horror when he saw that he had failed to disable his usual screen saver, which was a picture of Halle Berry in her Catwoman suit.

Grdankl the Strong looked at the screen, grunted, and said, in English, "Catwoman."

The four vice presidents nodded in agreement and said, "Catwoman."

Vrsk, relieved that nobody was going to hit him, at least for now, clicked the computer mouse and opened a Web browser. He was pleased to see that the Internet connection—it was the only one in Krpshtskan—was working. Manipulating the mouse, he opened a map site. An image of Earth, seen from space, came into view. Vrsk centered the window over eastern North America, then began to zoom in, closer and closer, until the sprawling metropolis of Washington, D.C., filled the screen. He zoomed in closer until individual buildings could be easily recognized. One by one, he showed the president close-up aerial views of the Capitol, the White House, and the Pentagon.

The president nodded. The four vice presidents nodded also.

Vrsk then zoomed out a bit and began to pan north on the screen window. He stopped over a Maryland suburb just outside the Washington city limit, then zoomed in until the screen was filled with a large building complex surrounded by parking lots and athletic fields.

"There," he said.

Grdankl the Strong frowned at the screen.

"You are sure?" he said. "This is the place?"

Vrsk checked a sheet of paper next to the computer. "I am sure," he said.

Grdankl the Strong nodded and turned to his vice presidents. "It is very close to the American government," he said, "just as Prmkt told us."

3

The vice presidents nodded in agreement. Grdankl the Strong turned back to Vrsk, and, pointing at the buildings on the screen, said, "Prmkt is there?"

"Yes," said Vrsk. "He works there, under a different name. He sends me e-mails from there."

Grdankl the Strong looked at the buildings, nodded, and turned back to his vice presidents. "He is very smart, Prmkt. Very smart."

The vice presidents agreed.

"If Prmkt is right," continued Grdankl the Strong, "if his plan works, then in one instant—*one instant*—the whole American government will stop, and America will be like a chicken with its head cut off, running around like . . . like . . ." He snapped his fingers, trying to think what it would be like.

"Like a chicken with no head?" suggested the first vice president.

"Exactly," said Grdankl the Strong. "Like a chicken with no head. And then the Americans will be sorry that they ever dared to insult the Republic of Krpshtskan. Very sorry." Grdankl the Strong started to laugh, thinking about America's impending doom. The four vice presidents also laughed. Vrsk also started to laugh, but he was stopped by a look from the fourth vice president, letting Vrsk know that this was strictly a high-level laugh.

Then Grdankl the Strong grew quiet, and immediately all laughter in the bunker ceased. Grdankl the Strong gestured toward the buildings on the computer screen.

"And the beauty of it is," he said, "if Prmkt's plan

works—and I am certain Prmkt's plan *will* work—the Americans will do it to themselves. The American *children* will do it. They will bring down their own country! It is genius!"

The four vice presidents nodded, agreeing on the genius of the plan.

Grdankl the Strong tapped the screen with a fat finger and asked Vrsk, "What is this place again?"

"It is a school," said Vrsk. "A public school. Its name is . . ." he consulted the piece of paper, then, in heavily accented English, said, ". . . Hubble Middle School."

Grdankl the Strong looked at the screen and smiled.

"The mightiest nation on earth," he said, "brought to its knees by children."

CHAPTER TWO

Toby Harbinger, backpack slung over his left shoulder, hurried through the halls of Hubble Middle School. His goal was to get to Gifted Science before the ME kids got there.

ME was short for Manor Estates, a development of giant houses that cost millions of dollars and had more bathrooms than people. Toby knew that, based on the law of averages, there should be at least one Manor Estates kid who was not a total jerk, but so far he had not met that kid.

The ME kids stuck together. Their families vacationed together at ski resorts and in Europe, Hawaii, and any other place where it cost a lot of money to be. On weekends, the ME kids went together to the mall, where

6

they used their personal credit cards to buy stuff they didn't need, like cell phones with even more unnecessary features than the cell phones they had bought three months earlier. They wore expensive clothes that were designed to look used. They made fun of kids who wore clothes that really *were* used.

Such as Toby. For years the ME kids had made fun of his freckled face, his apparent lack of biceps, and his high voice, which had recently begun to break, so that at times he croaked like a frog. But they'd moved on: now it was his clothes.

Toby reached the door to the Gifted Science classroom, took a breath, and went in.

Oh, no.

The ME kids were already there. They sat together, of course, right by the door, so Toby had to walk past them to get to his seat. Today they focused on his shoes, which, for a change, were new. They were a name brand, but not the *right* name brand. This was the kind of fashion error that ME kids, who had brand radar, always spotted immediately.

"Nice sneakers, Hardbonger," said Jason Niles, who had been calling Toby "Hardbonger" since third grade, and still, after five years, could not get over how hilarious this was. Toby ignored him, partly to send the message that he didn't care, and partly because Jason Niles was the size of a UPS truck.

"Oooh, Toby," said Haley Hess, making her voice sound like she thought Toby was cute, which of course she didn't, because she was Haley Hess. "I *love* them! They're so . . .

white! Did your mom get them at Discount Warehouse?"

Toby ignored her also, but his ears turned red, because, first, that's what always happened when Haley Hess spoke to him, and, second, his mom had, in fact, bought the shoes at Discount Warehouse. The ME kids would go to school dressed only in mud before they would wear clothing purchased from Discount Warehouse.

The ME kids insulted Toby's sneakers a few more times as he passed, then turned their attention to new victims. Toby slid into his seat at the back, between Micah Porter, who was his best friend, and Tamara Reilley, who was his best friend for a girl, although Toby tried not to stand next to her too much because she was four inches taller.

"Morons," said Micah, whose nose never stopped running, which is why he was known, unfortunately for him, as Mucus.

"Yeah," said Toby.

"I don't see why everybody says Haley Hess is so hot," said Tamara. "Do you think she's hot, Toby?"

"No," said Toby, lying.

"Of *course* he thinks she's hot," said Micah. "She's a moron, but she *is* hot. She's a hot moron."

"I think she looks like Kim Possible," said Tamara, whose name had never been used in the same sentence with hot.

"Exactly," said Micah. He noticed that Toby and Tamara were both staring at him. "What? You don't think Kim Possible's hot?"

"Please shut up," said Toby, who said this often to Micah.

The bell rang, and in walked the Gifted Science teacher, Mr. Neckstrom, a small, nervous-looking man with hair that grew unnaturally far down his forehead, threatening to merge with his eyebrows. He wore khaki pants and a brown shirt with large, permanent-looking wet spots under each arm.

"All right, settle down," he said. "Haley, stop texting and put away that phone."

"Sure," said Haley, continuing to text.

Mr. Neckstrom turned away so he didn't have to see her ignoring his order. "All right," he said to the class. "It's March first. Do you know what that means?"

"It's time for your monthly shower?" said one of the ME kids, just loud enough so everybody could hear, but just soft enough that Mr. Neckstrom could pretend he didn't hear, which was what he usually did when an ME kid said something. He had learned, as most teachers had, that it was better not to mess with ME kids, because if you did, you had to answer to their parents. And nobody wanted to do that.

The ME parents had money and power. They could have sent their children to private school; if they lived anywhere else, they would have. But it happened that Hubble Middle School was the best middle school in Maryland, and it fed its students into Spiro T. Agnew High School, which sent more of its graduates to Ivy League colleges than any other school in the United States. It was the best, and the parents of Manor Estates demanded the best.

So their children attended Hubble, and every one of

them got into the Gifted Program. This was not because they were all gifted; Jason Niles, for example, had the IQ of a zucchini. No, the ME kids all got into Gifted because it was the best program, so the ME parents made sure their children were in it. They did this in various ways— sometimes by making generous donations to the school; sometimes by threatening lawsuits, or worse. Some of the ME parents held powerful positions in the federal government, and they knew how to threaten. The teachers at Hubble did not want to mess with them or their children, and so Mr. Neckstrom pretended not to hear the remark about his monthly shower.

"March first," he reminded, "is the first day to register for the science fair. And thanks to the generosity of Mr. Swingle, first prize this year will be . . ." He paused, noting with pleasure that all of the students were paying attention. Haley Hess had actually stopped texting.

". . . five thousand dollars," said Mr. Neckstrom.

The classroom erupted with a chorus of *whoa*s. Even the ME kids were impressed by the prize amount, which was double the previous year's $2,500. The prize money came from a billionaire Hubble alumnus, Lance Swingle, who had started a hugely successful company, TranScent, based on a system he invented for sending smells over the Internet. Swingle credited his success in part to the scientific education he got at Hubble Middle. In gratitude, he donated a generous cash prize each year to be given to the winner of the science fair.

His goal, he said, was to create an interest in science.

What he had actually created was a near-maniacal interest in winning first prize. The Hubble science fair was *very* competitive. You did not win by hooking a flashlight bulb up to a battery to show how an electrical circuit works. No, to win the Hubble Middle School science fair, you had to do something really impressive. For example, the winner two years ago had built a robot that could do professional-quality French manicures. The winner last year had created, through genetic manipulation, a mutant gerbil with an extra pair of eyeballs located on its butt, so it could go through a maze either frontward or backward.

Both of these winners had been students from Manor Estates. In fact, every year since Lance Swingle had started offering cash prizes, the Hubble science fair had been won by an ME kid. They didn't need the prize money; sometimes they didn't even seem all that knowledgeable about their own projects. But they always won.

It was widely believed among the rest of the Hubble students that the kids from Manor Estates cheated. The teachers had their suspicions as well. In fact, six years ago, a veteran science teacher named Mrs. Feeney had gone so far as to reject a project brought in by an ME student, Taylor Niles, who happened to be the older brother of Jason Niles. Taylor claimed that he had made, all by himself, a powerful handheld laser. Mrs. Feeney doubted this, because—among other things—Taylor didn't know how to spell "laser."

Taylor's father, as it happened, was a very important man in Washington. Within a week, Mrs. Feeney had been

11

transferred to another school. On her last day at Hubble, she went out to the parking lot to discover that somebody had burned twenty-seven small circular holes through the steel body of her car. She was replaced at Hubble by Mr. Neckstrom, who never questioned anybody's science-fair project.

"Five thousand dollars," said Micah, as Mr. Neckstrom walked around the classroom, passing out the science-fair entry forms. "If I had that kind of money, I could—"

"You could wake up," said Tamara, "because you'd be dreaming. *You're* not gonna win. One of *them* is gonna win." She nodded toward the ME kids.

"She's right," said Toby. "We don't have a chance." As he spoke, Jason Niles turned around and looked at him.

"Hey, Hardbonger," he called. "When I win the five grand, maybe I'll buy you some decent shoes."

"If you win," answered Toby, "maybe I'll explain your project to you."

A bunch of kids laughed, including even some ME kids. Jason reddened, giving Toby a look that said: *You'll be sorry you said that.*

Toby knew he should have kept his mouth shut. But he was angry. Five thousand dollars meant nothing to Jason Niles's family, but it would mean the world to Toby's.

Especially now.

"I got an idea," said Micah.

"Uh-oh," said Tamara.

"No, really," said Micah. "I'm gonna win it this year."

"How?" said Toby.

Micah lowered his voice. "I'm gonna levitate a frog," he said.

Tamara shook her head sadly. "So young," she said, "and already on drugs."

"No, really," said Micah. "I read about it in Wikipedia. These Dutch scientists made a frog float in the air. It's called dia . . . diamagnetism. You just need a frog and a magnet."

"He's insane, right?" Tamara asked.

"Actually, no," said Toby. "Some guys did levitate a frog. But you need, like, a superpowerful magnet."

"So, Micah," said Tamara, "do *you* have a superpowerful magnet?"

"No," said Micah.

"I see," said Tamara.

"But I have a frog," said Micah. "His name is Fester."

Tamara turned to Toby and said, "He has a frog."

"Well, then," said Toby. "He's halfway there."

CHAPTER THREE

IT WAS LUNCHTIME in the Hubble Middle School cafeteria, and Toby, Tamara, and Micah were sitting at the same table they always sat at, with the same kids they always sat with. At tables all around them several hundred other students were doing the same thing.

Tamara examined the cafeteria's featured lunch entrée, which consisted of yellowish brown lumps.

"The menu says they're nuggets," she said. "But it doesn't say what *kind* of nuggets."

"Chicken," said Micah. He bit into one. "I think."

"Then why doesn't the menu *say* chicken?" said Tamara. "For all we know it's squirrel nuggets."

"If it's squirrel," said Micah, chewing, "it's not bad."

"Maybe," said David Wemplemeyer, whose nickname was Brad Pitt Wemplemeyer because he looked absolutely nothing whatsoever like Brad Pitt, "they don't say what kind of nugget because there's no meat at all. Maybe it's just a blob of fried grease, a pure nugget, uncontaminated by food of any kind."

"Or maybe," said Jennifer "Pencil" Wenzel—known as Pencil Wenzel, because she was very skinny, a redhead, and always wore yellow—"food scientists have created a new genetic mutant species of animal that's actually called a 'nugget.' It's this little hairless blob of meat that has no head or feet or anything, so it's real easy to prepare. You just hit it with a hammer and pop it into the fryer."

Everyone laughed except Tamara.

"I hear," said Brad Pitt Wemplemeyer, "that they're working on an improved nugget species that you don't even have to hit with a hammer. You just whistle, and it rolls into the fryer on its own."

"That's disgusting," said Tamara.

"Well, you're the one who's eating it," said Brad Pitt Wemplemeyer.

"Speaking of disgusting," said Micah, "what's your lunch today, Toby?"

Toby was peering into a paper bag. His mom always packed his lunch. His parents believed cafeteria food was unhealthy. In fact, as a general rule they believed that any food humans enjoyed was unhealthy. On Halloween, they gave out carrot sticks. The day after Halloween, there were

discarded carrot sticks all over their lawn and usually toilet paper on their house.

Toby reached into the bag and pulled out something wrapped in a paper towel. He unwrapped it and, sighing, set it in front of him.

Micah leaned over to have a look.

"Toby," he said, "did your mom send the wrong bag? Because that looks like a stool sample for the vet."

"It's a tofu enchilada," said Toby. Toby's mom believed that tofu had a near-miraculous ability to masquerade as any other kind of food—that if a lump of tofu was *shaped* like something, it would also *taste* like that thing. Thanksgiving in Toby's house was a nightmare.

He was about to attempt to eat his tofu enchilada when he felt something cold and slimy land on his neck, followed by laughter from the Manor Estates kids' table.

He did not turn around.

"What is it?" he said.

The others examined his neck.

"Yogurt," said Pencil Wenzel. "Peach, I think."

Toby tore off a piece of the paper towel that held his tofu enchilada and wiped his neck.

"Who threw it?" he said.

Brad Pitt Wemplemeyer looked over at the ME table and said, "Judging from how hard he's laughing, it's The Ferret again." The Ferret was Farrel Plinkett, who lately had begun amusing himself by flinging food at Toby's table. The Ferret was also one of the few ME kids not physically capable of beating Toby up.

"Okay then," said Toby. He picked up his tofu enchilada and walked to the line of garbage and recycling cans at the end of the cafeteria. Then, staying by the wall, he walked all the way around to the other side of the cafeteria, so he could approach the ME kids' table from the opposite direction. The ME kids didn't see him coming; they were deep in conversation, hunched forward over the table, heads close together. The Ferret had his back to Toby. As Toby approached, Jason Niles was talking, sounding angry. Toby stopped as he heard:

"Fifty *dollars*?" Jason was saying.

"That's what was in the note," said Haley Hess. "Cash, put the envelope in the regular place, get your plans tomorrow."

"But *fifty*," said Jason. "Last year it was twenty-five."

"Like you don't have fifty dollars," said Harmonee Prescott, who was considered to be almost as hot overall as Haley Hess, and hotter in some specific areas. "You just get the money from your dad anyway."

"I know," said Jason, "but . . ."

"Hey!" said Haley, noticing Toby. "What's *he* doing here?"

As the ME kids turned, Toby stepped forward and grabbed the back of The Ferret's pants. The Ferret liked his pants loose and baggy, so there was plenty of room for Toby to pull the waistband out, deposit his tofu enchilada, and let go.

"Hey!" shouted The Ferret, scrambling to his feet, hands groping his buttular area. "Hey!"

The rest of the ME kids were also on their feet, with the boys, especially the massive Jason, moving toward Toby. The commotion quickly spread as kids all over the cafeteria stood

to get a better view of what they hoped would be a fight.

Toby was very much hoping there would not be a fight, at least not between him and Jason, who was advancing on him like a tank, only larger. Toby had been thinking more along the lines of a confrontation with The Ferret, but The Ferret was fully occupied with the problem of getting the enchilada out of his pants, not an easy thing. Jason had just about gotten into striking range when a voice shouted:

"What is going on here?"

The voice belonged to Mr. Pzyrbovich, an algebra teacher who was always called Mr. P, for obvious reasons. He had a heavy accent, which a lot of kids said made him hard to understand, although to be fair some of these kids would never have understood algebra anyway. Mr. P was always in a bad mood, but it was especially bad when he had cafeteria duty.

"What is going on?" he repeated.

Pencil Wenzel stepped forward, a look of deep fake concern on her face.

"Mr. P," she said, "we're all worried about The Ferret here, because he seems to have pooped his trousers."

Everyone looked at The Ferret. A brownish glop was oozing from his right pants leg onto the floor.

"That's not poop," The Ferret said.

"It certainly *looks* like poop," said Brad Pitt Wemplemeyer.

"It's *not*," said The Ferret. He pointed at Toby. "He put it in there!"

"So what you're saying," said Pencil Wenzel reasonably, "is that *Toby* put the poop in your pants?"

"IT'S NOT POOP!" said The Ferret.

"Stop it! Stop all of this!" said Mr. P. He pointed at Toby. "Did you put that in his pants?"

"Yes," said Toby, "but he . . ."

"Quiet!" said Mr. P. "You will have three detentions, starting today."

"But . . ."

"Quiet!" Mr. P turned to The Ferret and said, "Go clean yourself up." The Ferret turned to go. He brushed past Toby, and as he did, he said, "You're dead, Hardbonger."

"Ooh!" said Toby, wiggling his hands to show fear. "Like on *The Sopranos*!"

"I told you, quiet!" said Mr. P. "Now everybody sit down!" He looked down at the remains of Toby's tofu enchilada, then yelled across the room: "Get over here and clean this floor!"

A tall, thin man with long hair, a scraggly beard, and a vacant stare, dressed in a janitor's uniform and flip-flops, shuffled across the cafeteria with a mop. This was J.D., which stood for Janitor Dude. J.D. was often held up to the students at Hubble Middle as an example of exactly why you should not mess with drugs. As he got to work, the students sat down, although the ME kids took the time to glare meaningfully at Toby. Finally, the cafeteria returned to its usual random clatter and conversation.

"Well," said Toby. "*That* went well."

"So you're not worried that The Ferret's gonna kill you?" said Brad Pitt Wemplemeyer.

"I'm more worried about Jason the Giant," said Toby.

"Speaking of which," he leaned in closer to the others, lowering his voice, "I heard him say something weird."

"What?" said Tamara.

"Something about fifty dollars," said Toby. "He and Haley were talking about it, and she said you had to put fifty dollars cash in an envelope, and put it some place, and then you'd get the plans."

"Plans for what?" said Micah.

Tamara was staring at Toby. "The science fair," she said.

"That's what I think," said Toby. "They buy their project plans from somebody."

"Who?" said Micah.

"They didn't say," said Toby. "Haley just said you put the money in the regular place, and you get the plans tomorrow."

"Do you think the regular place is here?" said Tamara. "At the school?"

"I don't know," said Toby. "But I gotta stay for detention anyway. I'll see if I notice anything."

"I would SO love to catch them cheating," said Pencil Wenzel, glancing over at the ME table.

Everybody nodded. They went back to their lunches, except for Toby, who had put his down The Ferret's pants.

"Nugget?" said Micah, offering a lump to Toby.

"Thanks," said Toby. He took a bite and chewed thoughtfully.

"I think maybe it *is* squirrel," he said.

Chapter Four

THE AFTERNOON WAS FADING, and the daytime clamor of Hubble Middle School had morphed into the quiet of evening. The main hallway was empty except for J.D., the Janitor Dude, who was swishing a filthy mop back and forth across the floor, thus making it wet but not actually cleaner.

Toby was in the detention room along with fourteen other detainees serving time for various crimes, ranging from talking in class to keeping an unauthorized snake in a school locker. These detainees were, in theory, being supervised by Coach Furman, known to generations of Hubble students as Herman Furman, because (a) it rhymed, and (b) he looked a little like the patriarch of the

Munster family. Coach Furman's supervision consisted entirely of yelling "Keep it down!" if he heard anybody say anything. He never actually looked at the students; his attention was fully focused on his laptop computer, on which he was playing Internet poker for real money. Depending on what cards he held, Coach Furman might not have noticed if the detention students were engaging in ritual human sacrifice.

This meant that Toby, sitting by the door, was free to observe the goings-on in the hallway outside the detention room. What was mainly going on was J.D. mopping the hallway.

"You want a piece?"

Toby turned and saw he was being offered a stick of gum by Malcolm Kornblatt, who held the Hubble School record for most detentions by a single student. He was always in for something, most recently an unsuccessful attempt to win a bet that he could flush an entire accordion down a boys' room toilet. He would be in detention for the next few decades. Chewing gum was a school offense and punishable by detention, so it only made sense to Malcolm to chew gum while *in* detention.

"No, thanks," Toby said. "If I put that in my mouth, they'd carry me out on a stretcher. I'm allergic."

"For real?" said Malcolm.

"I turn blue and can't breathe," said Toby. "It goes away pretty fast, but it's scary."

"Hey, you could get out of detention!" said Malcolm, holding out the gum stick again.

"Keep it down!" shouted Coach Furman, not looking up from the computer screen.

Toby waved the gum away and went back to watching the hallway. Every few minutes somebody walked past, and Toby had noted with interest that these evening passersby included quite a few ME kids, a group not known for hanging around after school. Sometimes they were alone, sometimes in pairs; Toby saw at least four carrying envelopes. They all passed left to right, then a few minutes later went in the other direction—without envelopes.

Toby thought about what was down that hall: some classrooms, a storage area . . .

. . . and the faculty lounge.

Toby frowned, trying to remember which teachers he'd seen since detention started. There'd been Miss Cooney, the French teacher who looked like she could be a student; Mr. Shroder, the science teacher; Mr. P, the algebra teacher; and Mrs. Cortinas, the Spanish teacher. But a lot of teachers were around after school, Toby knew; it might not mean anything.

The detention students were all watching the clock now; fifteen pairs of eyeballs were focused on the minute hand, wishing it ahead to 4:27 . . . 4:28 . . . 4:29 . . . and *finally* 4:30.

"Umm," said one of the braver detainees, "Coach Furman?"

"Keep it down!" yelled Coach Furman, not looking up from the poker hand on his screen. All he needed was a diamond, any diamond.

"But Coach . . ."

"I said KEEP IT DOWN!" He clicked his mouse, watched the card turn. A *spade*. He banged his fist on the desk so hard that all fifteen students jumped. He looked at the detainees. Several pointed at the clock.

"All right," said Coach Furman. "Get out of here."

Quickly, they did. The others headed left, straight for the exit, but Toby paused, then turned right toward the faculty lounge. He'd just reached the door when it opened and Mr. P stepped out. They stared at each other for a moment, then Mr. P said, "What are you doing here?"

"I'm . . . I mean, I was just . . . I'm . . . I had detention," said Toby.

"I know that," said Mr. P. "I gave it to you, remember?"

"Oh . . . yeah," said Toby.

"You want me to give you another one?" said Mr. P.

"No," said Toby.

"Then go," said Mr. P.

So Toby went. The last thing he heard as he exited the building was an angry roar echoing down the hall from the detention room, where Herman Furman had once again missed winning by one lousy card.

CHAPTER FIVE

NIGHT HAD FALLEN. Prmkt stood in the deserted main hallway of Hubble Middle School and listened for fifteen seconds; he heard nothing. He went to the bank of lockers next to the faculty lounge and, standing on tiptoe, reached up above the third locker from the end. His hand touched an envelope. He pulled it down, then another, then still more, until he had them all.

He unlocked the door to the faculty lounge, went inside, then closed and locked the door. He went to the big battered round table in the center of the room, where generations of Hubble teachers had drunk coffee and complained about generations of Hubble students. He set the envelopes on the table and, using a flashlight,

examined them. Written on the outside of each was a name and a number. He opened the envelopes carefully, counting the cash inside each one.

When he was done, he stuffed the money into his right-hand pants pocket. From his left-hand pocket he drew a sheaf of papers, each covered with writing and diagrams. He folded these carefully and placed one in each envelope, resealing the envelopes with tape. When he was finished, he arranged the envelopes in numerical order, reopened the door, stepped into the hall, and locked the door behind him. He looked around and listened; he saw nothing, heard nobody.

He looked down at the top envelope; the number next to the name was 107. He went to locker 107 and pushed the envelope through one of the vent slots in the door. He continued down the hall, slipping the envelopes into their corresponding lockers. In less than ten minutes he was done. He would e-mail his report to Vrsk tonight. The plan was working perfectly.

CHAPTER SIX

TOBY'S FAMILY LIVED in Woodland Meadows, an older development lacking both woods and meadows. Their house was a small brick ranch on Milkwort Court. It was dark when Toby got there, and his stomach was growling for food. But he didn't walk straight to his front door. Instead he stopped, keeping to the darkness away from the streetlights, and checked out the neighborhood, especially his yard. He was looking for two guys, one big, one bigger.

Darth and the Wookiee.

Those weren't their real names. But that's how Toby thought of them. They'd appeared the previous day outside Hubble Middle, right before school started, asking kids if they knew a Toby Harbinger. Nobody told them anything,

because they were weird. But word quickly got to Toby that there were two guys outside looking for him. Toby had spied on them from a classroom window: Darth, a tall bald guy, wore a black raincoat even though it was sunny out; the Wookiee, even taller and much wider, had hair shooting out everywhere and a thick beard that looked as if fairly large birds lived in it.

Toby knew right away who they were and why they were looking for him. What he didn't know was what to do about it. Ordinarily, he would have told his parents. But if he did that, he'd have to confess what he'd done.

He'd done it because he needed money. No, that wasn't right; he didn't *need* the money, the way poor people need money for food. He *wanted* the money so he could buy a decent gaming computer. His parents couldn't afford to buy him one, and even if they could, they never would. They'd given him their old Mac, and as far as they were concerned that was all the computer anybody needed, and when *they* were kids, they didn't even *have* computers, blah-blah-blah.

Toby didn't even try to explain that you couldn't be a competitive gamer with an old computer running the wrong operating system at the speed of a dead slug. His parents were clueless about electronic things. They still could not, on their own, get photographs out of their digital camera. When they wanted to show their pictures, people had to gather around and squint at the teeny camera screen, trying to figure out whether they were looking at a wedding, or the Chrysler Building, or what.

So Toby didn't waste time discussing his computer needs with his parents. Instead, he went down to the basement, which was mostly filled with all this supposedly valuable and sacred Star Wars junk collected by his parents. His parents were, to Toby's ongoing horror, major Star Wars geeks. They had actually met at the premiere of *The Empire Strikes Back*, which was the second Star Wars movie, although it was Episode V, which was one of many reasons why Toby thought Star Wars was stupid.

His mom had gone to the movie premiere dressed as Princess Leia, and his dad—Toby was glad he had not been alive then because he would have had to kill himself—had been dressed as C-3PO. Toby found this appalling. His feeling was, if you *have* to go out dressed as a Star Wars character, why wouldn't you at least be a human? And if you *have* to be a robot, why would you be the *dork* robot?

Fortunately, his parents were older now, and the Force was not as strong in them. But they still sometimes watched the movies, and they hadn't thrown out any of their sacred junk. There was so *much* of it, they couldn't possibly know everything they had. At least that's what Toby told himself when he went down there and took the autographed BlasTech DL-44 blaster pistol used in the Star Wars movies by Han Solo.

His father bought the pistol in 1978 and took it to the premiere, where he somehow managed to get it signed by Harrison Ford himself.

Or so he had always claimed.

Toby put the pistol up for auction on eBay, where, to his

utter amazement, it sold, after frenzied bidding, for $2,038. Toby set up a PayPal account to get the money; to make sure his parents didn't know, he used the Hubble Middle School address. When the money showed up in his account, he mailed the blaster pistol to the winning bidder, whose name—Toby later realized this should have made him nervous—was D. Arthur Vaderian. Using the money, Toby had bought, online, a totally screaming note-book gaming computer, the Tarantula Disemboweler 666X, which his parents, being clueless, did not realize was not his old Mac. For a short while, Toby was happier than he'd ever been, using his new computer to kill huge numbers of online enemies.

Then he got the e-mail from D. Arthur Vaderian.

Mr. Harbinger, it said. *The alleged signature of Harrison Ford on the BlasTech DL-44 you sent me is a fake. I demand that you send my $2,038 back immediately.*

Which was a problem, seeing as how Toby had already spent the money. Toby couldn't think of what to do, so he didn't do anything. He hoped D. Arthur Vaderian would go away. But D. Arthur Vaderian did not. He kept sending e-mails, each one angrier than the last. Toby didn't answer them. The last e-mail he had gotten said:

Since you have chosen not to respond to my e-mails, I am going to take direct action.

He didn't say *what* direct action. But when the two weird guys showed up at Hubble Middle asking about him, Toby knew right away who they were. He also knew it was only a matter of time before they found out where he lived.

They had his name, and there weren't that many Harbingers.

And so he paused at the dark end of Milkwort Court, checking the neighborhood for Darth and the Wookiee. Seeing nobody, he walked quickly to his front door and let himself in.

"Hi, honey," said his mother, Fawn Harbinger, who was sitting on the sofa. She actually did somewhat resemble Princess Leia, if Princess Leia had let her hair go gray and gained a little weight from pretty much never doing anything except Sudoku. "You're late."

"Yeah," said Toby. "I was busy working on my science fair project."

"I saved you some dinner," said his mom. "Tofu pork chops."

"Yum," said Toby.

"After you eat," she said, "your father needs some help packing shipments."

"Okay," said Toby. His parents operated a home-based business selling health products. His mom sat in the living room, taking orders and playing Sudoku; his dad worked in a corner of the basement, packing and shipping the orders. Their big seller was a product called HydroxyPulse 3000, which, according to the label, cured basically every human ailment. As far as Toby could tell, it was water.

He started toward the kitchen.

"Also, Mrs. Breetle called, from the school office."

Toby stopped.

"About what?"

"She said some man came by the school, wanting your home address. Something about winning some kind of Internet contest. She didn't give out your address, of course, but she got his name and number. He'd like you to get in touch with him. His name is . . . wait, I wrote it down . . . here it is: D. Arthur Vaderian."

Toby's stomach clenched. He started toward the kitchen again, though he was no longer hungry.

"Hey!" said his mom. "I just noticed something!"

"What?" said Toby.

"Well, D. Arthur Vaderian! If you take out some letters, it spells Darth Vader! Isn't that funny?"

"Yeah," said Toby. "Hilarious."

CHAPTER SEVEN

THE ME KIDS GATHERED every morning at a certain reserved spot in the hall near the front entrance to Hubble Middle School. It was a prime location because everybody had to walk past it, which meant (a) everybody saw the ME kids, and (b) the ME kids could observe all the other students and make note of their numerous flaws.

This morning, however, the ME students were formed into a close little clot, examining the contents of the envelopes they'd found in their lockers.

"Wow," said Harmonee Prescott, frowning at a piece of paper. "Mine has a lot of seriously big words."

"Mine, too," said Jason Niles. "Like, what's an alg . . . algri . . . What's this word?"

The Ferret glanced at Jason's paper. "Alligator," he said.

"Whoa," said Jason. "I need an alligator."

"Let me see that," said Haley Hess, snatching the paper from Jason. "You morons," she said. "It says algorithm."

"What's an algorithm?" said Jason.

"I have no idea," said Haley, handing the paper back. "But it's not an alligator."

"These are, like, *way* more complicated than last year," said Harmonee.

"Yeah," said Haley. "But it doesn't matter to us, does it?"

The others smiled.

"Whoa," said Jason. "Look at that."

They turned to watch a girl come through the front door carrying a tray, on which sat what looked like a big silver ball, nearly two feet across. As the girl drew near they realized that the ball was actually thousands of paper clips. From the look of it there was nothing holding the paper clips together—no glue, no tape. The girl clearly enjoyed the looks of astonishment from the other students.

"What is *that*?" said The Ferret.

"That," said Jason, "is the competition."

"It's a magnet ball," said Haley. "I read about one on the Internet. You charge all the paper clips until they're magnetized. Then they stick together and you make them into all sorts of stuff. It looks impressive, but it's pretty lame. No way that wins."

"She's already *done* with hers?" Harmonee said. "It was only announced yesterday!"

"I'm not worried," said Haley, tapping her piece of paper.

"So when do we go see our friend at the mall?" said The Ferret.

"Today," said Haley. "I can't wait to start learning all about"—she looked at her piece of paper—"co-resonant phase-shifted induction sequencers."

"Me, neither," said Jason. "And alligatorithms."

"Algorithms," said Haley.

"Whatever," said Jason.

"Uh-oh," said The Ferret, looking down the hall. "It's The Armpit."

Striding toward the ME kids was Assistant Principal Paul Parmit, Hubble's disciplinarian. The Armpit—as everyone, including teachers, called him, although of course not to his face—was a remarkably sweaty, prematurely bald man in his mid-thirties who always looked as though at least one of his eyeballs was about to explode. He spent the time before classes began patrolling the halls, telling clots of students to break it up. Nobody knew why The Armpit felt that it was so important for clots to break up, but he did.

"Hide the papers," hissed Haley. The MEs scrambled to put their papers away. Harmonee, finding nowhere to put hers, shoved it up the back of The Ferret's shirt.

"Break it up!" said The Armpit, bearing down.

Haley's paper slipped back out of The Ferret's shirt and fell to the slick hallway floor directly in front of The Armpit. "Let's break it UUUUUUNNHOOF!" he said, stepping on the piece of paper in such a way that his foot slid violently forward and the rest of him flew backward,

causing him to land hard on his butt, sweat spraying outward from his body in a small perspiration typhoon. The paper flew forward and into the air, directly into the face of Toby, who had just entered the school and was hoping to slip past the ME kids while The Armpit was breaking them up. Reflexively, he reached out and grabbed the paper.

"Give me that!" said The Armpit, scrambling to his feet, his face a deep, glistening red. He snatched the paper from Toby with one hand and grabbed Toby's shirt with the other.

"Do you think that was *funny*?" The Armpit yelled.

"Yeah, Hardbonger," said Jason. "Do you think that was *funny*?"

"But I didn't—" Toby began.

"Quiet!" said The Armpit. "You're going to come with . . ."

"Excuse me," said Haley, sweetly, putting her hand on The Armpit's arm. "But there's been a mistake."

"There has?" said The Armpit, softening, as all males did when targeted at close range by Haley's blue-eyed gaze.

"Yes," said Haley. "This paper belongs to Harmonee. She dropped it. Didn't you, Harmonee."

"I did," said Harmonee, batting her eyelashes at The Armpit. "And I am *so* sorry, Mr. Armp . . . Mr. Parmit." She, too, put her hand on The Armpit's arm, trying hard not to show how seriously grossed out she was by its dampness.

The Armpit looked at the piece of paper. "Ah!" he said, nodding. "I see." With an odd smile, he handed the paper to Harmonee. Then he turned to Toby and said, "Okay, break it up."

"But," said Toby, "I'm not—"

"Are you *trying* to get into trouble?" said The Armpit.

"No, sir," said Toby.

"Yeah, Hardbonger," said Jason. "Break it up."

Toby sighed, turned, and headed down the hall, ignoring the laughter of the ME kids behind him. His thoughts were on the brief glimpse he'd gotten of Harmonee's paper.

CHAPTER EIGHT

TOBY FOUND MICAH AND TAMARA at their regular morning spot, located down the hallway about fifteen yards—or, in Hubble Middle status distance, 287 million miles—from the ME kids.

"What'd you do to tick off The Armpit?" asked Micah, as Toby walked up.

"Well, first I was walking past when he slipped on a piece of paper," said Toby. "And then I didn't break it up."

"Break what up?" said Micah.

"I have no idea," said Toby. "But get this. I think the piece of paper was an outline for Harmonee Prescott's science fair project."

"Really?" said Tamara. "What was it?"

"I don't really know," said Toby. "I only saw it for a

second. But it was really technical, with all kinds of numbers and stuff."

"Harmonee?" said Tamara. "The lip gloss queen? Technical?"

"I know," said Toby. "There's no way she understands it. They're up to something." He told Tamara and Micah what he'd seen the previous evening during study hall—the ME kids walking past with envelopes, then returning without them, and his unsuccessful effort to investigate further, thwarted by Mr. P.

"Do you think Mr. P is helping them cheat?" said Micah.

"I dunno," said Toby. "I didn't see him holding any envelopes."

"Those *cheaters*," said Tamara, glaring at the ME kids. "I would so love to bust them. Or at least beat them, for once."

"Yeah," said Toby and Micah together.

"Did you see the paper-clip ball?" said Micah.

"Yeah," said Toby. "It looks cool, but it won't win. You have to be more original than that."

"Well," said Tamara, "my project is *very* original."

"You have an idea?" said Micah.

"Yup," said Tamara.

"Does it involve stinging insects?" said Toby. Two years earlier Tamara's project had been a cross-section of a bee-hive that Tamara believed had been abandoned by the bees. Unfortunately, not all of the bees had been informed that they were supposed to have left. One of them stung a

judge, who had an allergic reaction and had to be rushed to the hospital. Fortunately, he recovered, but as Tamara learned, even if your project does not actually kill a judge, you are still unlikely to win a prize for it.

"Ha-ha," said Tamara. "Very funny."

"So what is your project?" asked Micah.

"It's called, 'Packaging: The Deadly Killer in Your Home,'" said Tamara.

"Huh," said Micah.

"Seriously," said Tamara. "Think about it. You know how whenever you buy anything, it's sealed up inside that thick, hard plastic, and there's no way to open it, so you have to try to cut it with scissors or a knife, but it's really hard to cut, and it turns into these jagged pieces of plastic that are really sharp, and you end up cutting yourself?"

Micah and Toby both nodded.

"My aunt got my cousin a Barbie doll for Christmas," continued Tamara, "and by the time she got it out of the package, she needed eight stitches in her hand. There was blood all over Barbie. She looked like *Texas Chainsaw Massacre* Barbie."

"And this is a science-fair project . . . how?" said Toby.

"I haven't figured it all out," said Tamara. "But I'm gonna show how easy it is for package plastic to slice through human flesh."

"Whose flesh are you going to use?" said Micah.

"Ha-ha, very funny," said Tamara. "I'll use something to simulate flesh, like a canned ham."

"A canned ham," said Toby.

"Right," said Tamara. "Or baloney."

"Why don't you use a Barbie doll?" said Micah.

"That's actually not a bad idea," said Tamara. "It would be more dramatic. In fact, I have this old Barbie at home that would be perfect. My mom got it at a yard sale. Rollerblade Barbie. She has these pink booties with wheels that shoot out sparks when you roll them. It's really stupid."

"So," said Toby, "your science-fair project is going to be to show that plastic can slice luncheon meat."

"Or Rollerblade Barbie," said Tamara.

Toby sighed and turned to Micah. "What about you?" he said. "Still planning to levitate the frog?"

"Yup," said Micah. "Fester is ready. He's good to go. I just need a really strong magnet."

"Where're you gonna get that?" said Toby.

"That place at the mall," said Micah.

"The Science Nook," said Tamara. "With the weird guy."

"He's weird," said Micah. "But everybody says he can get anything. You guys wanna go with me after school?"

"Sure," said Tamara.

"I have detention," said Toby. "But I can meet you there after."

"Okay," said Micah. "Hey, what's your experiment gonna be?"

"I dunno yet," said Toby. "I need to think of one."

A really good one, he thought. Good enough to win.

Toby hadn't told Tamara or Micah—even though they were his closest friends—about the mess he was in. This

was partly because he didn't want them telling anybody else, but mostly it was because he was ashamed of himself. He wished he'd never taken the blaster, never sold it on eBay, never bought the computer. The only way out he could see was to somehow win the science fair and pay back the money to the Darth Vader guy.

That was the other thing on Toby's mind, every minute: where were Darth and the Wookiee? He'd had trouble sleeping the night before, fearing another phone call to his house, or worse, a knock on the door. But there had been nothing, and this morning Toby had seen no sign of the two creepy guys on his way to school.

Where were they?

Toby's unhappy thoughts were interrupted by the bell. The crowded hallway began to empty as students headed for their homerooms. From the distance came the voice of The Armpit, telling people to break it up.

"So," said Micah, as the three friends separated, "we'll go to the mall later and get my magnet?"

"Right," said Tamara. "And I'll buy something packaged in plastic."

"You're really gonna do that packaging thing?" said Toby.

"Absolutely," said Tamara. " 'Packaging: The Deadly Killer in Your Home.' You don't think that's a winner?"

"I think," said Toby, "you were better off with the bees."

CHAPTER NINE

NOTHING HAPPENED DURING detention except for Coach Herman Furman yelling at nobody in particular to keep it down.

When detention finally ended, Toby slung his backpack over his shoulder and hurried down the near-empty hallway to the front door. He burst out into a spring afternoon of sunshine, humid air, and the *thunk* of aluminum bats from the ball field, where members of Hubble Middle's baseball team—the Fighting Orbital Observatories, a.k.a the Foos—were practicing.

Toby started to cross the parking lot, the shortest route to the mall. He'd gone five steps when he saw an ancient yellow AMC Gremlin—with two faces staring at

him through the bug-stained windshield.

Darth and the Wookiee.

Toby froze for a moment, during which the Wookiee creaked open the passenger door and climbed out. For a big guy, he moved fast.

Toby turned and ran. A voice behind him shouted "Wait!" But Toby kept running, straight onto the baseball infield.

"Hey!" shouted a coach. "Off the field!"

"Sorry!" shouted Toby, not slowing down. He sprinted past the infielders into the outfield. He glanced back over his shoulder: the Wookiee, not daring to chase him onto the field and draw the attention of the coaches, had veered right and was running behind the bleachers alongside the first-base line. The detour slowed him down; Toby had gained some time. He crossed the outfield and, with effort, clambered over a six-foot wooden fence into a backyard. As he dropped down the other side, he glanced back and saw that the Wookiee was well behind.

That was the good news.

The bad news was that the yard contained a dog. A very, very large dog, wide and hairy, like a cross between a rottweiler and the Goodyear blimp. It was coming toward Toby, making an unpleasant sound deep in its throat, its lips pulled back to reveal two rows of drool-drenched daggers.

"Nice doggy," said Toby, although this was not his actual opinion of the Goodyear rottweiler. He backed up until he was pressed against the fence. He felt something behind him. *The backpack.*

He quickly peeled it off and dug down into it until he found the hummus-and-onion sandwich his mom had packed him for lunch. He had not eaten it; it smelled like a dead llama. He yanked it out and heaved it, still wrapped in aluminum foil, toward the dog, who snatched it from the air with a terrifyingly loud *clack* of its teeth and gulped it down, foil and all.

With the dog momentarily distracted, Toby slung the backpack onto his shoulder and turned, intending to vault the fence. He got his hands on top of it and was about to hoist himself over when he heard a snarl and felt himself being yanked violently backward by the shoulder strap, which was attached to his backpack, which was in the mouth of the dog, which apparently desired another tasty helping of hummus, onion, and aluminum foil.

Toby wriggled out of the backpack and staggered to his feet. He got his hands on the top of the fence again and, with a desperate, fear-powered leap, hurled himself over it headfirst. At exactly that moment, three feet to Toby's left, the Wookiee vaulted over the fence going the other way.

"Hey!" shouted the Wookiee. He reached out to grab Toby but missed, his momentum carrying him over the fence. As Toby tumbled to the ground, he heard the dog snarl and the Wookiee scream—a surprisingly high-pitched sound coming from a human that size. Toby scrambled to his feet and sprinted along the fence, going several more yards before he finally reached the street.

He turned and looked back. The Wookiee was

scrambling back over the fence, using one arm to climb and the other to beat the dog with . . .

Toby's backpack.

The Wookiee was over the fence now. Toby noted that his clothes were torn, and he was bleeding from his arms. This did not seem to have improved his mood. Seeing Toby, the Wookiee roared and began running, still holding the backpack. Toby turned, crossed the street, and ran down a driveway and into another backyard. He vaulted a low picket fence, crossed the connecting yard, and hurried out into the next street.

He glanced back: the Wookiee was gaining.

Toby sprinted across the street and plunged into a muddy slosh, a tangle of brambles and wild shrubs littered with trash. Just beyond lay the railroad tracks. Toby slogged through the mud, thorns scratching his arms, his new white Discount Warehouse sneakers sinking into the stink. He found firmer ground as he reached the railroad embankment. Behind him, he heard the Wookiee crashing through the brambles and cursing. He'd found the thorns, too.

As he neared the top of the railroad embankment, Toby saw two things—one good and one bad. The good thing was, a freight train was coming. A long one. If he could get across the tracks, the train might block the Wookiee and enable Toby to get away. The bad thing was, sitting directly across the tracks was a police car with a policeman inside.

* * *

Unlike his fellow officers, Lucius Broyle didn't mind Choo Choo Patrol. The assignment was to apprehend students who took the shortcut across the railroad tracks. Young people had done this for many generations; in fact, Officer Broyle had crossed these same tracks at this very spot many times in his own youth. Nobody had ever been hurt, but in recent years, track-crossing—like rock-throwing, tree-climbing, whittling, spitting, unsupervised play, and countless other things young people once did routinely— had been deemed too dangerous, and the Choo Choo Patrol had been instituted. It appealed to Officer Broyle because it mostly consisted of doing nothing. This gave him time to work on his secret hobby: knitting. At the moment he was in the middle of a very tricky section of a sweater pattern he'd found on a knitting blog called Needles on Fire.

Toby weighed his options. The policeman hadn't seen him yet; he seemed to be occupied with something in his lap. To Toby's right, the train was very close. Behind him, the Wookiee was charging through the bushes. In a few seconds he'd be on the embankment, and Toby would be caught.

The sound of the train broke Officer Broyle's concentration. He looked up and saw a boy standing by the tracks on the other side.

"Hey!" he shouted. He yanked the door handle and started to climb out, at the same time tossing the sweater

aside, knowing that this action could very well cost him an entire row of critical stitches. "HEY!" he repeated, his voice drowned out by the train.

The Wookiee, still holding Toby's backpack, crashed through the bushes and up the embankment. He roared in rage: the train was rumbling past, blocking him from following the boy. He stood next to the tracks, his face only a few feet from the freight cars, ready to dash across as soon as the train passed. He waited impatiently until he saw the green caboose approaching and then finally passing him. As it did, he ran around behind it . . .

. . . directly into the arms of Officer Lucius Broyle.

Toby, crouched in the bushes a few yards away, watched the Wookiee run into the policeman, the two of them almost falling over. There followed a heated exchange, in which the officer demanded to know where the boy was, while the Wookiee pointed out that he was clearly *not* a boy, and since when was it against the law to cross railroad tracks?

While they argued, Toby crept through the bushes until he was far enough away to dart across the tracks unseen. He hurried down the other side of the embankment and up the street to the Looper Avenue overpass, a concrete bridge that spanned State Highway 9. He was halfway across when something yellow flashed in the corner of his eye: the Gremlin. He glanced over and found himself looking at Darth, who was driving very slowly, keeping pace with Toby's trot, his passenger-side window cranked

down. Toby looked back at the road and resumed trotting.

"You owe me a refund," said Darth, in a voice that Toby realized, with horror, actually *sounded* like Vader's—deep and creepy. Toby took another glance and saw that the guy had some kind of black box, with a knob and switches, strapped to his mouth.

"Do not," Toby panted. The end of the overpass was only twenty yards ahead. Once clear, he could drop down the embankment and escape this lunatic.

"The autograph is a fake," said Darth.

"No, it's not," panted Toby. "My father got that at the premiere. He saw Harrison Ford sign it, in person."

"Your father is a *liar*," said Darth, jerking his head so angrily that he bumped the knob on his black box, changing the setting from Lord of the Dark Side to Chipmunk.

"You owe me $2,038," he said, sounding like Chip, or possibly Dale. Quickly he readjusted the knob back to Darth. "And you're going to give it to me," he said, "or you and your family will pay."

"But I can't . . ." Toby said.

"You WILL pay me!" said Darth, stomping on the accelerator, which, in the case of the Gremlin, mainly resulted in backfiring accompanied by a slight increase in speed. Toby stopped and caught his breath as he watched it disappear up the street.

He started walking, considering his plight. He had two maniacs chasing him; one of them had his backpack. The only way to get rid of the maniacs was to pay them a ton of money, and the only way to get *that* was to win the science

fair. And he had no project yet. And his new white sneakers were dark brown and smelled like a toilet. Other than that, things were going great.

Toby reached the end of the overpass, turned down the embankment, and began trudging toward the mall.

CHAPTER TEN

WANDERING OAKS MALL was considered to be one of the three or four most upscale malls in the Bethesda, Maryland, area. It had all of the major high-end department stores, including a Bergstram's, a Wentmickler's, a Plock & Hingle, a Frempner's, a Winkle & Curd, and a Storkbutters. Surrounding these retail giants were hundreds of smaller stores selling hundreds of thousands of upscale products that nobody actually needed. There was a store that sold just corkscrews (it was called Just Corkscrews) and two stores devoted entirely to fragrant little soaps shaped like animals.

Almost all of these stores were clean, brightly lit, and welcoming, with attractive, ever-changing merchandise displays. The lone exception was the Science Nook. It was

at the far end of the highest concourse, and it violated many of the Wandering Oaks tenant rules. It was open at odd hours, and some days it did not open at all. It was dimly lit and often emitted strange sounds and odors. The display window contained a bizarre collection of apparently random objects—a snorkel mask, a toilet plunger, a Hello Kitty vanity mirror, a spatula, and many deceased insects. The proprietor and sole staff member was a man named Neal Sternabite, who was never seen without sunglasses, and whose hair appeared to have been styled by crazed squirrels.

The store attracted little business; its customer base consisted of eccentric experimenters and science enthusiasts, many of them as odd as Sternabite himself. He tolerated the regulars but was generally rude to unsuspecting shoppers who wandered in. He disliked answering what he considered to be stupid questions—this meant most questions—and he routinely ordered shoppers who annoyed him to leave the store. He once threw his lunch (the number-six lunch platter from the House of China restaurant in the Wandering Oaks food court) at a man who attempted to return what he claimed was a defective circuit board.

"The BOARD is not defective," yelled Sternabite, as the man ran from the store with kung pao chicken dripping down his shirt. "YOU are defective!"

Many people wondered how the Science Nook was allowed to remain at Wandering Oaks. In fact, the mall had tried to evict Sternabite several years earlier. The mall

manager, a man named Dwight Craven, delivered the eviction letter to Sternabite personally. Sternabite read it, then handed it back to Craven and said, "You don't want to do that."

"Yes, I do," said Craven.

"All right," said Sternabite. Immediately the electricity went out in Wandering Oaks Mall. All the concourses and stores went dark; the air-conditioning system shut down; all the stores' computer screens went blank. Even the phones stopped working.

Except in the Science Nook. The lights stayed on there.

Craven looked out at the suddenly dark mall, heard the shouts of alarm from shoppers and the cries of fear from children. He turned back to Sternabite.

"What did you do?" he said.

"How could I do anything?" said Sternabite. "I'm standing here talking to you."

"We're not finished," said Craven, walking quickly from the store to deal with the emergency.

"No," said Sternabite, "we're not."

For the rest of that day, and all of the next day, engineers for the electric and telephone companies tried to restore power to the mall. They checked every connection and ran every test; the found nothing wrong. Yet the mall— except for the Science Nook—remained dark.

"We've never seen anything like this," one of the engineers told Craven. "It's almost like there's some kind of . . . *force field* in the mall, interfering with the grid. But of course that's impossible."

"Of course," said Craven.

On the third powerless day, with the mall stores losing small fortunes and threatening large lawsuits, Craven went to the Science Nook, where he found Sternabite sitting behind the counter, sunglasses on, reading a Stephen King novel.

"Turn the electricity back on," said Craven.

"How can I do that?" said Sternabite.

"I don't know," said Craven. "But if you do, I'll tear up the eviction letter."

"You could write another letter," said Sternabite.

"I promise I won't," said Craven.

"You'd better not," said Sternabite.

And the lights came back on.

Craven turned and looked, blinking, at his once-again brilliant mall. He turned back and looked at Sternabite, who had not, as far as Craven could tell, moved a muscle. Without a word, Craven walked quickly out of the Science Nook. He had never gone back in.

So the Science Nook stayed in business, serving its small, weird clientele. But once a year, at science-fair time, business improved as students from Hubble Middle showed up, lured by the rumor that the Science Nook sold things that were unavailable elsewhere—things that could be used to make a science-fair project that the judges would notice.

On this particular afternoon, the first students to arrive were Micah, who was carrying a Tupperware container, and Tamara. When they arrived, the Science Nook

appeared to be empty. They looked around the store for a minute, but there was little to see other than cardboard boxes scattered around the floor, some empty, some containing electrical components, and one filled with what appeared to be eggplants. Also, in a back corner of the store on a battered wooden cabinet, was a large stuffed owl.

"Do you think he's here?" said Micah.

"He must be," said Tamara. "The store's open."

"Maybe he's in the back," said Micah. He wandered over to the counter and saw a row of four buttons.

"There's some buttons here," he said. "Maybe one's a buzzer."

"Try it," said Tamara.

Micah pushed a button. Nothing happened. He pushed another. Nothing. He pushed a third. Instantly there was a loud *BANG*, as one of the eggplants exploded, sending eggplant innards all over the store, some clinging to the walls and ceiling. The rest of the eggplants were hurled out of the now-destroyed box and landed all around the store. As Tamara and Micah stood frozen, a door opened, and Sternabite came out of the back room.

"I'm sorry!" said Micah. "I didn't know . . ."

"Which button did you push?" said Sternabite.

"Th . . . this one," said Micah, pointing.

Sternabite looked at the button, nodded, and said, "Good."

There was a pause of about thirty seconds, during which nobody said anything. Finally, Micah realized that there

was going to be no further discussion of the exploding eggplant. He said, "I need a magnet."

"What for?" said Sternabite.

"To levitate a frog," said Micah.

If Sternabite found this unusual, he gave no indication. "Hubble science fair?" he said.

"Yes," said Micah.

"Did you bring the frog?" said Sternabite.

"In here," said Micah, setting the Tupperware container on the counter. "His name is Fester."

Sternabite removed the lid and looked at Fester. "Hmm," he said, more to Fester than to Micah.

"Do you have a magnet that'll work?" said Micah.

"I can sell you the magnet for forty dollars," said Sternabite. "That's not the problem."

"What's the problem?" said Micah.

"Power supply," said Sternabite. "You only get 110 AC in the Hubble gym. You need more than that. A *lot* more."

"So he can't do his project?" said Tamara, brushing eggplant innards from her hair.

"I didn't say that," said Sternabite. He turned to Toby. "Come back tomorrow," he said. "I've got an old cold-fusion reactor I can lend you. Weighs about two pounds, supplies 150,000 watts."

"Cold fusion?" said Micah. "I thought that was impossible."

Sternabite snorted. "It *is* impossible," he said, "for morons."

"But is it *safe?*" said Tamara. "All those watts?"

56

"He should be fine," said Sternabite, looking at Fester.

"I meant," said Tamara, "is it safe for *people*."

Sternabite thought about it. "Probably," he said.

Tamara was about to ask another question when from behind her came the distinctively whiny voice of Harmonee Prescott, saying, "What are *they* doing here?"

Tamara and Micah turned to see Harmonee, Jason Niles, Haley Hess, and The Ferret entering the store.

"Yeah," said Haley, frowning. "What *are* you doing here?"

"They're leaving," said Jason Niles, looming over Micah. "Aren't you, Mucus?"

Micah quickly resealed Fester's container, turned to Sternabite, and said, "I'll come back tomorrow."

"Right," said Sternabite, his eyes on the ME kids. Micah and Tamara headed for the door.

"Your hair looks nice, Tamara!" called Haley sweetly. "Is that eggplant?"

"I *hate* Haley Hess," said Tamara, once they were out in the concourse. "I hate her I hate her I HATE her."

"Oh, I'm sure she'd be nice enough if you ever got to talk to her alone," said Micah. "And she had a brain transplant."

Tamara was glaring back toward the Science Nook. "What do you think they're doing in there?"

"Same as us," said Micah. "Getting science fair stuff."

"They're up to something," said Tamara.

"There's Toby," said Micah, nodding down the concourse. Toby was trotting their way.

"Sorry," he said, when he reached them. "I got held up."

"Where's your backpack?" said Tamara.

"I . . . I left it somewhere," said Toby. Tamara frowned and started to say something, but Toby cut her off. "You ready to go to the science place?"

"We already did," said Micah. "The weird dude's gonna fix me up with a magnet and a cold-fusion reactor."

"There's no such thing," said Toby.

"That's what all the morons say," said Micah.

"The ME kids are in there now," said Tamara.

Toby perked up. "Really?" he said. "Doing what?"

"Dunno," said Micah. "They kicked us out."

"Interesting," said Toby. He started walking toward the Science Nook.

"What're you doing?" said Micah.

"I'm gonna have a look," said Toby.

"Niles is in there," said Micah.

"I'm not afraid of Niles," said Toby.

"Yes, you are," said Tamara.

"Yes, I am," said Toby. "But I'm gonna be stealthy."

"We'll wait for you here," said Micah.

"Stay away from the eggplants," said Tamara.

Toby looked back, frowning.

"She's serious," said Micah.

Toby walked to the Science Nook entrance, glanced at the strange window display, took a breath, and stepped inside. He saw nobody. He looked around, checking out the boxes and the stuffed owl. He noted with interest the eggplant splatter on the walls and ceiling, and the loose

58

eggplants on the floor. Hearing voices, he moved to a door along the back wall; it was open a crack. He put his ear close. A man was talking.

". . . Some unusual items this year," the man said. "For example, this . . ." There was a pause, and Toby heard paper rattling ". . . this item here, this is highly classified technology. Only certain government agencies are even supposed to know it exists."

A boy's voice—Toby recognized The Ferret—said, "How come *you* know it exists?"

"Because I'm smarter than the government," said the man. "But the point is, all of your projects this year involve classified technology. Who gave you these plans?"

"We told you, we don't know." That was Haley Hess's voice. "They just showed up, same as last year. But what do you care where they come from, as long as you get paid."

"Just curious," said the man. "But yes, as long as you pay my price, I don't care. I'm just saying some of these components are hard to get. *Very* hard to get. There are countries in the world that would *love* to get their hands on this technology."

The next voice belonged to Jason Niles. "Whatever it is, my dad can get it," he said.

"My dad, too," said another voice, which Toby recognized as Harmonee Prescott's. "If I tell my mom I need it for my project, she'll *make* him get it."

"So what's the deal?" said Haley.

"A thousand apiece," said the voice.

"A *thousand*?" said Jason. "That's a rip-off!"

"Fine," said the man. "Make your own project."

Jason mumbled something that Toby couldn't hear.

"Five hundred up front," said the man. "Five hundred when you get the project. You supply the parts I need. I circled them on your project sheets. Understood?"

There was more mumbling, and suddenly Toby realized that they were about to open the door. He had no time to get out of the store. He looked around frantically and saw the stuffed owl. In three quick tiptoe steps he was around the cabinet, crouching behind it.

He peered over the top and watched as the ME kids walked past, back out into the mall. The Ferret said something; they all looked back and giggled.

Toby was about to leave when Sternabite, whom Toby recognized as the store owner, came out of the back room. Toby almost showed himself but decided not to; after what he'd just heard, he didn't want this weird man to suspect he'd been listening. He decided to hold still for the time being, hoping Sternabite would go into the back room again, so he could escape.

Instead, Sternabite went out the door and pulled out a key ring. Toby's stomach froze.

He's closing up.

Sternabite walked over and pushed the middle button. Then he stepped outside, pulled the door shut, and put his key in the lock. Toby half rose behind the owl, wanting to yell, but afraid of what the weird dude might do.

The door lock clicked. As it did, the store lights went out.

And then the stuffed owl started to move.

Toby dropped back to the floor. Instantly the owl's head whipped around 180 degrees. Lying on his back on the floor, not breathing, Toby saw that the owl's eyes were glowing bright red. Two rays of red light shot out, causing two dots to appear on the wall.

Lasers, thought Toby.

The two dots scanned slowly down the wall; in a few seconds they would reach Toby. As quietly as he could, he felt around on the dark floor. His hand found something round and hard. An eggplant.

With the laser dots only inches away, Toby gripped the eggplant and, as quietly as he could, tossed it. It landed with a *thud* in the middle of the store.

Instantly, the owl spread its wings—to Toby, directly below, its wingspan looked gigantic. It flapped twice—Toby felt the air—and swooped off the perch. By the mall light filtering through the store window, Toby saw the owl pounce on the eggplant. There was an ugly wet *splat*. The owl stood there for a moment, and then, apparently satisfied that it had killed the eggplant, flapped its wings, took off, circled the room once, and returned to its perch.

Directly above Toby.

CHAPTER ELEVEN

★

TOBY LAY AS STILL AS POSSIBLE, his eyes on the owl—or whatever it was—perched overhead. Toby could see its talons gripping the perch. They glinted in the light coming through the store window from the mall concourse. Made of metal—steel, it looked like—the talons were at least six inches long, ending in curled, sharpened points. Definitely not a standard-issue owl.

Its laser eyes tracked back and forth, scanning the store. Toby studied the pattern: the twin red dots started up on the ceiling, then swept down to the floor. They continued across the tile to a spot right in front of the owl, and then the owl's head rotated slightly to the right as the beams flicked back up to the ceiling and the process started again. Each cycle was fast, taking only a second or

two, ceiling to floor. In no time—less than a minute—the red dots would fall on him, and the owl would do to him what it had done to the eggplant: turn him into sauce.

His instinct was to run, but to where? The front door was locked. That left the door to the back of the store . . . but what if it, too, was locked?

He fought his growing panic. The dots were coming right for him. He'd have to try the back door. But the owl, when it moved, moved *fast*. If the door gave him any trouble, slowed him down at all, the owl would attack. Toby tried to remember what, if anything, he'd seen at the front of the store that he might use to defend himself.

An image flashed into his mind.

It would have to do.

Carefully, he groped out with his right hand, hoping desperately to find . . . *There!* Another eggplant. With the moving red dots now only inches away, he threw the eggplant as hard as he could toward the back door.

Before the eggplant hit the wall, the owl was already moving, its huge wings lifting it off the cabinet perch. At the same moment, Toby rolled to his right, scrambled to his feet, and ran toward the store's front window. Behind him he heard the ugly *splat* as the owl landed on the eggplant.

As Toby reached the window, he looked back: the owl was on the floor, eggplant goo seeping from between its glinting talons. Its head was aimed directly at Toby.

Toby looked down: two red dots were centered on his chest.

The owl flapped its wings.

Frantically, Toby turned back to the window, looking for . . . *There it was*. As he felt the rush of air behind him he grabbed the Hello Kitty vanity and whirled, holding it in front of his face, mirror-side forward.

He staggered off balance as the owl's right wing brushed against him—the thing was *powerful*—and he peered around the side of the vanity to see that the owl had veered sharply left, following where the two red dots, now reflected by the vanity mirror, danced on the side of an old, dust-covered TV set.

The owl, talons raised in attack position, slammed into the TV, which in turn slammed into the wall, its tube exploding in a thousand shards of glass. Toby, still holding his Hello Kitty anti-owl vanity, ran to the back door. As he reached it, he heard the flap of wings and saw the owl—the thing was *indestructible*—swooping at him again. He lifted the mirror just in time to redirect the lasers and send the owl careening into the side wall with a crash so violent that it brought down ceiling tiles. Immediately, the owl turned, located Toby again, and flapped its huge wings.

Toby tried the doorknob. It was unlocked! He pushed the door open and slammed it shut just as the relentless owl slammed into it. Toby's relief lasted for perhaps two seconds; then the owl, which clearly had not given up, slammed into the door again—this time so hard that the wooden door frame began to give. Toby heard the huge wings flapping as the owl went airborne, evidently preparing for another lunge.

Frantic to get out of there, Toby looked around. He was in a back office lined with shelves full of tools and electrical components. A battered desk stood by the back wall, near the only source of light in the office. . . .

An exit sign.

Toby jumped as the owl, with another resounding *CRASH*, smashed into the door again; this time the door itself began to splinter as the points of the owl's steel-sharp talons pierced it. Toby, trying not to think about those same talons piercing him, ran toward the exit sign. As he reached it, he spotted a sheet of paper on the desk. Handwritten at the top was the word "Hubble." Beneath that was a list. Toby grabbed the paper and stuffed it into his pocket. He turned and slammed the panic bar on the door beneath the exit sign just as the owl burst through a hole in the office's wooden door. Toby heard an alarm sound as he slammed the metal door. A second later, the owl thudded into it.

Toby found himself in a wide, windowless corridor lit by overhead tube lights—a service hallway behind all the stores. He ran down the corridor, dodging cardboard boxes stacked outside the back doors of the stores. A dozen yards ahead he saw another exit sign.

"HEY! STOP!" a deep voice shouted from behind him.

Toby kept running. He reached the exit door, blasted through it, and was out of there, running from the mall as fast as he could into the approaching night.

Chapter Twelve

"I NEED A THOUSAND DOLLARS," said Jason Niles. "For the science fair."

Jason was eating dinner with his parents in their kitchen, which—in the style of Manor Estates homes—was the size of a volleyball court. It had two restaurant-quality stoves and a state-of-the-art refrigerator with a touchscreen, Internet-connected computer in the door that you could use to plan meals, generate grocery lists, and do many other helpful things, if you knew how to use it, which nobody in the Niles family did. The Niles family rarely used any of their vast array of advanced kitchen technology. Tonight they were eating—from designer ceramic plates that cost $280 apiece—takeout Mexican food from Mister Burrito.

"A thousand dollars?" said Jason's dad, Carl Niles, looking up from his BlackBerry, which he took everywhere, including into the shower in a special waterproof case. "For the science fair?"

"Yeah," said Jason. "That's what the other kids are spending."

"But a *thousand dollars*?" said Carl.

"If that's what he needs," said Jason's mother, Jeanette, "that's what he needs."

Carl Niles was an imposing, powerful man who had thousands of people working for him. He had no trouble disagreeing with generals, senators, even presidents. But he knew better than to disagree with Jeanette.

"Whatever," he said, looking back down at his Black-Berry.

Very few people argued with Jeanette Niles. She was an attractive, petite blond woman with perfect teeth and blue eyes capable of producing a gaze so intense that people felt as though she was burning holes in their faces. Jeanette sometimes sold real estate—always Manor Estates homes—but mostly she was a mom, an extremely *involved* mom, a mom who made certain that her son Jason, like his brother, Taylor, before him, had every possible advantage in what Jeanette viewed as the fierce, relentless, and critically important competition to always be ahead of all other children, and thus ahead in life.

Jeanette was very, very good at this competition. In elementary school, when Jason, along with the rest of his first-grade class, had to do a report on a country, Jeanette

had chosen Switzerland. On the day the report was due, Jason had arrived at school wearing authentic Swiss *lederhosen* and carrying a 124-page, professionally printed report that Jeanette had been up all night assembling in an attractive leather binder. Some of the other involved moms had also produced high-quality reports, but nobody else had broken the 100-page barrier. The rest of the kids—the ones who had actually done their own reports—showed up with a few stapled-together pieces of construction paper, on which they had pasted maps and pictures cut out from magazines. Jeanette could not imagine what kind of parents would allow such a thing to happen to their children. *Losers.*

Every school assignment Jason was given received a 110 percent effort from Jeanette, who had produced, over the years, dozens of detailed, well-researched, error-free, professional-quality reports. In addition, there was her beautifully crafted miniature medieval village, her rain-forest simulation complete with actual running water, and her solar-system model with planets that revolved *and* rotated, to name just a few of the projects she had done for Jason. She gave just as much effort, night after night, to Jason's homework. As he progressed through the grades, this had become more and more of a challenge for Jeanette; trigonometry, for example, did not come easily to her. But she had, through hard work and perseverance, mastered it. That's how involved a mom she was.

Jason's test scores, often below average, were her biggest headache. Jeanette was certain he was gifted—had *had* to be gifted—so she had concluded that he must have

some kind of learning disability. This she dealt with by hiring tutors for Jason and volunteering at his school, where she could keep an eye on Jason's teachers, who quickly learned the importance of always giving Jason the benefit of the doubt and then some.

Thus Jason had managed to compile an impressive academic record as he progressed through the grades. He was right on course to get into one of the best colleges, as his brother had. Jeanette would see to that.

"What's your project this year?" she asked Jason. "Do you need help with it?"

"Nah," said Jason. "The Science Nook guy is doing it."

"You mean he's helping you," said Jeanette. "Like a coach."

"Whatever," said Jason.

It bothered Jeanette, a little, that the strange man at the Science Nook was so involved with her son's project. But the strange man got excellent results—he'd done a marvelous job for Jason's brother—so Jeanette tried not to think about it.

"Oh, yeah," said Jason, pulling a folded sheet of paper from his pocket and handing it to his mother, "I need this stuff."

Jeanette unfolded the paper and read it. It was a list of technical words, meaningless to her. She tapped her husband, who looked up from his BlackBerry. She handed him the paper.

"Jason needs these things for his science-fair project," she said.

Carl looked at the paper, frowned, and looked up at Jason.

"Where did you get this list?" he asked.

"From some guy," said Jason.

"Can't you get him those things?" said Jeanette.

"I can get them," said Carl. "But this is highly restricted technology. This isn't supposed to be available outside of—"

"Oh, for heaven's sake, Carl," interrupted Jeanette. "It's for *your son's science-fair project.*"

Carl could feel his face burning under his wife's gaze. He turned to Jason.

"All right," he said. "But you have to get this stuff back to me as soon as the science fair is over."

"Whatever," said Jason.

Chapter Thirteen

THE NEXT MORNING, Toby squished through Hubble Middle's main doorway on sneakers still wet and mud-stained from the previous evening's Wookiee adventure. Toby had seen no sign of either the Wookiee or Darth this morning; that was good. Not so good was the fact that they had his backpack. Also not so good was the fact that Jason Niles was detaching his large self from the clot of ME kids to block Toby's path.

"Nice shoes, Hardbonger," he said.

"Good one, Niles," said Toby. "That must have taken all four of your brain cells."

Haley Hess, behind Jason, giggled, which made Toby secretly pleased and Jason openly infuriated. He stepped toward Toby and gave him a shove, sending Toby

staggering backward, directly into The Armpit.

"Hey!" said The Armpit. "Break it up!"

"But he—" began Toby.

"I said BREAK IT UP!" said The Armpit, giving Toby a shove with his sweat-slimed hands.

Toby stumbled forward past the smirking ME kids. He detoured around a ladder in the middle of the hallway occupied by J.D., the Janitor Dude, who was replacing a fluorescent ceiling lightbulb, a task that often took him more than an hour, because he spent long stretches of time staring into space. This spawned many jokes about how many Janitor Dudes it took to screw in a lightbulb.

Toby found his friends in their traditional hallway spot. As he walked up, Micah, Tamara, and Pencil Wenzel were gathered around Brad Pitt Wemplemeyer, who was telling them something that required a lot of arm motions.

"Hey," said Toby. "I found out—"

"Wait," said Micah. "You gotta hear what B.P.W.'s doing for his project."

"But I—"

"A nuclear Mentos!" said Tamara.

"A what?" said Toby.

"You know how, when you put a Mentos in a Diet Coke, it shoots up, *sploosh*, like a geyser?" said Brad Pitt Wemplemeyer.

"Yeah," said Toby, who'd seen video of this on the Internet. "It's like a chemical reaction."

"Wrong," said Brad Pitt Wemplemeyer. "It's a physical reaction. The Mentos lowers the surface tension of the

Diet Coke, so the dissolved carbon dioxide turns to gas really fast, *sploosh*."

"Okay," said Toby. "But how's that a science fair project? I mean, everybody's already seen the videos."

"Of *regular* Mentos, yes," said Brad Pitt Wemplemeyer. "But I'm gonna make a *huge* Mentos, a giant mint, and drop it into a whole tub of Diet Coke, like fifty gallons."

"What science thing would that prove?" said Toby.

"I dunno," said Brad Pitt Wemplemeyer, "but it's gonna be *awesome*. A nuclear Mentos. Think about it!"

"I'm not sure I want to," said Toby.

"You're just jealous," said Brad Pitt Wemplemeyer.

Before Toby could answer, Tamara said, "Hey, Toby, what happened at the mall? We waited, but you never came back."

Toby glanced back toward the ME kids, then, lowering his voice, said, "That's what I was trying to tell you. They're definitely cheating. The Science Nook guy is making their projects for a thousand each."

"A thousand *dollars*?" said Micah.

"Each," said Toby. "And that's not all." He reached into his pocket and pulled out the piece of paper he'd found on Sternabite's desk. The others gathered closer to look.

"What is this?" said Pencil Wenzel. "I don't understand most of these words."

"Me, either," said Toby. "But I heard the Science Nook guy tell the ME kids that it's classified stuff. They're gonna get their parents to get it for them."

"Classified, like, *classified*?" said Pencil Wenzel. "Like top secret?"

"That's what he said," said Toby.

"You sure you heard them right?" said Tamara.

"They were in the back," said Toby. "I listened by the door. I heard everything."

"So how'd you get the list?" said Micah.

"I took it," said Toby. "I was hiding behind the stuffed owl, and the Science Nook guy locked the store with me inside. Only it turned out the owl is this, like, *robot* that protects the store. So I ran into the back room and—"

"Waitwaitwait," said Micah, holding up a hand. "The owl is a *robot*?"

"Yeah," said Toby. "It has these laser eyes that track you, and these sharp pointy claws, and it flies *fast*."

"So how'd you get away from it?" said Micah.

"I threw eggplants," said Toby.

Tamara and Micah nodded, remembering the eggplants.

"So," said Pencil Wenzel, speaking slowly, "you escaped from a robot owl by . . . *throwing eggplants*."

"Right," said Toby.

"And you're mocking *me* because of nuclear Mentos?" said Brad Pitt Wemplemeyer.

"Watch it," said Micah. "Mr. P's coming."

Toby quickly folded the paper as Mr. Pzyrbovich, the algebra teacher, stalked toward them with the facial expression—normal, for Mr. P—of a man who had not gone to the bathroom for at least four days. As he passed, he glared at Toby's group. It seemed to Toby that Mr. P glared a little extra at him.

"So, Toby," said Tamara, after Mr. P had passed. "What're you gonna do about this? Did you tell anybody?"

"Just you guys so far," said Toby. "I thought about telling my parents, but . . . you know. They're weird."

The others nodded in unspoken confirmation of the weirdness of Toby's parents.

"Even if they believed me," continued Toby, "they'd come to school acting all weird, and nobody would believe *them*."

"So what're you gonna do?" repeated Tamara.

"I'm gonna tell Neckstrom," said Toby.

"I dunno," said Micah. "You think he'd do anything to the ME kids? He's like their personal slave."

"I know," said Toby. "But he's the science teacher and head of the fair."

"No," said Tamara. "Micah's right. You have to go over Neckstrom's head."

"You mean . . ." said Toby.

"Yep," said Tamara. "The Hornet."

The Hornet was Helen Plotz-Gornett, the principal of Hubble Middle, a short but terrifying woman. Nobody had ever seen her smile; nobody could say for sure that she even breathed. She knew everything about everybody in the school and could strike anywhere at any time without warning. You'd be doing something you shouldn't be doing, and you'd turn around, and *YIKES*, there would be The Hornet. *Even in the boys' room.*

"I don't want to go see The Hornet," said Toby.

"You have to," said Tamara. "She's the only one who's not afraid of the ME kids."

Toby's reply was interrupted by the ringing of the bell, and the approach of The Armpit, weaving wetly toward them through the corridor bustle. "Let's break it up!"

The little group began to break up, its members joining the throngs of students heading for their various homerooms. Tamara and Toby were the last to leave. She put her hand on his arm.

"Seriously," she said. "Do it. The ME kids have been cheating way too long. It's got to stop, and the only way to *make* it stop is for honest people to stand up to them."

"So you'll go with me to see The Hornet?" said Toby.

"Are you *nuts*?" said Tamara.

She turned toward her homeroom, leaving Toby to trudge, alone, toward the principal's office.

CHAPTER FOURTEEN

GRDANKL THE STRONG WAS UNHAPPY. He did
not like being interrupted at any time, but he especially
did not like it today, during one of the Republic of
Krpshtskan's most important national holidays, the
Tournament of the Fighting-Death Hamsters.

On this day almost everyone in the capital city of Krpsht
stopped working to gather in the national arena, where
a circle three feet in diameter—the Circle of Doom—
had been drawn in the middle of the concrete floor for
the death match. After the opening ceremony, which
concluded with the singing of the Krpsht national anthem
("Krpshtskan, My Country, for Now"), the audience fell
silent as two men entered the arena, each carrying a cage.

The men set the cages down on opposite sides of the Circle of Doom, then opened the cage doors and stepped back.

The crowd watched in anticipation as, from each cage, a legendary Krpsht Fighting-Death Hamster emerged. Or not. Sometimes the hamster wranglers had to shake the cages to get them moving. But eventually they came out and, with prodding from the wranglers, waddled into the Circle of Doom. Each hamster was dressed in a little tank top—one red, one yellow. The one wearing red, known as Lethal Thunder, was the five-time Fighting-Death Hamster champion and the favorite of Grdankl the Strong. The hamster in yellow—known as Harmful Killer—was the number one-ranked challenger.

The crowd watched expectantly for several minutes as the hamsters simply sat there, noses quivering. Then, as the crowd held its breath in anticipation, Lethal Thunder took a tiny step forward and pooped.

The crowd exhaled. The hamsters were once again motionless, as they would be for most of the death match. The one thing the Fighting-Death Hamsters never actually did—being hamsters—was fight. The death match was, in fact, more of a staring contest; the loser was the first hamster to leave the circle. But this could take hours. Days, even.

Nobody could remember how this event got its name, or why it become a national holiday. It was an ancient tradition, and the Krpshtskanis observed it for the same reason they did everything else; because they always had. Also, it was a day off work.

Grdankl the Strong especially liked the Tournament of the Fighting-Death Hamsters because he got to sit in the Presidential Chair, which was a recliner—in fact, the only recliner in the Republic of Krpshtskan. He enjoyed reclining it and normally fell asleep during the tournament.

Grdankl the Strong had been snoozing today when he was awakened by a tentative tap on his arm. He opened his eyes and glared angrily at the person who had dared interrupt his nap. This was the fourth vice president, formally known as Drmtsi the Medium-Sized, who had been assigned the unpleasant task of waking the president by the first, second, and third vice presidents, who were hovering nervously in the background.

"What?" snarled Grdankl the Strong, using the form of the word "what" that, in the Krpsht language, caused the speaker to eject as much as two ounces of saliva.

"I apologize with deepest sincere groveling regret, Your Utmost Excellency," said Drmtsi, wiping his face with his sleeve. "But there is a message for you." He lowered his voice. "From Prmkt."

Grdankl the Strong smacked Drmtsi the Medium-Sized.

"Why did you not tell me!" he roared, in a voice so loud that it echoed throughout the arena, causing Lethal Thunder to make weewee on his wrangler.

Drmtsi might have pointed out that he had, in fact, just told Grdankl the Strong about the message. But he was not that stupid.

"Where is the message?" said Grdankl the Strong.

"It is on the computer, Your Utmost Supreme Excellency."

Grdankl the Strong grunted unhappily. The only way to read the e-mail was to go look at the screen, as the Republic of Krpshtskan did not have a printer.

"Up!" he said.

Drmtsi pushed the lever that un-reclined the Presidential Chair; the first, second, and third vice presidents heaved Grdankl the Strong to his feet. He turned toward the hamster wranglers and bellowed, "Nothing may happen until I return!" Then, followed by his vice presidents, he waddled out of the arena and into the presidential limousine, a 1961 Checker that had once been a New York City taxi. For a change it started on the first try, and it soon arrived at the presidential palace, which was directly across the street.

Grdankl and his vice presidents entered the palace and descended into the bunker. Waiting nervously in front of the computer screen was Vrsk, the Krpshtskani minister of technology. He stepped aside as Grdankl the Strong waddled to the computer and, frowning deeply, read the e-mail on the screen. This took some time because Grdankl the Strong was a poor reader.

Finally he turned to the vice presidents.

"It is from Prmkt," he said.

The vice presidents nodded.

"There is a problem at the school," continued Grdankl the Strong. "A student has found out about our plan. Prmkt says he can deal with it, but he needs help."

Vrsk's eyes widened. He had read the e-mail, and Prmkt had in fact specifically stated that he did *not* need help. Grdankl the Strong had read the e-mail wrong. But Vrsk did not even consider correcting Grdankl the Strong; that would be suicide.

"It is a dangerous mission," said Grdankl the Strong. "Probably it means certain death. But we must help Prmkt. I will send two men." He pointed to Drmtsi. "You are one."

Drmtsi, looking like he had just eaten a live spider, managed to say, "I will not disappoint you, Your Utmost Supreme Excellency."

"If you do," said Grdankl the Strong, "I will make your liver into a pudding. The second man to go will be . . ." Grdankl the Strong looked around at the others, all of whom avoided his gaze ". . . you."

Vrsk realized, with horror, that Grdankl the Strong was pointing at him. Vrsk knew a lot about computers but absolutely nothing about helping a spy. He didn't even own a passport.

"You will leave now," said Grdankl the Strong. "Go! Do not be afraid! If you die, it is okay!"

Drmtsi and Vrsk, both pale, stumbled from the room. Grdankl the Strong and his remaining three vice presidents returned to the presidential limousine, which failed to start. This greatly displeased Grdankl the Strong, who ordered the chauffeur imprisoned, then walked, most unhappily, back across the street to the National Arena and the Tournament of the Fighting-Death Hamsters.

CHAPTER FIFTEEN

Toby had been sitting in The Hornet's outer office for twenty minutes, watching J.D. the Janitor Dude mop the same spot in the hall over and over, and listening to the semituneless humming of The Hornet's secretary, Mrs. Breetle. She was tapping on her computer and humming a song that Toby had finally figured out was "Oops! . . . I Did It Again." This surprised Toby because Mrs. Breetle did not strike him as a Britney Spears fan. Mrs. Breetle struck Tony as being, by a conservative estimate, one hundred and fifty years old.

Also in the office was Mr. P, who glared briefly at Toby before resuming whatever he was doing with the fax machine; and five students who were also waiting, unhappily, to face The Hornet. One by one they were summoned in to see The Hornet, emerging a minute or so

later looking as if they had just had dental work without anesthetic. Toby was about to abandon his plan when Mrs. Breetle pointed at him and said, "Your turn."

Toby stood and shuffled into The Hornet's office. The Hornet was sitting behind her desk, which had nothing on it but a letter opener the size of a bayonet. She looked at Toby with the expression of a person who had seen thousands of students standing in exactly the same spot and had not yet been impressed.

"Yes?" she said.

Toby found that his throat didn't work.

"Urg," he said.

"I see," said The Hornet. "Was there anything else?"

"Urg," repeated Toby.

The Hornet sighed. "Mr. Harbinger," she said, "I enjoy a good frog imitation as much as the next person. But if you've nothing else to say, I have work to do."

The amazing fact that The Hornet actually knew his name jolted Toby out of his paralysis.

"They're cheating," he blurted. "On the science fair."

"Who is?" said The Hornet.

"The ME kids," said Toby.

"Close the door," said The Hornet.

Toby closed the door.

"By ME you mean—"

"The Manor Estates kids."

"How are they cheating?" said The Hornet.

Toby told The Hornet about overhearing the ME kids talking in the cafeteria about envelopes and the fifty

dollars; about seeing ME kids after school in the corridor, first heading one way with envelopes in hand, then returning without; about picking up Harmonee Prescott's paper in the corridor and seeing that it was covered with technical terms; about listening outside the back-room door at the Science Nook and hearing Sternabite tell the ME kids that the price of a project was a thousand dollars, and that some of the components were classified technology. Toby then gave The Hornet the list he took from Sternabite's desk, telling her only that he picked it up while Sternabite wasn't looking. He didn't think now was a good time to mention the robot security owl.

The Hornet read the list, placed it on her desk, and frowned at the wall for a minute while drumming her fingers on her desk. Then she picked up her phone, pushed a button, and said, "Please have Mr. Neckstrom come to my office. Yes, now."

Two minutes later, Neckstrom entered The Hornet's office, looking every bit as nervous about being there as Toby did.

"Toby," said The Hornet, "tell Mr. Neckstrom what you just told me."

Toby did. As he spoke, Mr. Neckstrom's face got red, and then redder, and then very close to purple. When Toby was finished, Mr. Neckstrom glared at him then turned to The Hornet and said, "This is ridiculous. He's making it up."

"Why would he do that?" said The Hornet.

"It's obvious," said Mr. Neckstrom. "He wants to win

the science-fair prize money. He made up this story to eliminate his competition."

Toby started to say something, but The Hornet held up her hand. "What about this?" she said, sliding Sternabite's list across her desk.

Mr. Neckstrom picked up the list, looked at it for a moment, then tossed it back on the desk. "This is probably just technical-sounding gobbledygook he made up from words he found on the Internet," he said. "Who knows if these things even exist?"

The Hornet looked at Mr. Neckstrom, then at Toby, then back at Mr. Neckstrom.

"I'm going to talk to the other students," she said.

The color of Mr. Neckstrom's face went immediately from borderline grape to skim milk.

"Bu . . . but do you think that would be wise?" he said. "If you accuse them of cheating, it could be very . . . I mean, their *parents* . . ."

"I'm well aware who their parents are," said The Hornet. "But this is a serious charge, and I intend to . . ."

She was interrupted by the harsh electronic beeping of the Hubble Middle School fire alarm. As The Hornet rose to her feet, Mrs. Breetle appeared in the doorway.

"It's a locker," she said, "in the main corridor. Some kind of smoke or something. The fire department's on its way."

"Start the fire drill," said The Hornet. As Mrs. Breetle hurried away, The Hornet said, "We'll finish this later. Mr. Neckstrom, please see to your students. Toby, you'll

join your homeroom class out on the ball field."

Mr. Neckstrom, with a last glare at Toby, stalked out, followed by The Hornet, followed by Toby. The corridor echoed with the earsplitting sound of the alarm. Students were streaming from the classrooms in reasonably orderly lines, heading toward the main exit. Toby looked back down the corridor and saw the cause of the alarm: a cloud of what looked like bright green, glowing smoke was wafting from a locker just past Miss Cooney's classroom.

Toby frowned. He counted the lockers leading to the smoking one.

Three, four, five . . .

He felt a cold lump in his stomach.

It was his locker.

Chapter Sixteen

★

An hour later, the students still stood waiting on the ball field. The excitement of watching the fire trucks arrive, with sirens whooping, had gradually turned into the disappointment of realizing that the school was not, in fact, going to burn down.

Now, as they watched the firefighters load their gear back onto the trucks, most of the students were bored enough to actually be glad to hear it was time to go back into the school. The exception was Toby, who would have preferred to go anywhere else, including another planet. He had no idea why his locker had been emitting glowing green smoke, but he was pretty sure that whatever it was, it was not good for him.

As Toby's class filed through the main door, The Armpit was waiting.

"Harbinger," he said, "come with me."

Toby shuffled behind The Armpit down the corridor to where a small group of grown-ups had gathered around his locker. The Hornet was speaking softly to a fire-department guy. Mr. Neckstrom and Mr. Pzyrbovich were watching as J.D. mopped up something on the floor.

Each locker had a combination dial with a key slot in the center of the dial. The firefighters had taken a crowbar to Toby's locker rather than wait for the master key. His locker door was now badly bent and had been sprung open. In front of it, on the floor, was a pile of Toby's stuff: some random papers, a copy of *PC Gamer* magazine, an old banana that he'd forgotten about that was now a really gross banana-shaped mass of mold, some dead double-A batteries, a lone white sweat sock, and a baseball cap that Toby had been required to remove the day he wore it to school because it said BITE ME.

Included with Toby's stuff was a canister about eight inches tall made of brushed steel. Its screw-on lid was off and lying next to it.

"Toby," said The Hornet. "Is this your locker?"

"Yes," said Toby.

"A little over an hour ago," said The Hornet, "Mr. Pzyrbovich happened to be walking by and noticed that your locker was emitting some kind of smoke or gas. He sounded the alarm."

Toby looked at Mr. P, who was staring at him with an unreadable expression.

"The firefighters forced the locker open," continued The Hornet, "and found that the gas was leaking from

this." She pointed at the canister. "Toby, why was this canister in your locker?"

"I don't know," said Toby. "I never saw it before."

Mr. Neckstrom snorted.

"Really!" said Toby. "I swear I never saw it!"

"What about this?" said The Hornet. She handed Toby a piece of paper, on which was a brief printed note:

This is the plasma that will power the robot for your science project. You will get the robot and the instructions when you pay me the rest of the money. Keep the plasma in a safe place and KEEP THE CANISTER UPRIGHT OR IT WILL LEAK.

"I never saw this either," said Toby.

"Really?" said The Hornet. "It was also *locked* inside your locker."

"You didn't follow the instructions, Harbinger," sneered Mr. Neckstrom. "Your plasma leaked."

"It's *not mine*," said Toby. "I don't have a robot! I don't even have a science-fair project yet!"

"We have two serious issues here," said The Hornet. "First, we cannot have students bringing unknown substances to school. Fortunately, Chief Nichols"—she nodded toward the fire chief—"has determined that this . . . plasma is harmless."

"We don't *know* that," said Mr. Neckstrom. "Look what it did to that banana."

"That's *mold*," said Toby.

"So *you* claim," said Mr. Neckstrom. "But why should we believe somebody who cheats on his science-fair project?"

"But I didn't—"

"AND," continued Mr. Neckstrom, ignoring Toby, "tries to frame other students? *Good* students."

"But—"

The Hornet held up her hand, silencing Toby and Mr. Neckstrom. "As I was saying," she said, "the first problem we have is this plasma substance—where it came from and how it wound up in your locker. The second issue is your accusation of other students cheating on the science fair, when in fact the evidence seems to suggest that the cheater, Toby, is you."

Toby could feel his throat tightening and tears welling up in his eyes.

Don't cry. Not now.

"What I said before," he choked out, "about the Science Nook . . . that was *true*. I don't know if this," he said, indicating the canister, "has anything to do with that. But the rest of it is *true*. The stuff on that paper from the Science Nook . . . I bet that stuff is for real. I swear I didn't make it up."

"Just like you didn't know about the plasma in your locker," said Mr. Pzyrbovich.

"But I *didn't*," said Toby.

"That's enough," said The Hornet. "We'll sort this out in my office. Chief Nichols, thank you for your prompt

response. Mr. Neckstrom, Toby, come with me. Mr. Pzyrbovich, you may return to your students."

The Hornet led the way, followed by Toby, with Mr. Neckstrom behind. They passed through the outer office, where Mrs. Breetle was back at her computer, once again humming "Oops! . . . I Did It Again." The Hornet opened her office door and went inside, followed by Toby and Mr. Neckstrom.

The Hornet stopped, frowning at her desktop. She turned and went back to the doorway.

"Mrs. Breetle," she said, "did you remove a piece of paper from my desk?"

"No," said Mrs. Breetle. "I haven't been in your office at all."

The Hornet turned back to Toby and Mr. Neckstrom.

"I left that paper on my desk," she said.

They looked at the desktop, which was empty except for the letter opener.

"Somebody must have taken it," said The Hornet.

"It wasn't me," said Mr. Neckstrom. "It was here when I left for the fire drill."

The Hornet frowned, remembering. "Yes, it was," she said. "And I followed you out. Which means"—she looked at Toby—"you were the last one in here with it."

"I didn't take it," said Toby. "Why would I? I'm the one who brought it in the first place. It proved I was telling the truth about the Science Nook!"

"Perhaps," said The Hornet. "But it might also have proved you were lying."

CHAPTER SEVENTEEN

WHEN TOBY FINALLY LEFT SCHOOL—after a very unpleasant hour in The Hornet's office—he found Micah and Tamara waiting for him outside the main door.

"So?" said Tamara.

"I'm suspended," said Toby.

"Suspended?" said Micah. "From *school*?"

"No, moron, from Major League Baseball," said Toby. Shoulders slumped, he started trudging along the sidewalk, his friends walking on either side of him.

"How long?" said Tamara.

"The Hornet said three days, while she investigates," said Toby, "And then if she decides I'm guilty, I got expelled."

"Whoa," said Micah.

"Yeah," said Toby.

"But you didn't *do* anything!" said Tamara. She paused. "Did you?"

"No!" said Toby. "I don't know how that stuff got in my locker. Or that note."

"Well if you didn't put it there," said Tamara, "who did?"

"It had to be somebody with a master key to the lockers," said Toby.

"I think that's, like, a lot of people," said Tamara.

"Or somebody could have stolen a key," said Micah.

"True," said Tamara.

"So that narrows it down to . . . let's see . . . everybody in the universe," said Micah.

"I can narrow it down more than that," said Toby.

"What do you mean?" said Tamara.

"According to The Hornet," said Toby, "the person who discovered the stuff coming out of my locker was . . . guess who? Mr. P."

"Interesting," said Tamara.

"Yeah," said Toby. "Quite a coincidence, him being the one who discovered it, *and* him being around yesterday when the ME kids were dropping off their envelopes."

"So you think Mr. P put the stuff in your locker?" said Micah.

"Who else?" said Toby. "And maybe Neckstrom's in on it, too."

"But why would they do that?" said Tamara.

"I dunno," said Toby. "Maybe the ME kids are paying them, too."

"But they're *teachers*," said Tamara.

"Right," said Micah. "And teachers don't need, like, *money* or anything."

"Good point," said Tamara.

"The point," said Toby, "is *somebody* set me up, and somehow I gotta prove that to The Hornet."

"What about the paper?" said Tamara. "From the Science Nook?"

"It's gone," said Toby. "Somebody took it during the fire drill."

"Man," said Micah. "You are *dead*."

"I appreciate your support," said Toby.

"So what are you gonna do?" said Tamara.

"I'm going back to the Science Nook," said Toby.

"With the robot owl?" said Micah. "Are you *insane*?"

"That's where the proof is," said Toby.

"But what if the weird dude recognizes you?" said Tamara.

"He never saw me," said Toby.

"Yeah, but I bet he has a security camera," said Micah. "A guy who has a robot owl is gonna have cameras."

"I'll have to risk it," said Toby. "And I'll go with a distraction."

"What distraction?" said Micah.

"You," said Toby. "You're going back there, right? For the magnet for whatshisname? Your frog?"

"Fester," said Micah. "But that was before I heard about the robot death owl."

"C'mon, Micah," said Toby, "I really need to go back there."

"All right," said Micah. "But if the owl moves, I'm gonna point at you and yell, 'I'M JUST THE DISTRACTION!'"

"I appreciate your support," said Toby.

"So when are we going?" said Tamara.

"You're going, too?" said Micah.

"I can be distracting," said Tamara, batting her eyelashes.

"Is there something wrong with your eyes?" said Micah.

"Never mind," sighed Tamara.

They had reached the intersection, where, to get to their homes, Toby went right, and the other two went left. They agreed to meet at the Science Nook the next day after school, said their "see-yas," and split up.

By the time Toby got to Milkwort Court, night had fallen. He stopped at his front door and took a deep breath, bracing himself for the moment when he'd have to tell his parents about the suspension. Then he noticed that the house lights were off, and he relaxed a bit, remembering that his parents had told him they'd be at a seminar on vitamin B.

Toby opened the front door with his key and went inside. He had taken two steps into the darkened living room when he caught sight, through the archway, of a black-clad figure sitting at the dining-room table. He froze for a moment, then turned to run to the door. He froze again when he saw that his path was blocked by the massive form of the Wookiee.

"Hello, Toby," said D. Arthur Vaderian. He was talking through his electronic voice-changer again. "Please come sit down."

The Wookiee started moving forward, forcing Toby into the dining room. Toby saw that, in addition to the voice-changer, Vaderian had tucked a light saber into his belt.

He's completely out of his mind, thought Toby. *And he's in my house.*

The Wookiee pulled out a chair and pointed at it. Toby sat, his mind racing, trying to remember when his parents said they would get home.

"You know, Toby," said Vaderian, "you shouldn't leave your bedroom window unlocked. Anybody could get in." He chuckled in what he apparently thought was a Darth Vader manner. "Oh, and here's your backpack." He pointed to the backpack on the floor in the corner. "I found nothing interesting in it. Other than your address, of course." He chuckled again. He had clearly been working on the chuckle.

"What do you want?" said Toby.

"I want *brvvvrtt brrrrvvvppppp.*" The voice-changing device made a sound like a squirrel passing gas, then went silent.

"What?" said Toby.

Vaderian angrily yanked the device off his face and tossed it at the Wookiee, shouting, "I told you, *no more discount batteries!*" Without the device, Vaderian's voice was high-pitched, almost girlish. Toby could see why he wanted to change it.

Vaderian drummed his fingers on the dining-room table while the Wookiee changed the batteries in the device. When he was done, he handed it back to Vaderian,

who put it on and said, "What I want, Toby, is to know where you got the autographed BlasTech DL-44 you sold me."

"It's *real*," said Toby. "I swear I . . ."

"I know it's real," said Vaderian.

"You do?" said Toby.

"Yes," said Vaderian

"But you told me . . ."

"I know what I told you," said Vaderian. "I told you I thought the Harrison Ford autograph was a forgery. His signature is often forged, and the one on the blaster looks different from the others in my collection. But as a precaution, I e-mailed a photograph of the blaster to an autograph expert, and today I received his response. He says the signature is authentic. It looks different because Mr. Ford signed it on a curved surface, rather than on a piece of paper."

"So," said Toby, "you broke into my house to apologize and return my backpack?"

Vaderian chuckled again. It was getting on Toby's nerves.

"No, Toby," he said. "I'm here because I want to know what other items you can get me."

"What are you talking about?" said Toby.

Vaderian leaned forward. "That pistol wasn't yours, Toby. You're too young to own an item of such historic value."

"I don't get what you mean," said Toby.

"I mean that pistol belonged to a real collector, Toby,

97

and no real collector would have put such an item on eBay. Which means you stole it. That's why you didn't tell anybody when I came after you. I'm guessing that the owner doesn't know you stole it. Does he, Toby?"

"No!" said Toby. "I mean he . . ." He fell silent.

Vaderian nodded. "I thought so," he said.

"What do you want?" said Toby softly.

"I want more," said Vaderian.

"More what?" said Toby.

"You know what," said Vaderian.

"He doesn't have any more."

"You are a poor liar, Toby. Of course he has more. Only a serious collector would have had that blaster, in that condition. He has more items, and you're going to help me get them."

"No," said Toby.

"Would you prefer that I tell your father about the blaster you sold on eBay?"

Toby looked down.

"It was your father's, wasn't it?" said Vaderian.

Toby put his head in his hands.

"Show us where the collection is," said Vaderian, "or I call your father, anonymously, and tell him about your little eBay business."

"No," groaned Toby.

"Then tell us," said Vaderian. "It's in the house, isn't it? We noticed the basement was locked."

"It's my parents' business," Toby said. "They keep the stock down there."

Vaderian was about to say something when car head-lights shone through the living-room window, and a car pulled into the driveway.

Vaderian rose quickly. "I will be in touch with you soon," he said. "I will tell you where and when you will meet me with something else from the collection. Something valuable. If you don't cooperate, I *will* call your father." He drew the light saber from his belt and, in his most Vaderesque voice, said, "Do not disappoint me, young Toby."

With a flourish, he pressed a switch on the light saber. Nothing happened.

Vaderian whirled toward the Wookiee.

"No more discount batteries," he hissed.

There were footsteps at the door. Vaderian, followed by the Wookiee, hurried down the hallway to the bedrooms. As they disappeared, the front door opened, and Toby's parents entered. Toby's mom was first, followed by his dad, who looked the way Luke Skywalker would have if he got older and lost his hair and had that pasty, unhealthy appearance that comes from years of eating health food.

"Toby?" said his mom. She switched on the light and saw him sitting at the dining-room table. "What are you doing sitting there in the dark?"

"Nothing," said Toby.

There was a *clunk* as the window in Toby's room closed.

"What was that?" said his dad.

"Nothing!" said Toby, leaping up.

"Are you all right?" said his mom.

"Yes," said Toby. "No," he added.

"Toby," said his dad, "what's going on? Is there someone in your room?"

"No!" said Toby.

"Are you sure?" said his dad, moving toward the hallway. "Because I definitely heard . . ."

"I got suspended from school," said Toby.

"*What?*" said both of his parents.

"It's a mistake," said Toby. "I didn't do it."

"Didn't do what?" said his dad.

"Put the stuff in my locker."

"Stuff in your locker?" said his dad.

"Drugs?" said his mom. *"Are you doing drugs?!"*

"I'm not . . ."

"It's those video games he plays," said his father. "That's where this started."

"But it isn't . . ."

"What kind of drugs was it?" said his mom. "Was it pot? Ohmigod, was it *crack?*"

"*Crack?* Mom, no!" said Toby.

"So it *was* pot," she said.

"I didn't mean that!" said Toby.

"It was STP, wasn't it?" said his dad. "It's showing up in middle schools. I heard about this on NPR."

"You mean Ecstasy," said Toby.

"Ohmigod," said his mom, putting her hands over her mouth. "Ecstasy. Ohmigod."

"No, no, no!" said Toby. "I'm just saying that's the *name.* I'm not saying I'm *doing* it."

"Then what was it doing in your locker?" said his dad.

"It wasn't . . ."

"Who gave it to you?" said his mom.

"Nobody!" said Toby.

"Then how did you get it?" said his dad.

"You hear about this happening," said his mom, breaking down sobbing. "But you never think it's going to happen to you."

"It's okay, Fawn," said his dad, putting his arms around her. "We'll get him help. And we'll get rid of those video games."

"Listen!" said Toby. "Will you just please LISTEN for a minute?"

His parents, arms around each other, looked at him.

"First," said Toby, "there were no drugs in my locker, okay? No drugs."

"Then why did you just say there were?" said his mom.

"I DIDN'T SAY THERE WERE!" said Toby.

"Don't you shout at your mother!" said his dad.

Toby took a deep breath. "Okay, I'm sorry I shouted. I'm just trying to explain that they *didn't find any drugs in my locker*. They found some green stuff. Some kind of chemical or something. They think I put it there, but I didn't."

"Then who did?" said his dad.

Toby considered telling his parents his suspicions about Mr. P, but he decided that, for the time being, he would rather not have his parents charging into the school and trying to help him but basically just being weird while accomplishing nothing or managing to make things worse.

"I dunno," he said. "But whoever it was left a note, supposedly written to me, that makes it look like the green stuff was part of a science-fair project that I'm supposedly buying. They're making it look like I'm cheating."

"Are you?" said his dad.

"No! Of *course* I'm not!" said Toby.

"Then why are you suspended from school?" said his dad.

"It's just for three days," said Toby. "While The Hornet investigates."

"The who?" said his dad.

"Principal Plotz-Gornett," said Toby. "I'm sure she'll find out I'm innocent." He also decided not to tell his parents about his plan to go back to the Science Nook for proof that the ME kids were cheating.

"I think we need to speak to the principal," said his mom.

"No!" said Toby. "Please! I'm sure it'll be fine. It's just three days."

His parents looked at each other.

"Go to the kitchen and set the table while we discuss this," said his dad.

They called him out a few minutes later. His dad said, "Your mother and I have decided that you're going to be grounded during the suspension."

"Grounded?" said Toby. "Why?"

"If you're not at school, we want you here, studying," said his dad.

"What about after school?"

"You're still grounded," said his mom.

"But I didn't *do* anything!" said Toby.

"Watch your tone, young man," said his mom.

"And no video games," said his dad.

Toby argued some more, but it was no use. Once his parents had made a decision, they stuck to it, no matter how irrational it was. Toby was grounded.

They ate dinner (tofu foo yong) in silence. Toby spent most of the meal trying to figure out how, if he was grounded, he was going to get to the Science Nook. When dinner was over, he trudged to his bedroom. When he turned on the light, he saw dirty footprints on the bedspread next to the window—a reminder that, in addition to being suspended and in danger of being expelled, he was being stalked by a lunatic with a large, hairy assistant. He went to bed but spent the next hour and a half squirming restlessly, unable to stop his brain from thinking about his problems. But his thinking did no good: he came up with no answers.

The only consolation—and the last thought he had before he finally fell asleep—was this: *at least it can't get any worse.*

Chapter Eighteen

It took **Drmtsi and Vrsk** three days to travel from Krpshtskan to Washington, D.C.

They prepared for the journey in traditional Krpshtskani fashion by stuffing their pants legs with smerk, a very strong cheese that could be used as either food or wolf repellent. For money, they had four bills issued by the Krpshtskani treasury, each in the amount of one million purds. The purd was the official currency unit of Krpshtskan; one million purds, at the current exchange rate, was equal to about six dollars. As a backup, they also had some gold coins in a leather pouch.

With their preparations complete, Drmtsi and Vrsk set off by oxcart for Grdankl the Strong International Airport.

This was a weedy dirt strip next to a small, rundown wooden terminal building. On the side of the terminal was a sign in Krpsht that translated roughly to:

AIR KRPSHTSKAN
"IT IS GOING UP, THEN IT IS COMING DOWN IN DIFFERENT PLACE"

Parked next to the terminal was the Air Krpshtskan fleet, which consisted of a lone Russian-made World War II—era cargo plane. A goat was chewing on the tail. Drmtsi and Vrsk found the Air Krpshtskan pilot asleep in the cockpit, surrounded by the littered remains of several meals. Drmtsi shook the pilot awake and ordered him to fly them to the neighboring nation of Fazul, which had a larger airport. The pilot shooed the goat away and managed to get both of the engines started. He gestured for Vrsk to sit on the floor behind him. Drmtsi, fourth vice president of Krpshtskan, sat on a folding chair, which represented business class.

The pilot taxied the plane to the end of the rutted runway and then, after offering a brief prayer, advanced both throttles to full. The engines belched black smoke, and the plane lurched forward, causing the business-class chair to collapse, and sending Drmtsi tumbling backward. The plane gained speed, rattling violently. Vrsk got on his knees to look out the plane's windshield and saw they were rapidly approaching the end of the runway, beyond which was a wooden fence. The pilot, shouting another prayer, pulled back on the yoke. Slowly, the nose of the plane

began to rise. They were taking off! The pilot turned, smiling hugely, and gave his passengers a thumbs-up gesture.
At that moment there was a loud explosion, and something
fell off the right-hand engine. The pilot struggled with the
controls as the plane came back down, went off the end of
the runway, and plowed through a fence, plunging into a
field. It bounced along violently for a hundred yards,
finally shuddering to a stop. With a shrieking sound of
tearing metal, the right engine detached completely from
the wing and fell to the ground with a *whump*. A goat wandered over to the plane and began chewing on the tail.

The pilot turned to look at his passengers, who were
now both on the floor, their faces white.

"We are having slight mechanical delay," he announced.

With the Air Krpshtskan leg of their journey over,
Drmtsi and Vrsk traveled the rest of the way to Fazul by
oxcart. In Fazul they used some of their gold to purchase
tickets on Air Fazul (motto: "Very Reliable. Sometimes.")
to the Republic of Zerkistan. From there they flew Air
Zerkistan (motto: "At Least It Is Safer Than Air Fazul.") to
Paris. The flight lasted eight hours, during which they
were given nothing to eat except one stick, apiece, of Air
Zerkistan chewing gum. Drmtsi attempted to eat his, but it
was so hard that he cracked a tooth. Vrsk put his stick in
his pocket for later.

In Paris, Drmtsi and Vrsk were required, for the first
time, to produce passports. Solemnly, they handed their
documents to the French immigration official. These
were not actually passports: Krpshtskan did not produce

passports. Before they left, Drmtsi and Vrsk had gone into the government files and grabbed two official-looking pieces of paper. Drmtsi's was a 1937 wedding license. Vrsk's was a 1993 bill, unpaid, from a plumber who had unclogged the presidential palace toilet.

The French official frowned at these documents, then said something in French. Neither Drmtsi nor Vrsk spoke French. Vrsk, who had learned some English from the Internet, said, "Can you say in English, please?"

The French official sighed. "These passports," he said, "do not have pictures."

Vrsk translated this to Drmtsi, who replied, in Krpshtskani, "Why does he need pictures? We are standing in front of him! He can see us! Tell him he is stupid moron idiot with brain of salamander."

Vrsk translated this as: "Our country is very poor. We have no camera for picture."

"What is the purpose of your trip?" said the French official.

Vrsk translated this to Drmtsi, who replied, "Tell him we are on important secret mission that is none of his business."

Vrsk translated this as: "We are tourists."

The French official frowned at the documents some more, then said, "Your final destination is the United States?"

Vrsk translated this to Drmtsi, who said, "Tell stupid moron idiot if he asks any more stupid questions I feed his tiny idiot brain to pigs."

Vrsk translated this as: "Yes."

The French official frowned at the documents some more, looked at the growing line behind Drmtsi and Vrsk, sighed, then waved them through for the Americans to deal with.

Eleven hours later, Drmtsi and Vrsk, tired and hungry and smelling strongly of smerk, arrived at Dulles Airport outside of Washington. They shuffled along in a long line of people waiting to pass through immigration. When they reached the front, the immigration agent took one look at their documents and called for his supervisor. His supervisor, a woman named Wanda Lefkon, took them to a holding room for questioning.

"So, Mr. . . . Vrsk is it?" she said, frowning at Vrsk's plumbing bill.

"Yes, Vrsk," said Vrsk. "And this is Fourth Vice President Drmtsi. He is brother of Grdankl the Strong, president of Krpshtskan. He is very important man."

Lefkon looked at Drmtsi.

"Halle Berry," said Drmtsi, this being one of the very few things he could say in English.

"Excuse me?" said Lefkon.

"He is big fan," Vrsk said. "She is from here, yes? Halle Berry?"

"Yes," said Lefkon. "Now . . ."

"Catwoman," said Drmtsi.

"Right," said Lefkon. She rubbed her temples. "And you came from Kpr . . . Krt . . ."

"Krpshtskan," said Vrsk.

"Right, you came from there to here for what purpose?"

"Touristism," said Vrsk. "We are tourists."

"I see," said Lefkon. "And are there any particular sights you're planning to see?"

Vrsk thought about this. "No," he said.

Lefkon rubbed her temples again. The small room was starting to fill with an unpleasant aroma. As she watched in horror, Drmtsi reached into his pants and pulled out a greenish blob that smelled like a full Dumpster on a hot day. He thrust this toward Lefkon.

"Smerk?" he said.

"Is tradition," said Vrsk.

"No, thank you," said Lefkon. "Please wait here."

Lefkon spent the next several hours on the phone with officials at the State Department, the CIA, the FBI, and the Department of Homeland Security. Eventually it was determined that Drmtsi was, in fact, the fourth vice president of Krpshtskan, and that he and Vrsk would be admitted to the United States as diplomats. But it was also agreed that, because so little was known about Krpshtskan, and because the two men were so vague about the purpose of their visit, their activities would be closely monitored.

It was late afternoon when Drmtsi and Vrsk left the airport. They went to the taxi line, waited their turn, and got into a cab. The driver got one whiff of his passengers and immediately rolled down all four windows.

"We go to Hubble Middle School, please," said Vrsk.

"Where's that?" said the driver.

"Is near to Washington," said Vrsk.

"A lot of things are near Washington," said the driver.

"Yes," said Vrsk, "but we only want to go to Hubble Middle School."

The driver sighed, then radioed his dispatcher, who looked up the school and told the driver the address. The driver wrote it down, then said to Vrsk: "That's Maryland. You got money for the fare?"

"Yes," said Vrsk. He showed the driver one of the one-million-purd bills. It featured a picture of Grdankl the Strong wearing a traditional Krpshtskani fur headpiece. He looked like a man whose scalp was being attacked by a raccoon.

"What kind of money is this?" said the taxi driver.

"Is purds," said Vrsk.

"Purds?" said the driver.

"Purds," said Vrsk.

"I don't take purds," said the driver.

"What about gold?" said Vrsk, showing the driver a coin.

"Gold is good," said the driver.

"Halle Berry," said Drmtsi, to be part of the conversation.

"She's good, too," said the driver. With that, he put the taxi into gear and eased away from the curb. Traffic was heavy; it was rush hour. Neither the taxi driver nor his two tired passengers paid any attention to the white government-issue Ford sedan that began moving when the taxi did and was now following about one hundred feet behind.

CHAPTER NINETEEN

DANIELLE PRESCOTT MARCHED PAST the secretary into the large, modern office of her husband, Tim, and took a seat without asking if she was interrupting. Which, in fact, she was: Tim was on a conference call with some men in Taiwan who were about to pay Tim's company, PresTech Industries, fifty-three million dollars to build a surveillance satellite that could count the dimples on a golf ball from space. Although that probably wasn't what they planned to do with it.

"Excuse me for a moment, gentlemen," Tim said into the phone. He pressed the MUTE button. "Dani, you can't just . . ."

"Where's the thingie?" she said.

"The thingie?"

"The whaddyacallit," Danielle explained. "The computer thingie. For Harmonee's project."

Tim quickly rose from his desk, crossed the office, and closed the door.

"Dani," he said, "this is not something we should be discussing here."

"Yes, it is," she said. "Harmonee needs the thingie tomorrow."

"Yes, and I will—"

"So I thought I'd just pick it up now, since you might forget." Danielle checked her diamond-encrusted watch. "I have a nail appointment in fifteen minutes."

"This is . . . a delicate situation," said Tim. "It's not exactly"—he lowered his voice—"legal."

"This is the *science fair*," said Danielle, raising her voice. "Do you care about your daughter's education at *all*?"

"Of course I do."

"Well, I hope so." Danielle checked her watch. "Thirteen minutes." She drummed her flawless nails on her husband's desk. Tim wondered why nails that perfect needed a manicure, but he was way too smart to ask.

He looked at the phone, its light blinking to indicate that the fifty-three-million-dollar customers were waiting. He cleared his throat and said, "I'll meet you at the loading dock in ten minutes. Have the trunk open."

Danielle smiled a flawless smile. "You're *such* a good father, Timmy," she said. "Have I told you that?"

* * *

Carl Niles lugged the heavy aluminum case into the spacious, spotless, and fabulously ultramodern Niles kitchen, where his wife, Jeanette, and son Jason were eating food from Burger King. Jason was watching his video iPod. Carl set the case down gently on the floor. He tapped Jason's shoulder to indicate that he wanted to talk. Reluctantly, Jason removed one of his earbuds.

"What?" he said.

Carl pointed at the case. "Be very, very careful with this," he said.

"Yeah, whatever," said Jason, starting to put the earbud back in.

Carl gripped his son's shoulder. "I'm *serious*," he said.

"Ouch," said Jason.

"Carl, you're hurting him!" said Jeanette.

Carl let go, took a calming breath. "Okay," he said. "But he needs to understand that this"—he gestured toward the case—"is an extremely sophisticated piece of technology. If anybody found out it was in civilian hands . . ."

"I'm sure Jason will be very careful," said Jeanette, scraping the breading off a chicken nugget. "Won't you, dear?"

"Sure," said Jason.

"And above all," said Carl, "tell the . . . tell your guy to follow the power-supply specifications. This is very important, all right? If he exceeds them, this thing could . . . It would be very bad. You understand, Jason?"

"Yeah," said Jason.

"Then tell me what I just said," said Carl.

"You said he shouldn't exceed . . . something."

"The power-supply specifications!" said Carl, gripping Jason's shoulder again. "This is *very important*."

"Ouch," said Jason.

"Carl, stop hurting him!" said Jeanette. "I'm sure it will be fine. Jason will tell the science coach what you said. Won't you, Jason?"

"Yeah," said Jason, reinserting the earbud, his eyes on the iPod screen.

Carl looked at his son for a moment, then at the metal case, then at his wife.

"I need a drink," he said.

CHAPTER TWENTY

DRMTSI AND VRSK STARED OUT through the taxi windows at America, their mouths wide open like groupers. Everything they saw astonished them, starting with the sheer number of cars—more cars on just this street than there were in all of Krpshtskan. And these were *new* cars, cars that actually worked, driving at amazing speeds on smooth roads as wide as the Krpshtskani presidential palace.

The taxi whizzed past forests of fantastic buildings, new and clean and spectacularly high, some of them looking as though they were made entirely of glass. And then there were fields of houses, *big* houses; Drmtsi and Vrsk assumed that houses this grand must be occupied by the

rulers of America. But there were so *many* of them, and every one had a car out front. Sometimes *two* cars. Just *sitting* there. The houses were surrounded by grass, big swaths of it, green and lush. Drmtsi and Vrsk saw no livestock; they assumed that the cows and goats were kept inside the houses, let out to eat the grass at night. Much different than the Krpsht system.

Drmtsi turned to Vrsk, and, speaking Krpsht, said, "Is large country."

"Yes," replied Vrsk, also in Krpsht. He was thinking, *Maybe it is not such a good idea to attack this country.*

"Where are you from?" said the taxi driver.

"Krpshtskan," said Vrsk.

"Gesundheit," said the driver.

"What?" said Vrsk.

"Gesundheit," said the driver. "It's a joke."

"Ah," said Vrsk. "Ha-ha. Thank you." He did not actually understand the joke. But in Krpshtskan, where people had little else to give each other, a joke was considered sort of a present. If somebody told you one, good manners required that you tell one in return. Vrsk frowned, trying to think of a Krpshtskani joke he could translate into English. Finally, he settled on one that was popular with Krpshtskani children. He said to the driver, "How are you keeping chicken out of toilet?"

"What?" said the driver.

"How," Vrsk repeated slowly, "are you keeping chicken out of toilet?"

"You need a toilet?" said the driver.

"No, no," said Vrsk. "*Chicken* is trying to get into toilet."

"Chicken?" said the driver.

"Yes," said Vrsk. "Chicken."

"*What* chicken?" said the driver.

"Is not real chicken," Vrsk assured him.

The driver eyed Vrsk in the rearview mirror.

Drmtsi said to Vrsk, in Krpsht, "What are you saying to him?"

"I am telling him joke about chicken and toilet," said Vrsk.

"Ha! Good one!" said Drmtsi, roaring with laughter and pounding his thighs hard enough to send powerful puffs of smerk smell billowing through the taxi.

"Is there a problem back there?" said the driver.

"No problem," said Vrsk. "Is joke."

"You think it's funny, stinking up my cab?" said the driver.

"Ah," said Vrsk. "Is not stink. Is smerk."

Recognizing the word, Drmtsi reached into his pants and held a reeking green glob out toward the driver.

"Smerk?" he said.

"Get that *away* from me!" said the driver, almost swerving off the road.

"He says he is not hungry," Vrsk said to Drmtsi.

They rode the rest of the way in silence, the driver darting suspicious glances at his aromatic passengers in the rearview mirror. By the time they pulled into the Hubble Middle School driveway, dusk had fallen. The taxi stopped in front of the enormous, two-story brick building, which

appeared deserted. Drmtsi and Vrsk got out and gave the driver a gold coin. He grunted—he was pretty sure the coin was worth far more than the fare—and drove away, keeping all the windows open to rid the taxi of smerk stench.

Drmtsi and Vrsk approached the school's large, glass front doors. They pushed and pulled on the handles; the doors were locked. They pounded on them and waited; nothing happened. They pressed their faces against the glass and peered into the dark corridor. They saw nobody.

Drmtsi and Vrsk looked at each other. They hadn't given much thought to what they would do when they got here. They'd just assumed that they would find Prmkt. But there was no Prmkt here, and it was dark, and they were both very tired and very hungry. Drmtsi frowned. As fourth vice president, he knew it was his responsibility to come up with a plan.

"Perhaps," said Vrsk, "we should find a place to sleep and come back to school in morning."

"Quiet," said Drmtsi. "I am thinking of a plan."

"Sorry," said Vrsk.

Drmtsi frowned some more. It was hard work. After a minute he said, "I have a plan."

"Yes?" said Vrsk.

"Right now," said Drmtsi, "we find a place to sleep."

"Ah," said Vrsk.

"Tomorrow," said Drmtsi, "we come back here and look for Prmkt."

Vrsk nodded. "It is a good plan," he said.

"Yes," said Drmtsi. "Follow me."

With Fourth Vice President Drmtsi in the lead, the two Krpshtskani agents began walking along the school driveway. When they reached the street, they turned right, toward the business district.

They did not notice the white Ford sedan creeping along the street about fifty feet behind them.

The two occupants of the Ford—both wearing starched white shirts and dark suits—were not thrilled to have pulled this duty. They'd followed the cab from the airport into the suburbs, only to realize—as the two targets started *walking*—that it was going to be a long night.

With all their attention on the two in front of them, they did not notice the man following them—a man who had emerged from Hubble Middle School a minute behind Drmtsi and Vrsk. A man keeping an eye on the Ford as well as the two men the Ford was following.

A man with a plan of his own.

CHAPTER TWENTY-ONE

FOR THE HUNDREDTH TIME on this endless day, Toby looked at his watch. Six-thirty p.m. *Finally.* He was meeting with Micah and Tamara at the mall at seven p.m. Time to put his escape plan in motion.

Toby took a deep breath and blew a final lungful into the full-scale Luke Skywalker blow-up doll that was a central part of his parents' cherished memorabilia collection. He closed off the valve and pulled up the bedcovers so that when the room lights were off it would look as if he were asleep—as long as nobody looked too closely. Next, he slipped his iPod's extension speaker inside the pillowcase right next to Luke's head. The speaker was connected to his laptop computer over on his desk via a concealed wire. Finally, he tested the small wireless

microphone taped above the door by speaking into it.

"Testing . . . one, two . . ."

A small light blinked on the computer, confirming that it was receiving the microphone's signal.

Hope this works, Toby thought.

He went out to the living room, where his parents were watching an infomercial for gluten-free pasta products.

"I'm going to bed," he announced.

"Now?" said his dad.

"Is something wrong?" asked his mom.

This was the tricky part. Toby, who normally fought to stay up past the eleven o'clock news, had to convince his parents that he wasn't feeling well. He had to sound tired enough to go to bed but not so sick that they would try to force him to take some of their natural remedies. Toby still had nightmares about the time they'd decided that the best treatment for his sore throat was a mustard enema.

"No, I'm cool," he said. "Just kind of tired is all."

His mom's eyes brightened. He could hear it coming. . . .

"I have a wonderful avocado-smoothie recipe. The ginseng helps to promote—"

"No, thanks! Really, Mom, I'm okay. Just tired." Toby yawned a big fake yawn. "So, g'night then."

"Good night," said his dad, glued to the television.

But his mom looked concerned. Toby knew that look: she would check on him later.

Which was why he'd rigged his bed.

He returned to his room. He double-checked that the microphone was still picking up a signal and that the

shareware voice-recognition program was up and running. He decided he'd done all that he could.

Then, after listening at the door to make sure his parents weren't coming down the hall, he turned off the lights, quietly raised the window, and climbed out, pulling the curtains closed before sliding the window shut. Hunching down low and crawling below the living-room window, he skirted around the house to the street and started trotting toward the mall.

A few minutes passed. As Toby had anticipated, his mother had to check up on him. She went to his bedroom door and tapped lightly. There was no answer, so she opened the door a crack. The room was dark.

"Toby?" she said softly.

"I'm trying to sleep," said Toby's voice, coming from the speaker under the pillowcase. Toby had recorded this and other phrases on his computer, which now played back his own voice in response to his mom's voice triggering the wireless microphone. He'd programmed the software, downloaded from the Internet, to listen for certain key words and phrases. He pretty much knew what his mother would say to him.

"Are you all right?" asked Toby's mom.

Toby had expected this question. The computer had no trouble with how to answer.

"I'm fine," said Toby's recorded voice on the computer. It added, "I'm trying to sleep."

"Are you hungry?" said Toby's mom.

The computer recognized "hungry." There was a moment's hesitation as the program found Toby's recorded answer and played it.

"No thanks," said the computer.

"I could make you some herbal tea," said Toby's mom.

The program did not recognize any of the key words in this phrase. There was a longer hesitation this time. Then it played the default response that he'd recorded just for this situation: "I just want to sleep, okay?"

"I know, but herbal tea is relaxing," said Toby's mom.

"I just want to sleep, okay?"

"I *know* that," said Toby's mom. "I'm trying to help."

"I just want to sleep, okay?"

"You don't need to take that tone with me, young man," said Toby's mom.

"I just want to sleep, okay?"

"Well *fine*, then," said his mom. "Good night." She closed the door with a bit of a thump.

The computer hesitated for a second, then said "Good night," to the door.

Chapter Twenty-two

Drmtsi and Vrsk were turned away by three chain hotels that did not take either purds or gold. Finally they found an old motel called the Shady Inn Motor Court, whose owner, a coin collector, quickly agreed to give them a room for three nights in exchange for just one of their coins.

He was definitely getting the better of the bargain. The room he assigned to Drmtsi and Vrsk was seedy and drafty, with an ancient heater/air conditioner that clattered like a clothes dryer filled with rocks. The wallpaper was peeling; the carpet was worn; the toilet ran constantly; and the bedspreads appeared to have been laundered in radioactive waste.

Drmtsi and Vrsk thought it was fabulous. They had

never known such luxury. Not only did the room contain two beds—*two beds!*—but it also had electric lights, a working telephone, and—most amazing of all—a color television. It took Vrsk a while to figure out how to operate the remote control, but once he did, he and Drmtsi could not take their eyes off the TV screen.

In Krpshtskan there was only one station, which broadcast speeches by Grdankl the Strong alternating with long periods of static (the static was more popular). But the TV in the Shady Inn Motor Court had dozens and dozens of channels, showing every kind of program—including drama, comedy, news, sports, weather, cartoons, people talking, people exercising, people shouting at each other, and a courtroom show in which people were tongue-lashed by an angry lady judge, who frankly terrified Drmtsi and Vrsk.

They were sitting on their beds watching this show, when the telephone rang. They looked at each other. Drmtsi nodded toward the phone. Vrsk picked it up.

"Hello," he said in English.

"Let me speak to Drmtsi," said a voice in Krpsht.

"Who is this?" said Vrsk, switching to Krpsht.

"Prmkt," said the voice.

Vrsk handed the phone to Drmtsi. "It is Prmkt," he said.

"Where are you?" barked Drmtsi into the phone.

"I am . . . nearby," said Prmkt. "What are you doing here?"

"We are watching the television," said Drmtsi. "The

angry-woman-judge show. Have you seen it?"

"No," said Prmkt, "I mean, what are you doing in America?"

"We are here to help you destroy the American government," said Drmtsi.

"I don't need your help," said Prmkt.

"Yes, you do," said Drmtsi. "You sent a message asking for help, so we come here to help. I will, of course, take charge. These are orders from Grdankl the Strong."

There was a sigh, then a silence. Then Prmkt said, "All right."

"Good," said Drmtsi. "Now, first thing we must do is . . ." He paused, because that was as far as his thinking would take him. Besides, the lady judge was shouting again.

"Perhaps we should meet," said Prmkt.

"Yes," Drmtsi said decisively. "We will meet. These are orders from Grdankl the Strong."

There was another pause, then Prmkt said, "Would you like me to find a safe place for meeting?"

"Yes," decided Drmtsi. "You will find a place for meeting. These are orders—"

Prmkt interrupted. "Yes, *sir*. I will call again in morning."

"I suggest you call me back in the morning," said Drmtsi, peering over at Vrsk. He grunted into the phone, hung up, and looked back at the TV. The scary woman judge was now snarling at an unhappy-looking man. Drmtsi turned to Vrsk, who was watching intently, remote control in hand.

"Change the channel," ordered Drmtsi, a man in charge.

Chapter Twenty-three

As Toby arrived at the mall, Micah and Tamara were already waiting for him by the main entrance.

"Did you bring your laptop?" Toby asked Micah.

Micah indicated his backpack. "Right here," he said.

"Good," said Toby. He wrinkled his nose. "What's that smell?"

"It's her," said Micah, pointing at Tamara. "She put perfume on so she could be a distraction."

"It's called Fruit of Passion," said Tamara, leaning forward. "Like it?"

Toby recoiled from the wave of powerful aroma.

"How much did you put on?" he said.

"Just half a bottle," said Tamara.

"You smell like you took a bath in Hawaiian Punch," said Micah.

"Thank you," said Tamara, batting her eyelashes.

"Okay, listen," said Toby impatiently. "When we get to the Science Nook, you guys need to distract the weird guy, so I can figure out where to put this." He reached into his jacket pocket and pulled out a cantaloupe.

"That's a cantaloupe," observed Tamara.

"My parents didn't have any eggplants," said Toby.

"I see," said Tamara.

"You do?" said Micah.

"No," said Tamara.

Toby sighed. "I cut it in half, hollowed it out and put the webcam inside, and glued it back together," he said. He showed them the camera lens peeking out one side of the cantaloupe. "I figure with all the other junk in the Science Nook, he won't notice this."

"It just might work!" said Tamara.

"You really think so?" said Toby.

"No," said Tamara.

"Well, it's the best I could do," said Toby. "Come on."

The three friends rode the escalator up to the highest mall concourse and walked to near the end. The Science Nook was open; they walked inside. Toby, in front, looked warily over to his left, where the robot owl sat motionless on its perch. Suddenly, Toby heard a humming noise to his right. He jumped backward, along with Tamara and Micah, as a canister vacuum cleaner zipped past them. It went to a corner of the store, extended its hose, and began rapidly

darting this way and that, vacuuming the random Science Nook clutter.

"Who's operating that thing?" said Micah.

"I dunno," said Toby. There was no one in sight. The door to the back room was closed.

"Hello?" Toby called toward the door. "Is anybody here?"

Immediately, the vacuum zipped over to them. It raised its hose and pointed its nozzle at Toby, as if studying him. It looked like a snake about to strike.

"I think we should go," whispered Micah.

"It's just a vacuum cleaner," whispered Tamara.

"Yeah," whispered Micah. "The vacuum cleaner from *The Exorcist.*"

The hose darted over to Micah, who made a small squeaking noise and took a step back. He was getting ready to sprint when the nozzle spoke to him. It spoke in Sternabite's voice, loud and clear.

"Frog Boy," it said.

Micah stopped, frozen.

"You need an electromagnet and a major power supply for the science fair," said the nozzle. "Correct?"

Micah remained frozen.

"Say yes," hissed Tamara. Instantly the nozzle darted in front of her. It moved close to her neck, then said, "Are you wearing Hawaiian Punch?"

"Fruit of Passion," said Tamara.

"I like it," said the nozzle. It zipped back to Micah and said, "Did you bring the money?"

"Y . . . yes," said Micah, finally finding his voice.

"Wait here," said the nozzle. The vacuum cleaner zipped toward the door behind the counter, opened it with its nozzle, and went through into the back room. A moment later Sternabite emerged, wearing sunglasses, as usual. He was carrying two cardboard boxes, which he set on the counter. He looked at Toby for a moment, then turned to Micah.

"Forty dollars," he said.

Micah dug into his pocket and handed Sternabite the money.

"The money is for the electromagnet," said Sternabite, pointing to one of the boxes. "The trouble is, it draws a huge amount of power. You'll blow every breaker in the school. So I'm lending you the cold-fusion power supply." He reached into the other box and pulled out what looked sort of like a miniature Slurpee machine.

"Come here so I can show you how it works," said Sternabite.

Reluctantly, Micah approached the counter. Toby caught Tamara's eye and nodded his head toward Sternabite, mouthing the word "distraction." Tamara followed Toby over and stood near Sternabite, who was demonstrating the reactor to Micah.

"It's pretty basic," he was saying. "The power source is this plug. You'll connect your magnet here, once it's up and running. To power it up, you flip this switch, and then watch this temperature gauge until the electrolyte reaches eighty-three degrees. You with me so far?"

Micah nodded and said, "Eighty-three degrees."

"This is *fascinating*," Tamara said to Sternabite, batting her eyelashes.

"Is there something wrong with your eyes?" he said.

"No," sighed Tamara.

"All right," said Sternabite, turning back to Micah. "When it's at eighty-three degrees, you turn this knob to— I'm gonna say—ten percent, to start the reaction. Then you watch your voltage meter, here on this readout. Still with me?"

"Ten percent," said Micah.

"Okay," said Sternabite. "Pay attention, because this is where it can get tricky." As Sternabite continued to give Micah instructions for operating the reactor, Toby edged behind his back and looked around for a place to put his cantaloupe. He settled on a cluttered shelf behind the counter, where there was an opening between an accordion and what looked like either a clump of moss or a very old sandwich. Toby tiptoed over, keeping an eye on Sternabite, and set the cantaloupe on the shelf, with the lens pointing outward. From there the camera would take in most of what happened in the store, and the microphone would pick up whatever was said in the vicinity of the counter. Toby edged away from the cantaloupe.

"Whatever you do," Sternabite was saying, "don't let this meter read higher than forty thousand. Dial it back closer to five percent if you see it approaching forty K."

"What happens if it goes past forty?" said Tamara.

Sternabite aimed his dark glasses at her.

"Have you ever seen lightning strike?" he asked.

"Yes," she said.

"*Inside* a gymnasium?" he said.

"Oh," she said.

Sternabite turned back to Micah. "Okay," he said. "Take this stuff and get out. I have other customers coming." He put the reactor back into its Slurpee box. "And make sure you bring this back after the science fair."

"Okay," said Micah. Then he frowned and said, "Can I ask you a question?"

"What?" said Sternabite impatiently.

"How come you're letting me use this thing for free?"

Sternabite stared at him for a long moment. Then he said, "Two reasons. Mainly, I think it's high time there was some real competition in the science fair."

"You mean for the ME kids," said Tamara.

"Exactly," said Sternabite.

"But don't you *help* them?" said Toby. Sternabite turned toward him. Several seconds passed. Toby worried that he'd gone too far.

Finally Sternabite spoke. "Maybe I do," he said. "But that doesn't mean I'm on their side."

"What's the other reason?" said Micah.

Sternabite turned back to Micah. "This will serve as an excellent field test for the reactor."

"Test?" said Micah.

"Field test," said Sternabite.

"So you're saying it's never actually been tested?" said Micah.

Sternabite studied Micah for a moment.

"Just do what I told you, Frog Boy," he said, "and you'll be fine."

Micah started to say something, but Tamara, looking out into the mall concourse, interrupted. "The ME kids are coming," she said.

"Let's go," said Toby. "Come on, Micah." He handed Micah one of the boxes and grabbed the other.

"But . . ." said Micah.

"Come *on*," said Toby, dragging Micah out of the store after Tamara. They turned right on the concourse, heading away from the approaching ME kids. Toby glanced back into the Science Nook to make sure the webcam cantaloupe was still in position. Sternabite was facing him, his eyes unreadable behind his dark glasses.

Toby quickly turned away and followed his friends.

Chapter Twenty-four

DRMTSI AND VRSK LOVED all the TV channels at the Shady Inn Motor Court, except for the one with the scary judge lady. But their favorite channel, the one they kept returning to, was the shopping network. Such excellent merchandise! Such friendly hosts! It was as if they were talking to Drmtsi and Vrsk personally, wanting so much to make their lives better by giving them an opportunity to own these wonderful products.

No matter what the friendly hosts were selling—exercise equipment, jewelry, clothing, cookware, home beekeeping equipment—Drmtsi and Vrsk found that they wanted to buy it. Drmtsi was especially smitten with a smiling blond woman who was selling a cappuccino machine for only $489, which you could pay for in three

convenient installments. After watching her explain the benefits of this machine for twenty minutes, with Vrsk translating, Drmtsi could contain himself no longer. He ordered Vrsk to call the toll-free number.

Vrsk called. A nice lady told him that the shopping network did not take purds or gold; only credit cards. Vrsk said he did not have a credit card. The nice lady said this was not a problem; she'd be happy to take an application for the official shopping-network credit card. In half an hour, both Drmtsi and Vrsk had been approved. The cards would not arrive for a day or so, but they would be given special account numbers that they could use right now. They could begin shopping immediately!

Drmtsi and Vrsk could hardly believe it. Such a generous country! So trusting! Drmtsi returned his attention to the smiling blond woman on the TV screen. Vrsk translated what she was saying: the cappuccino machine had been reduced to just $419! An amazing price, according to the smiling woman. But there were only a few left! Drmtsi ordered Vrsk to buy one—no, *two*—cappuccino machines. Vrsk picked up the phone again, and in minutes the order was placed. They paid extra to have the machines delivered to the Shady Inn Motor Court by overnight delivery. It was $80 more, but Drmtsi decided it was worth it.

Vrsk hung up the phone and gave Drmtsi the good news. They shared a smile of accomplishment. The mission was going well. Two cappuccino machines! Neither Drmtsi or Vrsk knew what cappuccino was, but they were sure it was a good thing.

They turned back to the TV. The smiling blond woman had been replaced by two new hosts who were selling a large, miracle rubber ball that could be used for many purposes, including toning the thighs. It was only $49.95! Drmtsi leaned forward with interest, his eyes on the screen, his ears taking in Vrsk's running translation. He was tempted to order the miracle ball right away, but his instinct told him that if he waited, the price might drop. So he held off, biding his time, waiting for just the right moment to strike. He could feel the pressure. But he was an agent in the field; pressure was his business.

CHAPTER TWENTY-FIVE

TOBY, TAMARA, AND MICAH set up Micah's laptop on a table in a deserted corner of the mall food court. They hoped it was close enough to the Science Nook to get a decent signal from the Cantaloupe Cam. Micah booted up the laptop, worked the keyboard for a few moments, then said, "There."

The image on the laptop screen was a little dark, but clear enough. Standing at the Science Nook counter, facing the camera, were four ME kids: Haley Hess, Harmonee Prescott, Jason Niles, and Farrel "The Ferret" Plinkett. Sternabite was also visible, his back to the camera. He finished placing some cardboard boxes on the counter and some larger ones on a hand truck. Then he opened and looked into some envelopes, which appeared to contain cash.

"Can we get sound?" asked Toby.

Micah increased the volume. There were some rustling noises as Sternabite finished checking the envelopes. Then his voice came through the laptop speakers, surprisingly loud and clear.

"Okay, it's all here," he said.

"So how do we, like, set the projects up?" said Haley.

"The instructions are inside the boxes," said Sternabite. "Nothing complicated."

"All right," said Haley. She turned to Jason and The Ferret. "You guys carry the heavy ones, okay?"

"It might be a couple of trips," said Jason, eyeing the boxes.

"Whatever," said Haley. "Just get started." She and the others began picking up boxes.

"Hold on a minute," said Sternabite.

The ME kids looked at him.

"Is this important?" said Harmonee. "Because *Celebrity Cage Fight* is on in a half hour."

Indicating the boxes, Sternabite said, "These components . . . some of them are very . . . sophisticated."

"You told us that already," said Jason Niles.

Sternabite nodded. "And I've been thinking more about it," he said. "There's a potential situation that concerns me about these projects."

"Are you saying they won't work?" said Haley.

"No," said Sternabite. "They work. I built them."

"Then what's the problem?" said Jason.

Sternabite paused, then said, "I'd like to talk to

whoever designed these plans—whoever gave them to you."

"We told you," said Haley. "We don't know."

"What difference does it make who gave them to us?" said Jason. "We bring you the stuff, we *pay* you, and you make the projects. Same as always."

"No," said Sternabite. "It's not the same as always. The others I've done . . . those were always separate, very different projects. They didn't relate to each other. But these"—he gestured at the boxes—"there's a possibility . . . the combination. It's . . . troubling."

"Troubling, why?" said Haley.

Sternabite paused. "I . . . can't . . . say exactly," he finally muttered, sounding as though it caused him physical pain to speak these words. His voice returned to normal. "I haven't worked it out yet. Not completely. But I will. I'm just worried that in the meantime, should these technologies be used in combination, it could be . . . interesting. Potentially *very* dangerous."

"Potentially," said Haley. "*If* it's used wrong. But it won't be. It's just for the science fair."

"I still don't like it," said Sternabite. "I'm thinking maybe I shouldn't even . . ."

"Listen," interrupted Jason. "We need these projects. You can't back out now."

"Yeah," said The Ferret. "You took our money."

"That's right," said Haley. "You took our money. *And* you told us to bring you all the classified stuff."

"*I* didn't tell you to bring it," said Sternabite. "Whoever

designed these did. *You're* the ones who brought *me* lists."

"That's *your* story," said Haley. "The four of us might remember it differently, if, say, the police got interested. It could look very bad, an adult tricking innocent kids into getting him dangerous classified technology." She turned to the other three. "Isn't that right?"

"That's right," said The Ferret.

"Yeah," said Jason.

"What are we talking about?" said Harmonee.

Haley sighed and turned back to Sternabite. "I think," she said, "that the best thing for everyone would be if you just forgot about your little worries. When the science fair is over we'll return everything and it'll all be fine. Okay?"

There was a long pause. Then Sternabite nodded reluctantly.

"Okay!" said Haley brightly. "Bye!"

The ME kids moved the boxes out of the Science Nook and out of range of the Cantaloupe Cam. Sternabite was motionless for a few seconds, then left, apparently going to the back room.

Toby, Tamara, and Micah continued staring at Micah's computer screen. Tamara broke the silence.

"Wow," she said.

"Micah," said Toby, "did you by any chance record that?"

"No," said Micah. "Was I supposed to?"

Toby shook his head ruefully and said, "I should've thought of it before. This is unbelievable. They're using *classified* technology."

"*Dangerous*, classified technology," said Tamara. "Potentially *very* dangerous. What do you think he meant by that?"

"I dunno," said Toby. "But we have to tell somebody about this."

"Who?" said Micah.

"The FBI?" said Toby.

"Oh, sure!" said Tamara. She held an imaginary phone to her ear. "Hello, FBI? I want to report that the guy in a shopping-mall science store used classified technology to make something very dangerous. . . . No, I don't know what it is, but I saw the whole thing on a camera hidden inside a cantaloupe. . . . Hello? FBI? Hello?"

"Okay, so maybe not the FBI," said Toby.

"Then who?" said Micah.

Toby thought. "The Hornet," he said.

"Are you *insane*?" said Tamara. "No, let me rephrase that. You *are* insane."

"Listen," said Toby. "She loves the school. She would never let anything bad happen there. Plus, she's a human rottweiler. If I can convince her that Sternabite knows something, she *will* make him tell."

"How're you going to convince her?" said Micah. "She already thinks you're a lying cheater."

"Right," said Toby. "But she doesn't think *you* are."

"You want *us* to tell The Hornet," said Tamara.

"Just tell her what you saw and heard on the computer," said Toby. "She'll have to check it out. I'll back you up."

"Oh, *that'll* help," said Tamara. "Being backed up by a lying cheater."

"Come on," said Toby. "We gotta do this. If we don't go to The Hornet, these morons could end up blowing up the school. Is *that* what you want?"

Tamara looked down, then shook her head. Micah just stared at Toby.

"Well *is* it?" said Toby.

"I'm thinking," said Micah.

CHAPTER TWENTY-SIX

★

IT WAS DARK BY THE TIME TOBY returned to Milkwort Court. He paused out on the street for a moment, watching his house. Through the living room window he saw the TV on, which meant his parents were still up. He hoped they hadn't discovered that he'd snuck out. But it was equally important they not hear him sneak back in.

So he tiptoed across the yard cautiously and around the side of the house to his bedroom window. He peered inside: thankfully the room was dark and the door closed. *Good.* He reached for the window to raise it.

"Hello, Toby," spoke an electronically distorted voice from directly behind him.

Oh, no!

Toby spun around: stepping out from the shadows were

Vaderian and the Wookiee. Vaderian was dressed in full Darth Vader costume, including helmet. He was holding a glowing light saber—apparently he'd replaced the batteries—which he now pointed at Toby's chest.

"So, young Harbinger," he said, "we meet again." He emitted an electronic chuckle, as though he had said something witty.

"What are *you* doing here?" said Toby.

"As I told you last time," said Vaderian, "I want more from your father's collection."

"I can't get you anything now," said Toby, glancing nervously at the house. He whispered: "My parents are home!"

"Fine," said Vaderian. He produced a cell phone from inside his cloak. "Then I'll call them and tell them you stole the Han Solo blaster."

"No!" said Toby. "Don't call them!"

"Then get me something else."

"But . . ."

"Now." Vaderian held up the phone. "I'll count to ten. One, two . . ."

Toby's mind raced.

". . . three, four . . ."

He rubbed his face, trying to think of a way he could get out of his room and past his parents, down to the basement. . . .

". . . seven, eight . . ."

Then Toby remembered: *his room.*

". . . nine . . ."

"Stop!" said Toby. "I have something for you."

"What?" said Vaderian.

"A Luke Skywalker blow-up doll."

Vaderian almost dropped his light saber. "You *have* one?" he said. "An *original*?"

Toby nodded glumly, racked by guilt.

"That's more like it," said Vaderian eagerly, putting away the phone. "Where is it?"

"I'll get it," said Toby. "But you have to stay out here."

"All right," said Vaderian. "But don't try anything stupid. If you don't come right back here with the Luke doll, I'm calling your parents, understand? I might even ring the doorbell and introduce myself."

"No, no, I'll bring you the doll," Toby said. "Just don't make any noise, okay?"

He turned, slowly raised his bedroom window, and climbed onto the sill. In the darkness, he felt around with his foot, locating the Lego castle he'd built when he was nine. He didn't want to step on it, so he reached his foot out farther, shifting his weight into the room.

Too far. Toby's foot missed the edge of the bed. He tumbled into the room and landed on the floor with a loud *thump*, followed by a louder *BAM* as the window, which he'd let go of as he fell, slammed shut. A moment later he heard voices from the living room and the sound of footsteps coming his way. He quickly rolled under his bed.

The bedroom door opened, flooding the room with a soft light from the hallway. Through the small gap between his dangling bedspread and the floor, he saw his mom's silhouette in the doorway.

"Toby?" she said. "Are you all right?"

Toby was about to answer when his voice, coming from the speaker under his pillow, said, "I'm fine. I'm trying to sleep."

"We heard a noise," said his mother. "It sounded like it came from your room."

The computer, not recognizing these words, hesitated, then said, "I just want to sleep, okay?"

"Yes, but it was quite a loud noise," said his mother.

"I-fell-out-of-bed-but-I'm-okay!" said Toby, talking fast, to beat the computer.

"I'm fine. I'm trying to sleep," said the computer.

His mother hesitated.

"Are you sure?" she said. "You sound . . . strange."

"I'm-fine-really-Mom-thanks!" Toby said quickly.

"I'm fine. I'm trying to sleep," said the computer.

His mother hesitated again. Under the bed, Toby held his breath.

"All right, then," said his mother. "Good night."

"Good night!" Toby said quickly.

"Good night," said the computer.

His mother closed the door. Toby waited a few moments, listening to her footsteps recede. He crawled out from under the bed and turned off his computer, then pulled the Luke Skywalker doll out from under the covers. Carefully, he raised the window again. Vaderian and the Wookiee emerged from the shadows. Toby pushed the doll through the window. Vaderian took it eagerly, and, after inspecting it for a moment, he giggled softly and handed

the doll to the Wookiee. Toby started to lower the window, but Vaderian's black glove stopped it.

"What now?" Toby whispered angrily. "I gave you your stupid doll."

"I'm going to need more," said Vaderian.

"I can't," whispered Toby. "You've got enough. You're not even *paying* for that! Just . . . leave me alone. Please."

"I see," said Vaderian. "So you prefer that I tell your father who's been raiding his collection?"

Toby hung his head. "No," he whispered.

"Good," said Vaderian. "I'll be in touch." He made a point of breathing heavily through the electronic device, like Darth Vader, before lowering the window. And then he was gone.

With a groan, Toby flopped onto his back. Somehow, he had to get rid of this maniac *and* convince The Hornet he was telling the truth about the kids' science-fair cheating . . . not to mention the involvement of classified technology. Toby stared up at the darkness, begging his overworked, overworried brain to produce an answer, or at least an idea. . . .

In the living room, Mr. and Mrs. Harbinger were discussing their son's odd behavior.

"It was the strangest thing," Fawn was saying. "He said everything twice, and he spoke . . . oddly."

"How so?" said Roger.

"Like he was distracted," said Fawn. "Worried about something."

"It's this suspension," said Roger. "You know how kids are at that age. They think everything's a huge crisis."

"True," said Fawn, smiling at the cluelessness of the young. "He'll feel better after some sleep." She yawned. "I could use some sleep myself. I'm going to bed."

"Me, too," said Roger. He rose and went to the window and started to close the blinds, then suddenly stopped, pressing his face to the window.

"What is it?" said Fawn, coming over.

"Just for a second there, I thought I saw something," said Roger.

"Saw what?" said Fawn.

"It's nothing," said Roger, peering out. "It's just shadows. But for just a second, out there past the street-light, I thought I saw . . . this is *so* ridiculous . . ."

"Saw *what*?" Fawn repeated.

Roger looked sheepish. "Darth Vader," he said.

Fawn laughed out loud.

"You *do* need sleep," she said.

CHAPTER TWENTY-SEVEN

★

THE PHONE JANGLED. Vrsk jerked awake. In the other bed, Drmtsi groaned.

The TV was still on, tuned to the shopping channel. Vrsk and Drmtsi had finally fallen asleep around four a.m., but not before using their new credit cards to purchase a variety of items to go with their two cappuccino machines, including jewelry, clothing, shoes (men's and ladies'), exercise equipment, a set of ovenware, an Air Hockey table, and an eight-foot inflatable gorilla pool toy.

The phone jangled again. Vrsk fumbled for the handset.

"Hello?" he said, in English.

"It is Prmkt," said Prmkt, in Krpsht.

Vrsk, switching to Krpsht, turned to Drmtsi and said, "It is Prmkt."

Drmtsi groaned again.

"Men are watching you," said Prmkt.

"What men?" said Vrsk.

"I don't know yet," said Prmkt.

Vrsk turned to Drmtsi and said, "Men are watching us."

Drmtsi opened one bloodshot eye.

"What men?" he said.

"He doesn't know yet," said Vrsk.

Drmtsi rubbed his face. His head hurt.

"I will find out who these men are," said Prmkt. "I will call later."

Before Vrsk could relay this, Drmtsi said, "Tell him to find out who these men are and call later."

Vrsk, speaking into the phone, said, "Drmtsi says find out who these men are and call later."

"I just said that," said Prmkt.

"Exactly," said Vrsk.

The line went dead. Vrsk hung up the phone. On the TV screen, a perky woman was selling a kitchen appliance that could toast bagels *and* play DVDs. The price had just dropped twenty dollars, to $179.99. Despite their exhaustion, both Vrsk and Drmtsi sat up to watch. This could be big.

CHAPTER TWENTY-EIGHT

★

TOBY GOT A BREAK the next morning: both his parents left home to attend an all-day seminar on curing baldness with zucchini oil. That meant Toby didn't have to think up a new way to sneak out of the house.

The trick was getting into school. He'd agreed to meet Tamara and Micah at The Hornet's office at 8:20, just before the homeroom bell. But Toby was still suspended. He was afraid one of the teachers might spot him and kick him out before he could get to The Hornet and help his friends convince her—they *had* to convince her—about the science-fair cheating plot. As he left his room, he grabbed one of his baseball caps and pulled the brim low to cover his face, hoping this would be enough of a disguise.

On the way to Hubble Middle he kept a wary eye out for

the maniac Vaderian and his hairy sidekick; to his relief, he saw neither. He entered the school at 8:19, the hallways quickly emptying as students headed for their home-rooms. Keeping his head down, Toby hurried toward the main office. Nobody stopped him. He reached the office just as the bell rang. Ducking inside, he was relieved to see Tamara and Micah in the outer room, sitting on the bench, not looking thrilled to be there.

"Does The Hornet know we're here?" Toby asked.

"Mrs. Breetle just went in to tell her," said Tamara.

"We still have time to escape," said Micah.

"Micah, we have to do this," said Toby.

"Remind me exactly *why* we have to do this," said Micah.

"Because of what Sternabite said," Toby explained, "about the projects being dangerous."

"But that's just his opinion," said Micah.

"But he's really smart about science," said Toby.

"Right," said Micah. "He's also a lunatic with a robot attack owl."

Toby was trying to think of a good comeback for that when The Hornet's office door opened and Mrs. Breetle came out, holding an armful of papers.

"Principal Plotz-Gornett will see you now," she said. "But she only has a minute." Mrs. Breetle bustled off toward the copy machine.

Prodded by Toby, Micah and Tamara shuffled into The Hornet's office. Toby stopped just outside the doorway, fearing that if he went in, The Hornet would immediately

banish him. His plan was to eavesdrop and then step forward when he was needed.

Micah and Tamara continued into the office. The Hornet was sitting behind her desk, looking even more irritated than usual.

"What is this matter that's so important?" she said.

Micah and Tamara looked at each other, both too nervous to speak. Finally Micah cleared his throat and said, "We, um, found out something that we, ah, found out about. So we, ah, came here." He stopped there, his brain apparently frozen by The Hornet's gaze.

"I see," said The Hornet.

"Good," said Micah.

"That was sarcasm," said The Hornet. "In fact, I have no idea what you're talking about."

"Oh," said Micah.

"The science fair," blurted Tamara. "We saw them cheating."

The Hornet turned her gaze on Tamara, who now felt her own brain freezing. Finally, The Hornet said, "Whom?"

"Whom what?" said Tamara.

The Hornet sighed. "Whom," she said, "did you see cheating?"

"The ME kids," said Tamara. "Jason Niles, Haley Hess, Harmonee Prescott, and The Fer . . . I mean Farrel Plinkett."

The Hornet's eyes narrowed.

"And how, exactly, were they cheating?" said The Hornet.

"They're hiring the guy at the Science Nook to make their projects," she said. "They're paying him. They're not working on them themselves."

The Hornet's eyes narrowed even more.

"Did Toby Harbinger tell you to say this?" she asked.

"Yes," said Tamara. "I mean, no. I mean, he told us to tell you, but we were there. We saw them. And we heard the Science Nook guy say the projects were dangerous."

"Very dangerous," said Micah.

"So you were in the Science Nook when this happened?" said The Hornet.

"Yes," said Tamara. "I mean, no. Not exactly."

"Excuse me?" said The Hornet.

"I mean," said Tamara, "we were in the food court."

"You were in the food court," said The Hornet.

"Right," said Tamara. "But we saw them."

"Through the Cantaloupe Cam," added Micah.

"You saw them," The Hornet said slowly, "through a cantaloupe?"

"Through a camera *in* a cantaloupe," said Tamara. "Yes."

"We didn't have an eggplant," added Micah.

"I beg your pardon?" said The Hornet.

Before Tamara or Micah could answer, Toby, realizing that things were not going well, took a deep breath and stepped through the door. The Hornet fixed him with a stare that could stop a rhino.

"What are *you* doing here?" she said.

"Please listen," he said. "This is my fault. I asked them to come here because I didn't think you'd believe me. But

they *saw* it. They saw the ME kids talking to the Science Nook guy about their projects. He got all freaked out, because he said they were using classified technology and that it could be dangerous."

The Hornet's office was utterly quiet for five long, scary seconds. Then The Hornet said, "Mr. Harbinger?"

"Yes," said Toby.

"First," said The Hornet, "you will remove that disgusting hat."

Toby snatched the hat off his head and realized, with horror, that it was the one that said BITE ME.

"Ohmigod, I'm sorry," he said. "I—"

"Be quiet," said The Hornet. "I am deeply disappointed in you, Mr. Harbinger. *Deeply.* It was bad enough that you accused your fellow students of cheating, when it appears that *you* are the one who is cheating."

"But—"

"I said *be quiet*. But then you compound your transgression by getting your friends to back up your accusations, thus not only causing them to embarrass themselves with this pathetic story about cantaloupes and eggplants, but also exposing them to serious disciplinary action."

Micah and Tamara looked at Toby. Toby looked away.

"I didn't mean to—" he began.

The Hornet cut him off. "Whatever you meant to do," she said, "you have managed to make a bad situation far worse for yourself *and* your friends."

Toby started to speak, but The Hornet held up her hand. "Before you say any more," she said, "I'm going to bring

Mr. Neckstrom here, since he is in charge of the science fair that you seem so determined to sabotage." She pressed the intercom button on her phone and said, "Mrs. Breetle, please tell Mr. Neckstrom I want to see him in my office immediately. I also want Jason Niles, Haley Hess, Harmonee Prescott, and Farrel Plinkett to report to the outer office and wait there until I call them in."

Two uncomfortable minutes later, there was a tap on the door and Mr. Neckstrom entered The Hornet's office, closing the door behind him. Catching sight of Toby, he glared and said, "I thought he was suspended."

"He is," said The Hornet. "He has returned to the school, without permission, to bring new accusations concerning the science fair. He and his friends now claim that not only are some of the children purchasing their projects from this mall store, but that these projects may involve classified technology and could be dangerous."

Mr. Neckstrom's face was now exactly the same shade of red as a baboon's behind.

It took him a moment to control his anger enough so that he could speak.

"That's *ridiculous*," he spat.

"I agree," said The Hornet. "But since he is now raising the issue of safety, I am obligated, as principal of this school, to inform you of it and ask if you have any reason to believe there is any truth to it."

"Absolutely not," said Mr. Neckstrom, glaring at Toby. He's still trying to save his own skin, and he doesn't care who he hurts."

The Hornet nodded. She pressed her intercom button. "Mrs. Breetle," she said, "please come here and bring your notebook."

The office door opened. Mrs. Breetle stood in the doorway, notebook in hand. Behind her, Toby saw the ME kids sitting on the bench. He also saw Mr. P by the copy machine, apparently making copies. For an instant their eyes met. Mr. P looked away.

"Mrs. Breetle," said The Hornet, raising her voice. "Please take this down and prepare it for my signature and inclusion in the files. I want to note for the record that today these three students—Toby Harbinger, Tamara Reilley, and Micah Porter—came to me with new allegations regarding their fellow students and the safety of the science fair. I have discussed this matter with Mr. Neckstrom, and our preliminary finding is that these allegations are unfounded. However, because of the safety issue, I am instructing Mr. Neckstrom to investigate this matter further, as I intend to do myself."

The Hornet paused for a few moments while Mrs. Breetle scribbled furiously to catch up.

"Also," The Hornet went on, "as of now, I am placing all three of these students on indefinite disciplinary suspension from Hubble Middle School."

Tamara and Micah gasped.

"But they didn't do anything!" said Toby. "I'm the one who—"

"*Be quiet*, Mr. Harbinger," snapped The Hornet. "They did indeed do something. They listened to you. Perhaps in

the future they will think twice before they make that mistake."

Toby hung his head.

The Hornet resumed dictating to Mrs. Breetle: "During this suspension," she continued, "these students are banned from attending school and from participating in *any* school activities."

"In . . . including the science fair?" said Micah.

"*Especially* including the science fair," said The Hornet.

"But I need to go into the gym!" said Micah. "Tamara and I already set up our projects, and Fester's going to be hungry."

"Fester?" said The Hornet.

"My frog," said Micah. "He's in my project. It's about . . ."

"Mr. Porter," interrupted The Hornet, in a voice that sounded the way a cold shower feels.

"Yes?" said Micah.

"Be quiet," said The Hornet.

"Okay," said Micah, "but Fester . . ."

"I said *be quiet*," said The Hornet. "You will not go to the gymnasium. The three of you will wait in the outer office while Mrs. Breetle contacts your parents to come pick you up."

All three children looked stricken. *Their parents.*

"That's all," said The Hornet, dismissing them. "Mrs. Breetle, send in the four students waiting outside. Mr. Neckstrom, please remain here while I question them."

As he turned to leave The Hornet's office, Toby felt his stomach churning. This had gone horribly, horribly

wrong. The room seemed to be swirling around him as he stumbled blindly through the doorway, almost knocking over a bucket being used by Janitor Dude to mop the outer-office floor. A wave of filthy water sloshed against his legs, drenching his pants and shoes. The ME kids roared with laughter. They were still snickering as they filed past Toby, Tamara, and Micah. They didn't seem a bit worried about facing The Hornet and Mr. Neckstrom. As he passed, Jason Niles deliberately stepped hard on Toby's right foot.

Wet and hurting, Toby stumbled to the bench and sat down on the end. He noticed that Tamara and Micah sat on the other end.

"I'm sorry," Toby said, his voice hoarse. "I didn't think . . . I never thought . . ."

"No," said Tamara, "you didn't."

Toby wanted to say something more, but he didn't know what, and Micah and Tamara obviously didn't want to hear it anyway. Toby looked around the office. Mr. P was taking some papers from the copier. His eyes met Toby's again for a moment, then he left. At her desk, Mrs. Breetle was on the phone. She apparently had just gotten through to Tamara's mother.

"Yes, Mrs. Reilley," she was saying, "suspended."

Tamara's shoulders shook; she was weeping.

Toby leaned over and put his face into his hands, hoping his own tears would not leak through.

CHAPTER TWENTY-NINE

Toby was in his room, instant messaging Micah, who was in *his* room, since both of them, along with Tamara, had been grounded for all eternity, if not longer.

Toby was in the midst of yet another apology for causing the suspensions when he heard the doorbell ring. He froze, fearing that Darth and the Wookiee were back. He listened intently, his fingers hovering over his laptop keyboard. He heard the front door open, then close, followed by footsteps heading for the kitchen. Toby relaxed; it was his mom returning from errands. A minute later he heard the angry whine of the blender. His mom was experimenting with a brussels-sprout-yogurt-protein facial cream.

Turning back to the keyboard, he typed:

my rents r 4 real ths tme

mine 2, answered Micah.

im srry

u shud b

The door to Toby's bedroom opened behind him. Toby started to turn, annoyed that there'd been no knock.

"Mom," he said, "I thought we agreed that . . ."

He cut himself off as he spun around. The door stood ajar, but his mother wasn't there.

brb, he typed. He got up and peered into the hallway—nobody. He could hear his mom in the kitchen. Frowning, he closed the door and turned around.

Sternabite was sitting in his chair.

Toby screamed. He didn't mean to; it came out before he could stop himself.

"Calm down," said Sternabite calmly.

There were quick footsteps in the hall, then pounding on the door. For once, Toby's mom was observing the knock-first agreement.

"Toby?" she said. "Are you okay?"

Toby glanced at Sternabite, then the door. *What to do?* He looked back at Sternabite.

Except Sternabite wasn't there.

Toby blinked.

Sternabite wasn't there.

"Toby?" said his mom. "May I come in?"

"Um, yeah," he said, still looking at his empty chair.

His mother came in, looking worried. She smelled like brussels sprouts. "Are you all right, sweetheart?"

"I . . . ah . . . yeah," he said. "I'm fine." He frowned at the chair, noticing something. The chair was leaning back. *By itself.*

"Are you sure?" said his mom. "Because I heard you yell."

"Yeah," he said, tearing his eyes away from the chair. "I guess this, ah, being grounded thing is getting to me."

His mom gave him a disgusted look and shook her head. "Nice try," she said, closing the door.

Toby waited until her footsteps had receded. Then he turned back to the chair.

"I know you're there," he said.

"Just don't scream again," said Sternabite's voice.

That was weird enough. What followed was weirder: the light in front of the chair flickered, and suddenly . . . there was Sternabite again. He wore a baseball cap, sunglasses, a dark sport coat, khakis, and running shoes. He had an iPhone clipped to his belt, in the front. His hair was all over the place, sticking out of the cap as if he'd grabbed a live wire.

"How did you *do* that?" Toby asked.

"Quantum mechanics," said Sternabite. "You'll study it in high-school physics. *Applying* it, though . . ." He reached down, touched the iPhone, and disappeared.

"Whoa," said Toby.

Sternabite reappeared, his hand again on the iPhone.

"Whoa," Toby said again.

"It was you, wasn't it," said Sternabite, "in my store that night."

"What?" said Toby.

"Don't act stupid. You took a list of science-fair components, yes?"

"Yes," admitted Toby.

"How did you evade the owl?"

"I used the Hello Kitty mirror," said Toby.

Sternabite nodded approvingly. "Not bad," he said.

"What would the owl have done?" said Toby. "If it had caught me, I mean."

"We wouldn't be having this conversation," said Sternabite.

Toby started to ask another question, but Sternabite held up his hand. "It was your locker, wasn't it," he said.

"What?"

"Where the firemen found the plasma."

"Oh, yeah," said Toby. "But I didn't put it there."

"Of course not," said Sternabite. "You'd have no way to obtain plasma. I assume it also wasn't you who returned the component list to me."

"You got that back?" said Toby.

"Somebody slid it under the door to my store," said Sternabite.

"Not me," said Toby. "I took it to The Horn . . . to the principal. It disappeared from her office."

"And why," said Sternabite slowly, "did you steal that list and take it to the principal?"

"I wanted to show her that the ME kids were buying

their science fair projects from . . ." Toby's voice trailed off.

"From me," said Sternabite.

Toby nodded. He could feel Sternabite's gaze from behind the dark sunglasses. He tensed as a thought flashed through his mind: *He's here to kill me.*

"Calm down," said Sternabite. "I'm not going to kill you."

"Why *are* you here?" said Toby.

"Because something's wrong," said Sternabite. "Whoever gave the plans to these idiot rich kids is up to something, and he's using me to accomplish it. And I don't like being used."

Toby hesitated, then said, "You didn't mind last year, and the year before that."

"True," said Sternabite. "In fact, I enjoyed messing with Hubble's precious science fair, and that idiot Lance Swingle."

"Idiot?" said Toby. "He made billions from TranScent, and he . . ."

"He stole that idea from me," snapped Sternabite.

"What?" said Toby.

"Ten years ago," said Sternabite, "he came into my store looking for help, with this vague notion of sending smells over the Internet. But he was clueless about the science of it. It took me ten minutes to figure out the basic idea and another five to draw up a rough schematic. He paid me fifty dollars for my time; said he was just doing it for fun. Then he went on to start his company and make his billions and

claim all the credit. He's never once mentioned my name."

"So why don't you sue him?"

Sternabite waved his hand. "I hate lawyers," he said, "and I don't need his money. I don't *do* science for money. I do science because it *amuses* me. And it amuses me greatly that every year, the great Lance Swingle, when he gives his big award for first prize at his famous science fair, is giving it to a rich cheat—just like himself—for a project done by *me*." Sternabite smiled at the thought. "That's why I do the projects for those idiot rich kids."

"Where do the project plans come from?" said Toby.

Sternabite's smile faded. "That's the troubling thing," he said. "For the first few years, the ideas were mine. These kids would come in looking for help, and I'd whip something up that I knew would win. Then five years ago they started coming in with plans of their own. Some of the science was pretty sophisticated, actually. I asked the rich kids where they got them, but they claimed not to know. That bothered me a little, but I assembled the projects, because I didn't see why not, and to be honest I found them interesting. Until this year. This year, I found them disturbing."

"So why did you make them?" said Toby.

Sternabite looked sheepish, or as sheepish as he knew how. "Because," he said, "I didn't see it at first. I had suspicions, but it wasn't until late last night, *after* I gave the projects to the idiot rich kids, that I figured it out." He stopped, shaking his head.

"Figured what out?" asked Toby.

"What he plans to do," said Sternabite. "Whoever's behind this . . . he's clever, I'll give him that. Brilliant, actually. He had obviously been testing his plan in the previous science fairs, seeing if he could use idiot rich kids' insanely competitive parents to get classified technology, and then using me to assemble the projects. And it all worked." Sternabite's face reddened. "And now he's ready to put his plan into effect, unless we stop him."

"Why don't you just tell the police?" said Toby.

"The police?" Sternabite snorted. "Let's say they believed me, which I doubt they would. But say they do. Who are they going to arrest? Who put the projects together?"

"You," said Toby.

"Right," said Sternabite. "I'm the first person they'd arrest. No, no police."

"But what . . ." Toby stopped at the sound of footsteps in the hall and another knock on the door. Sternabite put his hand on the iPhone, preparing to disappear.

"Time for lunch," said Toby's mom through the door. "I made beef tacos."

"With actual beef?" said Toby.

"Don't be silly," said his mom.

"Five minutes, okay?" said Toby.

"Five minutes," said his mom, walking away.

Toby turned back to Sternabite. "So what do the projects—"

Sternabite interrupted. "No time. I need to show you how this works." He began to untie his sneakers.

166

"How *what* works?" said Toby. "Why're you taking off your shoes?"

"You need these," said Sternabite, carefully pulling what looked like a blue insole out of each shoe. He set these on the desk along with his ball cap. Then he pulled an iPhone from his jacket pocket and set it inside the hat. Stepping closer, Toby could see that there were thin, transparent wire filaments connecting the insoles and the cap to the iPhone.

"Okay," he said, pointing to the insoles. "You put these in your shoes. The switch is on the iPhone—it's this magic-wand icon. You have to be careful with the fiber optics"—he pointed to the filaments—"because they break easily, and then you're not invisible anymore. Of course, you're not really invisible anyway."

"I'm not?" said Toby.

"Of course not," said Sternabite, relacing his sneakers. "You're still there. This is just bending the light so it goes around you. You know how polarized sunglasses remove glare? The glare's still there, but you don't see it. This works on a similar principle. In fact, anyone wearing polarized sunglasses can see you. You need to remember that. I'm giving you two sets of the fiber optics, so you have a spare. You put the phone on your belt, and . . ."

"Waitwaitwait," said Toby, holding up both hands. "Why are you giving me this thing?"

Sternabite looked at him for a moment, then said softly, "Because you're the key to finding whoever's behind this."

"*What?* Why me?"

"Because he knows you know. And he's at your school. He has to be. He put the projects in the kids' lockers. He found out that you went to the principal. He stole the components list from the principal's office and gave it back to me. Did you see anybody suspicious around when you went in to see her?"

"Yeah," said Toby, thinking back. "A teacher, Mr. P. He's also the one who supposedly found the plasma stuff leaking from my locker."

"Then I would say he's definitely a suspect," said Sternabite. "Because whoever took the list from the principal's office also put the plasma in your locker to frame you. But whoever he is, we're going to need solid proof to get him. We need to force him to make a move. That's your role. This guy sees you as a threat. As far as he knows you're the only person who knows about the science fair. If you show up at the school again, causing trouble for him, he'll try to get rid of you again."

"So . . . you want me to go back to school," said Toby.

"Right," said Sternabite. "You sneak in, invisible. Then you do something to draw this guy out."

"Like what?"

"The science fair," said Sternabite. "It's being set up in the gym, right?"

Toby nodded.

"Okay, then that's where he'll be," said Sternabite. "He'll be watching the rich kids' projects, I guarantee you. He can't let anything happen to them. If he sees you

poking around, he'll figure you're going to sabotage them, and he'll have to show himself. So you go to school today, at the end of the day. The school will be mostly empty, and you'll be invisible. You go into the gym and make sure everybody's out of there. Then you make yourself visible, and you fool around with the projects I built. The next person you see—and you *will* see him—is the guy behind all this."

"Then what do I do?" said Toby.

"Then you call me. Press the sunglasses icon on the iPhone. I'll be there in seconds."

"How can you be there in seconds?"

"Trust me," said Sternabite. "I'll be there. Plus, if you get scared, all you have to do is press the magic wand on the phone, and you're invisible again."

"So basically," said Toby, "you want to use me as bait."

"Exactly," said Sternabite.

Toby thought about it for a moment, then shook his head. "I don't think so," he said. "I'm already in way too much trouble."

Sternabite shifted closer, his sunglasses only inches from Toby's face. "Trouble?" he said. *"Trouble?* You don't have *any idea* what trouble is, kid. If we don't stop this maniac's plan—if we let this science fair go ahead—this whole *country* will be in trouble. The whole *world*. Do you understand?"

"No," said Toby. "I don't. What's going to—"

Toby was again interrupted by his mom's footsteps and sharp rapping on the door.

"Toby!" she said. "It's past five minutes!"

"But . . ."

"Now."

The footsteps receded. Sternabite rose quickly and opened Toby's window.

"Wait," said Toby.

But Sternabite was already climbing out. "Remember," he said, "when he shows himself, press the sunglasses icon. And be careful not to break the fiber optics."

Before Toby could say anything else, Sternabite had lowered the window and was gone.

Toby's laptop beeped. He'd forgotten his IM conversation with Micah, who had grown impatient and typed dozens of lines of question marks. Toby went to the keyboard and typed, sorry got 2 go

r u ok? typed Micah.

Toby hesitated, then typed: u wd NOT blve

?? typed Micah.

Toby was about to answer when his mom shouted, "TOBY HARBINGER YOU COME TO LUNCH *RIGHT NOW*!"

"Coming!" he called, opening his door and leaving a growing string of question marks on his laptop screen.

CHAPTER THIRTY

TOBY WAS JITTERY DURING LUNCH, barely chewing his food before he swallowed, which was probably the best way to eat tofu tacos anyway. All he could think about was trying out Sternabite's invisibility device. He pretended that he was chewing for a few minutes and then excused himself, leaving his mother to continue her work on the brussels sprouts facial cream.

Back in his room, Toby carefully clipped the iPhone to his belt. He then put a blue insole into each of his shoes and laced them up. Finally he put the ball cap on his head. He made sure that the fiber-optic filaments from each shoe and from the cap were attached to the coupler plugged into the iPhone.

He was ready.

Heart pounding, he stood in front of his closet-door

mirror, held his breath, looked down, and touched the magic-wand icon on the phone. Then he looked up at the mirror.

He wasn't there. He could see the opposite wall of his bedroom. He backed up, mesmerized, and stumbled on a footstool. The footstool moved in the mirror; the blanket came off the end of the bed as he reached out and grabbed it to break his fall. But there was no boy in the mirror. No Toby.

"Awesome!" he said.

He looked down to turn the device off, but couldn't see the iPhone. Couldn't see his hand. Couldn't see *anything* but the floor of his room. How could he push the magic wand on the phone if he couldn't see the iPhone in the first place?

His throat tightened as he panicked.

Then he remembered: polarized sunglasses. He pulled open his desk drawer—and *that* was weird, the drawer opening as if by itself—and found his shades. He put them on, and sure enough: he could see himself. And the iPhone. He made a mental note of where the wand icon was: the lower righthand corner of the screen.

He pressed the icon, and there he was. He slipped the sunglasses into his shirt pocket. He opened his door and called, "Is it okay if I watch some TV?"

"Okay, honey," his mother called back. Toby preferred the massive television set in the basement, the one his parents watched all the Star Wars movies on. It had a big old comfy couch in front of it and surround sound. If Toby was lucky, his mom wouldn't call him upstairs until dinner was ready; he'd have time to get to school and back.

He opened the door to the basement and, without going

through, shut it loudly. Then he tiptoed back to his bedroom, quietly closed his door, touched the magic wand on
the iPhone, and sneaked out his bedroom window. As he
closed the window, a car pulled into the driveway next door;
it was Mrs. Penin, their neighbor. She stopped no more
than twenty feet from where Toby stood, and as she got out
of the car she looked in Toby's direction. He waved his arms
at her—no reaction. Toby grinned an invisible grin.

Now he turned his attention to his mission. The fastest
way to get to school would be on his bike, but he figured a
bike riding itself would raise some eyebrows. So he set off
at a trot. From time to time, out of habit, he glanced at his
watch, only to realize each time that he couldn't see it. He
didn't pass many pedestrians, and he swerved wide
around the few people he did encounter. One man heard
Toby's trotting footsteps and looked around curiously;
Toby stopped and held his breath, and after a moment the
man, frowning, moved on.

In less than a half hour Toby was within a block of his
school. He didn't know the time exactly, but he figured it
was just about right. So far, so good. If Sternabite's plan
worked, he'd be . . .

"Hey!"

Toby froze. The voice came from a side street to his left.

Toby looked and saw a Gremlin parked at the curb, facing away from Toby. The Wookiee was leaning against the
rear of the car.

He was wearing . . . *sunglasses*.

"Get over here, kid!" He pounded on the roof of the car.

Through the window Toby could see Vaderian's head slumped to the side, apparently dozing.

"The kid's here," said the Wookiee, still pounding. Vader's head snapped up. He turned toward the Wookiee. Vaderian *wasn't* wearing sunglasses.

Toby had a quick decision to make: if he ran, the Wookiee would chase him; he'd have to abandon his mission to get into the science fair, as Sternabite had asked. So he felt forced to talk to them.

But if Vaderian got out of the car and saw Toby—or, rather *didn't* see him—he and the Wookiee would figure out that Toby had something even better than the Star Wars collection. They'd want the invisibility device. Toby couldn't let them get it.

Vaderian had opened the car door and was climbing out. He looked pretty stupid in the cape. Toby felt for the iPhone and touched what he prayed was the lower right-hand part of the screen. Vaderian was now out of the car, looking Toby's way.

"There you are," he said.

Toby looked down and saw with relief that he was, indeed, there. He checked his watch: 4:25. The school doors would be locked for the night in five minutes. He had to get rid of these lunatics quickly.

"Hey," he said.

"So, young Toby," said Vaderian. He was about to say more, but then he remembered something. He reached into his pocket, pulled out his voice-changer, and clapped it over his mouth.

174

"So, young Toby," he said, his voice now distorted. "We meet again."

Toby rolled his eyes and looked at his watch: 4:26.

"I'm kind of in a hurry," he said.

"Are you, now?" said Vaderian. He electronically chuckled as though this was the single cleverest thing anybody had ever said. He chuckled so hard that it turned into a cough, which continued until the Wookiee pounded Vaderian on the back, which stopped the cough, but which also sent the voice-changer clattering onto the sidewalk, where it came apart, spilling its batteries.

"Idiot!" Vaderian yelled at the Wookiee. "Pick it up!"

The Wookiee scrambled to reassemble the voice-changer. Toby rolled his eyes again, and for the hundredth time berated himself for getting involved with these morons. He looked at his watch: 4:27.

Finally Vaderian was ready to speak again. "You did well, young Harbinger, giving me the Skywalker doll."

"Like I had a choice," said Toby.

"I'm glad you understand that you *don't* have a choice," said Vaderian. "Because I want the rest of the collection."

"*What?*" said Toby. "You can't . . ."

"Yes, I can," said Vaderian. "And you'll help me, unless you want me to tell your parents what you've already stolen from them."

Toby was shaking his head. "I can't."

Vaderian lowered his electronic voice to what he apparently thought was a soothing tone. "It will look like a burglary," he said. "We'll do it when nobody's home. All

you have to do is leave a door open for us and tell us where the collection is."

Toby was still shaking his head.

"So you'd prefer that I called your parents?" said Vaderian.

"No," said Toby. "Please."

"Then cooperate. The collection is in the basement, isn't it?"

Toby, feeling trapped, looked down and nodded once. He couldn't believe that this was happening, that he was helping this lunatic. But he could see no way out of this. He just wanted it to be *over.*

"That's better," said Vaderian. "And will it all fit into this car?"

Toby glanced at the car. He was surprised it even fit the two men. He shook his head.

"Excellent!" said Vaderian. "We'll bring a truck. And when should we bring it?"

Toby thought about this for a few seconds, then said, "Tomorrow night. There's an event at school. A science fair." He was hoping, desperately, that by the next day he'd be reinstated at school.

"Good," said Vaderian. "The sliding glass door at the back of your house. Leave it unlocked."

"You've been to the back of my house?"

"Just leave it unlocked."

"But my parents check the doors before we go out."

"You'll think of something. You're a smart boy."

Toby looked at his watch and flinched at what he saw: 4:32

"I gotta go," he said, turning.

Vaderian grabbed his arm. "The door *will* be unlocked, right, Toby?"

"Okay. Okay," Toby said. He shook off Vaderian's grip and hurried away.

4:33.

He turned and ran. He rounded a corner and headed toward the school. As he neared it, he looked around. Seeing nobody, he touched the magic wand on the iPhone. Invisible now, he ran toward the school. He thought he saw a shape move across the glass of the front doors.

They were locking the doors.

He sprinted.

Up the sidewalk. Up the steps.

He grabbed the door handles.

Locked.

He sprinted around the side of the school to the gymnasium doors.

Locked.

Toby took a step back, then slumped down on the concrete walkway, trying to think of what to do next. Nothing came to mind. He'd failed in his mission to get into the school. He'd failed Sternabite and his friends. He'd been a traitor to his own parents. And he had no idea, none at all, how to make any of this right.

He leaned forward and put his invisible face into his invisible hands. He muffled a sob. A tear, then another, leaked through his hands. The tears became visible in midair, just before they splattered onto the hard concrete.

CHAPTER THIRTY-ONE

THE PHONE RANG in the crowded room at the Shady Inn Motor Court. Vrsk stumbled toward it through a cloud of steam, banging into empty cardboard boxes.

The steam was coming from the two cappuccino machines that Vrsk and Drmtsi had purchased from the TV shopping show. The machines had arrived by express delivery an hour earlier; Vrsk had been trying to get them to work. He still had no idea what cappuccino was, but he had produced a *lot* of steam. The cloud was so thick that Drmtsi had to sit right in front of the TV, his face only inches from the screen, so he could monitor the status of the item currently being sold—a set of eight deluxe tiki torches, propane-fueled, with electronic ignition. The price was currently $89.95, but Drmtsi was sure he could get them for under $70.

The phone rang again just as Vrsk reached it.

"Hello?" he said.

"It is Prmkt," said Prmkt, speaking Krpsht.

Switching to Krpsht, Vrsk said to Drmtsi, "It is Prkmt."

"Not now," said Drmtsi, his eyes glued to the screen. The price had just dropped to $75.99. *Any minute now . . .*

"Drmtsi is very busy," said Vrsk into the phone.

Prmkt sighed. "Tell him I have arranged a meeting. You must go to Jungle Norman's Pizza Party Place."

"Where?"

Vrsk repeated the name slowly: "Jungle. Norman's. Pizza. Party. Place. It is on Wackmore Avenue, seven blocks north of your motel. Meet me there in one hour."

"What about the men watching us?" said Vrsk, remembering Prmkt's warning from the night before.

Prmkt hesitated, then said, "These men are gone."

"Gone? But didn't you say—?"

"Not to worry about them," interrupted Prmkt. "Just meet me at Jungle Norman's in one hour. When you arrive, you will give the special signal, and I will come to you."

"Special signal?"

"Yes. You will lift up the hat from the head of the gorilla."

"The *what*?"

"The gorilla. You will lift up its hat."

"The gorilla wears a *hat*?"

"It is not a *real* gorilla," said Prmkt impatiently. "It is a robot gorilla that sings 'Happy Birthday.'"

"I . . . see," said Vrsk, although this was not entirely true.

"When you lift up the hat, I will come to you. One hour.

You must be there on time. Do not fail. The mission depends on you."

"We will not fail," said Vrsk, but Prmkt had already hung up. Vrsk turned and peered through the ever-denser fog of cappuccino-machine steam at Drmtsi, who suddenly leaped to his feet and shouted, "Sixty-nine ninety-five! I knew it!"

Vrsk pointed to the phone. "Prmkt says we must meet him in one hour."

"Where?"

"Jungle Norman's Pizza Party Place," said Vrsk, speaking the name slowly.

"What is this place?" said Drmtsi.

"I do not know," said Vrsk. "But it is seven blocks from here. We are to lift the hat of the gorilla."

"The gorilla?" said Drmtsi.

"It is not a real gorilla," said Vrsk. "It is a robot gorilla, for singing 'Happy Birthday.'"

Drmtsi and Vrsk eyed each other through the steam, both thinking the same thing: America was a mysterious place.

"All right," said Drmtsi. "We will go to the meeting. But first"—he pointed at the screen, where two enthusiastic women were admiring the set of deluxe propane-fueled tiki torches with electronic ignition—"you must call and order this item."

Vrsk picked up the phone and dialed the number, which he now knew by heart. Drmtsi watched him, then looked back at the TV screen. Then he made a command decision. He was going out on a mission; there was no telling what might happen out there. He turned back to Vrsk.

"Order *two* of this item," he said.

Chapter Thirty-two

★

TOBY CLIMBED QUIETLY through the window and into his bedroom. His plan was to sneak down to the basement, where he was supposed to be watching TV. But as he crossed his room, he heard the beep of an instant-message box popping up on his computer. He glanced at the screen and stopped when he read the message.

SecretAgentMan: Hello, Toby. Enjoying your suspension?

Toby's first thought was that it had to be Micah or Tamara messing with him. But neither of his friends bothered with the formalities of capitalization, punctuation, or spelling when they IM'd. Besides, this was a new name on his Buddy List. How could someone have gotten onto his Buddy List

without him putting them there? Toby frowned, then sat down at the computer and typed a response.

toby: who r u?

SecretAgentMan: I am the one person who can help you with your problems.

toby: wht do u mean?

SecretAgentMan: The plasma in your locker? The list you left on the principal's desk? I think you know what I mean.

toby: but y? who *r* u?

SecretAgentMan: Go to Jungle Norman's Pizza Party Place 30 minutes from now, at exactly 5:45. I will meet you there and give you proof of who is behind this.

toby: y shud i trust u?

SecretAgentMan: That is for you to decide. Stay suspended if you want. But if you want to resolve this, be at Jungle Norman's at 5:45. Stand next to the gorilla. This is your only chance. I won't make this offer again. Good-bye.

Before Toby could answer, SecretAgentMan signed off. Toby's mind raced. SecretAgentMan could be the person behind the science-fair plot; he could be setting a trap. But he'd picked a very public place to make trouble. Besides, a trap could be laid both ways. Toby had just tried, and failed, to draw out whoever was behind all this; now maybe that very person was offering to meet him. And if SecretAgentMan had a trap planned, Toby figured he had a surprise or two of his own: the invisibility device and Sternabite.

Toby made up his mind: he'd go to Jungle Norman's. As soon as SecretAgentMan revealed himself, Toby would press the sunglasses icon on the iPhone to summon Sternabite. If there was trouble, he'd also press the wand icon and disappear. And as a precaution, he'd let somebody know—somebody other than Sternabite—where he was going to be, so if worse came to worst they could tell his parents. Toby started to dial Micah's cell phone but then changed his mind; Tamara was more levelheaded. She answered on the first ring.

"Are you calling to see if I still hate you?" she said. "Okay, since you ask, yes."

Toby winced. "That's not why I'm calling," he whispered.

"Why are you whispering?"

"I don't want my mom to hear. I need to tell you something."

"Well, whatever it is, make it quick, so I can get back to doing nothing for the rest of my entire life except be grounded."

Toby winced again. "Listen," he said. "I'm going to Jungle Norman's."

"Is that why you called? I'm afraid I can't join you, because, as I believe I mentioned, I'm grounded for the rest of my entire—"

"No," interrupted Toby. "I just want somebody to know where I am, in case."

"In case what?" said Tamara, her voice suddenly serious.

"In case . . . something happens," said Toby.

"Like what?"

Toby briefly summarized Sternabite's plan to draw the enemy out, Toby's failure to get into the school, and his IM exchange with SecretAgentMan about the meeting at Jungle Norman's.

"You're not actually going to *meet* him, are you?" said Tamara.

"Yes, I am," said Toby. "What if he can help us?"

"You can't possibly think that's for real! He's obviously planning to do something bad to you!"

"Maybe," said Toby. "But there'll be tons of people around at Jungle Norman's. And Sternabite's gonna back me up."

"Sternabite's insane," noted Tamara.

"Insane," agreed Toby, "but smart. He gave me this device."

"What device?"

"A device that makes me invisible."

"*What?*"

"For real. It uses an iPhone."

184

There was a pause, then Tamara said, "Have you been experimenting with your parents' vitamin supplements?"

"Tamara, I swear, this thing is amazing! People can't see you! Unless they're wearing polarized sunglasses."

"Sunglasses?" said Tamara.

"Really!" Toby looked at his watch. "Listen, I gotta go. If anything happens, remember I was going to Jungle Norman's, okay?"

"Toby—"

"Gotta go." Toby disconnected. The phone rang again almost immediately. Toby looked at the screen and saw it was Tamara calling back. He ignored it and went back out the window. He looked at his watch again: he had to be at Jungle Norman's in twenty minutes. No way he'd make it on foot. He grabbed his bike, which was leaning against the side of the house, and hopped on. He was about to start pedaling when he realized that his mom might see him out the kitchen window. He decided he had no choice but to become invisible, even though this meant somebody might see the bike apparently riding by itself. He tapped the wand on the iPhone.

Next door, the Harbingers' neighbor, Mrs. Penin, was having a glass of wine and watching the TV news. She glanced out the window and saw a bicycle pedaling furiously out of Milkwort Court.

She didn't see anybody riding the bicycle.

Mrs. Penin rose, walked to the kitchen sink, and poured her wine down the drain.

Chapter Thirty-three

INSIDE THE WHITE, government-issue Ford sedan parked across the street from the Shady Inn Motor Court, the mood was less than perky. The aroma wasn't so great, either. The two FBI agents—Iles and Turow—had been living in the car for two days now, watching Room 17 and surviving mainly on Red Bull and Cheez-Its, food purchased from a nearby convenience store. They were tired, grumpy, and increasingly smelly.

They were also bored. Almost nothing had happened since they'd begun the stakeout. The only action had been the delivery of two boxes to the suspects' motel room. Iles and Turow had reported this to their supervisor, hoping he would tell them to arrest the suspects or question the delivery man, or *something*. But he had ordered them to

continue the stakeout. And so they had, taking turns sleeping and watching the door to Room 17, while their white shirts and dark suits slowly turned orange from Cheez-It dust.

Currently, Agent Turow was on duty, staring dully out the window and listening to Agent Iles snore. Turow wondered how his partner could sleep through the racket he was making; the man sounded like a defective chain saw.

Then the door to Room 17 opened.

"Hey," said Turow, nudging Iles.

Iles sputtered awake. "What?"

Turow pointed at the door. Drmtsi and Vrsk were coming out of their room, surrounded by a billowing white cloud.

"Is that *smoke*?" asked Iles.

"Steam," said Turow. "I hope."

"What are they *doing* in there?" said Iles.

"No idea," said Turow.

The agents slouched low in their car as Drmtsi and Vrsk headed across the parking lot in their direction. At the sidewalk, they turned toward the main street. When they reached it they hesitated, then turned right and set off at a brisk pace. Iles started the Ford and eased it away from the curb. Turow flipped his cell phone open and hit the speed dial.

"They're moving on foot," he said. "North on Fenster, toward downtown. Right. Okay." He closed the phone, turned to Iles, and said, "He said to stay with them."

"Duh," said Iles. He turned right on the main street,

staying about twenty-five yards behind Drmtsi and Vrsk, who were still walking fast.

"You snore, you know," said Turow.

"That's what my wife says," said Iles. "I don't hear it."

"I think people in Baltimore could hear it."

"It's that bad? Really?"

Turow was about to answer when his phone chirped. He flipped it open. "Hello?"

Turow listened for a few moments, then said, "Still northbound on Fenster Avenue. Uh-huh." He said "Uh-huh" a few more times, then "Okay," and he flipped the phone closed.

"Whoa," he said.

"What?" said Iles.

"The bureau got a call," said Turow. "Anonymous, from a pay phone around here. The caller says these two"—he pointed at Drmtsi and Vrsk—"are trafficking in classified technology. *Highly* classified. Caller says they're on their way to an exchange right now."

Iles snorted. "Classified technology? *These* clowns? It has to be a hoax."

"That's what they thought at the Bureau," said Turow. "Except the caller gave them the name and serial number of some kind of highly specialized computer chip. So the Bureau checked it out with the Defense Department. And guess what."

"It's real?"

"It's not only real, but it's supposed to be top secret. And guess what else?"

Iles opened his mouth to speak, but Turow answered his own question. "The chip with that particular serial number is missing. Nobody is supposed to know that. So Defense is very interested in this. *Very.*"

"Whoa," said Iles. "So what do we do now?"

"First," said Turow, "we do *not* lose these guys."

Iles drove the Ford a little faster.

"Easy," said Turow. "We also don't want to spook them. If there's gonna be an exchange, we let it happen."

"Then we take them down?" said Iles hopefully. A high-profile espionage arrest could do a lot of good for an FBI agent's career.

"Dream on," said Turow. "Everyone wants a piece of this. Half the Bureau's gonna be here in five minutes, not to mention about nineteen other agencies."

"Oh, man," said Iles, looking down at his Cheez-It–colored suit. "All that brass coming, and we look like traffic cones."

"We don't smell so great either," said Turow.

"Look," said Iles. "They're stopping."

Drmtsi and Vrsk had stopped in front of a strip shopping center in the middle of which was a large building whose walls were covered with mucus-colored fiberglass panels. Apparently, the panels were supposed to look like grass, so that the building resembled a giant mutant grass hut. A fiberglass giraffe poked its long neck through the roof, its grinning giraffe head hovering over a huge neon sign that read, JUNGLE NORMAN'S PIZZA PARTY PLACE.

Drmtsi and Vrsk studied the building for a moment,

then crossed the parking lot and went inside. Turow grabbed his cell phone and hit the speed dial again.

"It's Turow," he said. "Hey, we just observed the suspects entering twenty-thirty-eight North Fenster. An establishment called Jungle Norman's. Yes. J-u-n-g-l-e." He listened for a moment, nodded, then said, "Copy that." He closed the phone.

"Copy what?" said Iles.

"We're going to cover the exits," said Turow. "I'll take the back. We are not to enter the premises, not to engage the suspects until directed."

Iles said a bad word.

Turow said, "There's an insertion team in a chopper on its way." As he spoke, they heard the *whup-whup-whup* of an approaching helicopter.

"*That* was fast," said Iles, yanking the Ford over to the curb. The two agents quickly climbed out. Turow headed around back of the shopping center; Iles jogged toward the front door of Jungle Norman's. As they ran, both men brushed their dark suits, trying, without much success, to get rid of the Cheez-It dust.

Chapter Thirty-four

★

It was a typical Friday evening at Jungle Norman's Pizza Party Place, meaning it was a cross between a school recess and a prison riot. There were fourteen birthday parties going on simultaneously, and the huge room echoed with the earsplitting din of dozens of sugar-crazed children running, shoving, laughing, shouting, shrieking, crying, and fighting for turns on the various video games, at least half of which were out of order.

Toby, having made himself visible again, covered his ears as he picked his way through the chaos toward a group of long tables swarming with more shrieking kids and tended by harried waiters wearing safari outfits. The tables were littered with pizza crusts, fries, ketchup blobs, spilled

drinks, and giant gooey smears that had once been birthday cakes. An air war had erupted between two of the tables, with a party of eight-year-old boys hurling chicken nuggets at a party of seven-year-old boys, who retaliated by throwing cupcakes, one of which had just knocked the princess tiara off the head of a sobbing five-year-old birthday girl at a third table. Parents at all three of these tables were shouting at their children, at other people's children, and at the parents of other people's children. None of this shouting had any effect on anybody.

The tables were grouped around a low stage, on which was Toby's objective, the centerpiece attraction of the Jungle Norman experience: the Jivin' Jungle Jammers. This was a band made up of five large, brightly colored robot animals: Ernest Elephant on drums, Harriet Hippo on keyboards, Gina Giraffe on guitar, Leon Lion on saxophone, and Gordon Gorilla, the MC and lead singer, who wore a purple top hat. Every few minutes the band would come to life and go through its computerized routine. First, Gordon Gorilla told some stunningly unfunny jungle jokes. ("Why are bananas never lonely? Because they hang around in bunches!") Then the band performed "Happy Birthday," followed by some songs that had been popular, or at least vaguely familiar, several decades earlier, when Jungle Norman's had first opened.

As Toby neared the stage, the Jivin' Jungle Jammers were performing an anemic version of the Pointer Sisters' "Jump (For My Love)." A wedge of pepperoni pizza soared gracefully over three party tables and landed on Harriet

Hippo's nose. Toby, remembering SecretAgentMan's instruction, got as close as he could to Gordon Gorilla. He turned and quickly ducked as a cupcake whizzed past. Then, with his back to the stage, he scanned the crowd, not sure what or who he was looking for. He glanced down to make sure he had the iPhone clipped to his belt; he hoped the fragile fiber-optic filaments hadn't been damaged as he pushed his way through the crowd. He resumed scanning, watching, waiting.

"Toby!"

Toby, startled, turned and saw Tamara and Micah working their way through the crowd toward him.

"What are *you* doing here?" he said, as they reached the stage.

"We're here for the pizza," said Micah. He pointed at the slice on Harriet Hippo's nose. "Is anybody eating that?"

Toby looked at Tamara. "I told you not to come."

"Right," said Tamara. "And your plans have been working out *so well*."

"But your parents . . ."

"They already grounded us for life," said Micah. "What're they gonna do, ground us for the *after*life?"

Toby allowed himself a small grin. "Okay," he said. "Thanks for coming. You guys're good friends."

"Shut up," said Micah.

"No, really," said Toby. "I mean it."

"Me, too," said Micah. "Shut up."

"Enough," said Tamara. "Have you seen your mystery guy?"

"Not that I know of."

"So what's your plan?" said Tamara.

"I'm supposed to stand by the gorilla," said Toby.

As he spoke, the Jivin' Jungle Jammers, having finished "Jump (For My Love)," launched into "Jeremiah Was a Bullfrog."

"Maybe," said Micah, "he's planning to kill your brain cells with this music."

"Who're those guys?" said Tamara. She pointed at two men working their way through the crowd. One was young, thin, and intense-looking; the other was older and heftier, with a thick beard. Both men wore ill-fitting brown polyester suits festooned with stains. Both looked overwhelmed by the chaotic mobs of children swirling around them.

"They don't look like birthday boys, either," said Toby.

"They're coming toward us," said Tamara.

As the men approached, Toby glanced down at the iPhone clipped to his belt. He located the sunglasses icon that would, he hoped, summon Sternabite.

"Okay," he said to Tamara and Micah. "Let me handle this."

"Handle *what*?" said Tamara.

"I have no idea," said Toby.

"It is food!" Vrsk said to Drmtsi, in Krpsht. "They are *throwing food*!" Such a thing would *never* happen in Krpshtskan. For one thing, food there was scarce; for another thing, what food there was tended to be heavy.

"Really?" said Drmtsi. Like Vrsk, he had eaten nothing

but smerk for days; there was only a little left in his pants. "They are throwing *food*?" As he spoke, a half-eaten, ketchup-drenched nugget landed on his lapel. He picked it off, sniffed it, and ate it. "Not bad," he said.

They were almost to the gorilla, which was singing about joy to the world. Vrsk scanned the crowd, looking for Prmkt. But the only people near the singing gorilla were three teenagers, who stared at Vrsk and Drmtsi as they approached.

"They're coming right at us," said Tamara.

"Yeah, I can see that," said Toby.

"What is that *smell*?" said Micah.

Tamara sniffed, wrinkled her nose, and said, "I think it's coming from the fat guy's pants."

"That is *gross*," said Micah.

Vrsk and Drmtsi reached the edge of the stage. The teenagers watched them closely, but nobody else at Jungle Norman's seemed to be paying any attention. Drmtsi, showing excellent quickness for a man his size, caught a slice of pizza in midair and took a bite.

"Where is Prmkt?" he said in Krpsht, through a mouthful of cheese.

"Prmkt said he will come to us when we give the special signal," said Vrsk.

"What is the special signal again?" said Drmtsi, taking another bite.

"We lift the hat of the singing gorilla," said Vrsk.

Drmtsi, chewing, studied Gordon the Gorilla for a few seconds, then made a command decision.

"You do it," he said.

Jungle Norman's Pizza Party Place was now swarming with heavily armed federal agents wearing black SWAT-team uniforms. Most were from the FBI, but there were also personnel from a half-dozen other agencies, including two men who were with the CIA, although if questioned they would claim they were with the Department of Agriculture. The various agents had formed a perimeter around the stage area, taking cover behind video games. A few parents and staff members had noticed them but thought they were there to entertain one of the birthday groups. In the general wildness of Jungle Norman's, the agents had not yet created much of a stir.

The agents were under the command of a veteran field operative named Blount. He was monitoring the situation on night-vision binoculars from behind the Dance Dance Revolution machine. Blount raised his wrist to his mouth and spoke quietly into a microphone, which would transmit his voice to earpieces worn by the agents inside, as well as those outside on the barricaded street and others in cars and in the helicopters—there were now four of them—hovering overhead.

"The two individuals have approached the gorilla," he said. "There are three other individuals in the vicinity of the gorilla. We wait for the exchange, people. I repeat, *we wait for the exchange*. We move *only on my command*."

Both Agent Turow and Agent Iles clipped their FBI identification shields to their orange-crusted suit coats at about the same time. On opposite sides of the same building, they grabbed the door handles, ready to rush inside. They'd spent two days following these suspects; they wanted to be part of the takedown.

Toby, Tamara, and Micah watched as Vrsk put his foot up on the stage, as if preparing to get on it. The man looked around nervously. Toby was convinced this guy and his friend had something to do with the IMs he'd received. Why else would he be here, hanging around the gorilla?

Vrsk now was up on the stage. His eyes scanned the crowd and met Toby's. Toby made a decision and stepped up on the stage with him.

"Are you looking for me?" Toby asked.

"What?" said Vrsk. "Who? Me?"

"Are you SecretAgentMan?"

"Who are you?" said Vrsk. He said it in Krpsht, so it came out sort of like spitting.

"Hey!" said Toby, wiping off his shirt. Tamara and Micah quickly climbed up onto the stage to back up their friend.

"Sorry," said Vrsk, switching to English.

Now Drmtsi was also clambering up onto the stage. "Who is this?" he said in Krpsht, waving his pizza slice at Toby.

"Hey!" shouted a voice from the crowd. "You're not allowed on the stage!"

Toby, Tamara, Micah, Vrsk, and Drmtsi looked down to see a waiter in a safari outfit glaring at them.

"I said, off the stage!" the waiter hollered over the music. "You're not allowed to . . . *uhhh.*"

The waiter staggered sideways as his right buttock was penetrated by a small but potent tranquilizer dart fired from behind a Skee-Ball machine by an FBI sharpshooter acting on orders from Field Commander Blount. As the five people on the stage watched, the waiter staggered sideways with a puzzled look on his face, smiled, then slumped into a chair, unconscious and drooling.

Toby turned back to Vrsk and repeated, "Are you SecretAgentMan?"

"What is boy saying?" Drmtsi asked Vrsk, indicating Toby.

"He is asking if I am a secret agent," said Vrsk.

"Admit nothing!" said Drmtsi. "Tell him we are tourists."

"We are tourists," Vrsk said to Toby.

"Smerk?" said Drmtsi, smiling at Toby and his friends while reaching into his pants.

"Ick!" said Tamara.

The drama on the stage had started to attract attention. People were pointing; several more safari-outfitted waiters were coming. Vrsk sensed that things were getting out of hand.

"Excuse me," he said. "I must go to gorilla." Pushing Toby aside, he started toward Gordon Gorilla, who had just launched into the Jivin' Jungle Jammer's big finale, Lee

Greenwood's patriotic anthem "God Bless the USA."

"Wait a minute," said Toby, grabbing Vrsk's arm. "Who are you? Why are you here? Do you know Mr. P?"

"Please to let go!" said Vrsk. He struggled toward the gorilla, with Toby still tugging on his arm. Tamara and Micah stepped forward to help Toby. Drmtsi stepped forward to help Vrsk. Vrsk, determined to carry out his mission, dragged Toby to Gordon Gorilla, reached up with his free hand, and lifted the top hat. It took some effort—the hat was attached to Gordon's head with duct tape—but it popped off. A small package wrapped in brown paper, which had been concealed under the hat, fell out and tumbled onto Gordon Gorilla's shoulder. Vrsk grabbed for the package, but at that instant Gordon Gorilla sang "I'd proudly stand UP!" and raised his powerful robotic right arm to wave an American flag. Gordon's fist slammed into Vrsk's jaw, and Vrsk went down like a sack of rocks. As he fell, Toby reflexively grabbed the tumbling package.

That was all Field Commander Blount needed to see.

"GO!" he yelled into his wrist microphone. "GO! GO! GOGOGO!"

In an instant, Jungle Norman's became even louder and more chaotic than it usually is, as two dozen agents charged. One of them went down immediately as he ran face-first into the path of an entire airborne basket of nachos. Another hit a nasty patch of vanilla frosting on the floor and lost control, slamming into two other agents, the three of them knocking down a row of classic Space Invaders games, which fell like dominos, one crashing

into another, video tubes exploding, glass shards flying everywhere. There was some applause, which quickly changed to shouts and screams as excited partygoers and their parents realized this wasn't a show. The crowd dove frantically out of the way of the burly black-clad men charging the stage, where Gordon Gorilla and the Jivin' Jungle Jammers were hitting the dramatic final notes of "God Bless the USA."

The humans on the stage—Toby, Tamara, Micah, and Drmtsi (Vrsk was on the floor, unconscious)—watched in stunned incomprehension, still as stones, as the first wave of men reached them and, without slowing down, tackled them. They went down like bowling pins, only faster; Toby lost hold of the package. Tamara managed a short scream, but that was the only sound any of them had time to make before they were lying under a minimum of two agents apiece, unable to breathe, let alone shout.

In seconds their hands were behind their backs as all of them, including Vrsk, were handcuffed. Toby, his face smushed against the stage, watched as one of the agents picked up the package he'd been holding, shouting, "I got it! I got it!" He pointed at Toby. "This one here had it."

"That's not mine!" Toby said, fighting to get the words out with two agents—Turow and Iles—sitting on him.

"But you *were* holding it," said Iles.

"But I don't even know what it *is*," said Toby.

"We'll sort that out later," said Turow.

"But what did we do?" said Toby. "What is this *about*?"

"We'll sort that out later, too," said Turow. Toby felt the

weight come off him as Iles pulled him to his feet. He looked around the vast room. It was emptying quickly as the partygoers and their parents streamed toward the front door, leaving a chaotic mess of overturned chairs and tables, with food and drink spilled everywhere. At the front door, a TV crew was forcing its way in past the crowd, lights blazing. Some agents ran to intercept it, but the camera was aimed at the stage already, focusing on Toby and the others in handcuffs.

"This can't be happening!" said Tamara. "I have to be home in twenty minutes! My parents think I'm in my room!"

"They'll probably stop thinking that when they see you on TV," said Micah, nodding toward the camera.

"Ohmigod," said Tamara. "Ohmigod, *we're on TV*. Toby, what's gonna happen? What are we gonna *do*?"

Toby looked at his friends.

"I don't know," he said. His eyes were burning. He looked down at the floor.

"I don't know," he said again.

CHAPTER THIRTY-FIVE

INSIDE TOBY'S HOUSE ON MILKWORT COURT, Fawn Harbinger was in the kitchen cooking dinner, which involved pickled seaweed. She poked her head through the doorway to the family room, where Toby's dad was reclining on his recliner, watching the local news.

"Roger," she said, "could you please call Toby up for dinner? He's in the basement watching TV."

"Just a second," said Roger. "The helicopters we're hearing?" He pointed at the TV. "Look at this."

Fawn moved closer to the screen, which had the words LIVE AND BREAKING across the bottom. She frowned as she recognized the building.

"Isn't that Jungle Norman's?" she said.

"Yup," said Roger. "There's some kind of huge federal

raid going on. There are FBI agents and SWAT guys all over the place."

"That's less than two miles from here!" she said. "What on earth happened?"

"No one's saying much." Roger threw a lever, and the recliner lurched forward, nearly ejecting him. "The reporter said the FBI *allegedly* busted some kind of spy ring that was stealing defense secrets."

"At *Jungle Norman's*?" she said.

"I know!" said Roger.

As he spoke, the TV news camera showed four men coming out the front door of Jungle Norman's beneath the giraffe head, carrying something large toward an FBI van. The image jumped around for a few seconds, as the camera person was jostled by the mob of newspeople shoving each other for a closer look. Finally the camera stabilized, and Roger and Fawn got a look at what the agents were carrying.

"Is that the singing gorilla?" said Fawn.

Roger nodded. "Gordon," he said.

"But why on earth would—"

Roger held up his hand and said, "They're bringing out the suspects."

There were shouts, and again the image went jerky. For a moment, Roger and Fawn could see only a blur of bodies and faces. And then, all at once, there he was, filling the screen.

"Ohmigod," said Roger.

"Toby!" screamed Fawn, staggering backward.

Their son was being half carried through the surging crowd by two men in dark suits flecked with orange dust. For just a moment, Toby's pale and terrified face filled the screen. The next shot showed him being hustled into the van along with Gordon Gorilla. The van doors were slammed shut and the van roared away. The camera swung back to pick up . . .

"That's Micah and Tamara!" Fawn gasped.

They were being hustled toward a second van. But by then Roger and Fawn were no longer looking at the screen; they were staring at each other, speechless, their faces slack with shock. Finally, Fawn found words.

"He was supposed to be in the basement," she said.

"Yeah?" said Roger. "Well, guess what?"

Chapter Thirty-six

★

GRDANKL THE STRONG, president for life, lumbered unhappily into the bunker deep beneath the presidential palace. Waiting for him were his first, second, and third vice presidents, who were gathered around the lone working computer in the Republic of Krpshtskan. They appeared nervous.

"Well?" said Grdankl the Strong.

The first and second vice presidents stared at the third vice president, indicating that he was going to have to do the talking. He cleared his throat and said, "The red flag is up."

"What red flag?" said Grdankl the Strong.

"On the little mailbox," said the third vice president, pointing to the computer screen. Grdankl leaned over and frowned at the mailbox, then rose up, looking displeased.

"You disturbed my presidential nap for *this*?" he said.

The first and second vice presidents edged away from the third vice president, who quickly said, "The flag means we have e-mail."

"How do you know this?" said Grdankl.

"Vrsk told me," said the first vice president. Vrsk had given him a hasty lesson on the computer before leaving for America with Drmtsi.

Grdankl nodded. "E-mail," he said. "It must be from Prmkt. What does it say?"

"In order to read it," said the third vice president, "we must first open it."

"Then open it!" said Grdankl the Strong.

All eyes were now on the third vice president, who was sweating as he tried to remember his lesson.

"To open it," he said, "we must press on the mailbox."

As the others watched, Grdankl the Strong reached toward the screen and aimed for the little mailbox, pressing a meaty, sausage-shaped forefinger against the glass of the computer monitor. Nothing happened. Grdankl glared at the third vice president, who was sweating harder now as he racked his brain, trying to remember. . . .

"The mouse!" he said, startling the others.

"What mouse?" said Grdankl, looking at the floor.

"Here," said the third vice president, pointing at the computer mouse. "We must use this to press on the mailbox."

Grdankl the Strong picked up the mouse and pressed it against the computer screen.

"No!" said the third vice president, quickly adding, "What I mean to say, Your Supreme Democratically Elected Excellency, is that you do it like this." He gently took the mouse from Grdankl the Strong, set it on the computer table, and slid it back and forth. "See? It moves this little arrow on the screen."

Grdankl looked at the mouse, then at the arrow. "It is a stupid system," he said.

"Yes," agreed the third vice president. "Stupid." He put the arrow over the mailbox and pressed the mouse button. An e-mail header appeared on the screen. "Your Exalted Highness is correct," he said. "It is from Prmkt." He clicked on the header, and the e-mail filled the screen.

"Let me see," said Grdankl. He leaned forward and read the e-mail slowly, his lips moving. He grunted in surprise, then read some more. When he was done, he faced his vice presidents.

"Drmtsi and Vrsk have been captured by the Americans," he said. "In a jungle."

The vice presidents gasped.

"America has a jungle?" asked the first vice president.

"Yes," said Grdankl the Strong. "It is called Norman."

The vice presidents nodded.

"What will the Americans do to Drmtsi and Vrsk?" asked the first vice president.

"They will hang them by their ears," said Grdankl, "and poke them with sticks." Grdankl did not know this for a fact, but it's what he would have done.

"It is terrible!" said the second vice president.

"Yes," agreed Grdankl, although he did not seem particularly upset.

"Does this mean," the first vice president said cautiously, "that our plan to destroy America has failed?"

Grdankl the Strong smiled. "No," he said. "The Americans *think* they have stopped the plan. But Prmkt"—Grdankl pointed at the e-mail—"says they do not know the *real* plan. Everything is still in place. We will still destroy the United States."

"Excellent!" said the first vice president.

"But . . ." the second vice president began.

"But what?" said Grdankl the Strong.

"What about Drmtsi and Vrsk?" said the second vice president.

Grdankl the Strong waved his hand, indicating this was not a major problem. "I will name something for them. A street, perhaps. A nice one, without too many mud holes."

The vice presidents applauded the generosity of Grdankl the Strong. He bowed, graciously acknowledging their praise. Then he sat down in front of the computer screen, put his hand on the mouse, and turned to the third vice president.

"Now show me," he said, "how to find Catwoman."

CHAPTER THIRTY-SEVEN

★

A KEY TURNED IN THE LOCK of the cell door, startling Toby out of his snooze. He jerked up and said a bad word when, for the fifth or sixth time, he banged his forehead into the ceiling only inches from his face.

Toby was in the upper bunk of a bunk bed in a cell in a building somewhere near Washington, although he had no idea where. Micah was sleeping in the lower bunk. The other bunk bed in the small cell was occupied by the two weird foreign guys who had been arrested with them at Jungle Norman's. Toby was pretty sure that the cell had microphones and cameras hidden in it and that the feds had put them all together so they would talk. But they hadn't talked, because the weird foreign guys were not

good at English. They also emitted a funky odor: the cell smelled like a cross between old cheese and dirty laundry.

Both foreign guys were snoring. The big foreign guy was in the upper bunk, where he had insisted on sleeping even though it took him five minutes to climb up there. The little foreign guy was in the lower bunk; he had a bandage on his chin where he'd been decked by Gordon, the singing robot gorilla.

Toby glanced at the clock: it was almost noon. They'd been in the cell a few hours after being kept up all night getting fingerprinted and questioned. The feds had taken away their belts and personal belongings—including Toby's special iPhone and the special hat. Then the suspects were placed in this cell and instructed to get some sleep. Thanks to the snoring, Toby hadn't gotten much.

The door opened, and in came FBI Agent Turow, who apparently had not gotten much sleep either. His face was stubbled with beard growth; he still had orange dust on his suit. Wrinkling his nose at the smell in the cell, he nudged Micah and the two foreign guys.

"Wake up," he said. "Time to move."

"Move to where?" said Toby.

"Interrogation," said Turow.

"Again?" said Toby.

"Oh, yes," said Turow, with the hint of a smile, but not a friendly one. "There's gonna be *lots* more."

"I want to talk to my parents," Toby said.

"Me, too," said Micah, adding, "I don't mean I want to talk to *Toby's* parents. I want to talk to *my* parents. But if I

can't talk to mine, I want to at least talk to his. But I'd rather talk to—"

Turow cut Micah off. "As I told you both last night," he said, "your parents have been contacted. They know you're in custody. You'll see them later."

"How much later?" said Toby.

"Later," said Turow.

"Where are we?" said Micah.

"You're in a government facility, in what we like to call an undisclosed location," said Turow.

"But don't we . . ." began Toby, "I mean, don't we get to talk to a lawyer?"

"Where'd you get that idea?" said Turow. "From TV?"

"Yes," admitted Toby.

"Well, guess what, Toby?" said Turow. "This isn't TV. This is real life, and in real life you *don't* get to talk to a lawyer if it's deemed a matter of national security."

Toby blinked. "National security?" he said.

"Oh, yes," said Turow. "Call us a crazy federal law-enforcement agency, but when we at the FBI find somebody holding stolen highly classified defense technology, which he's apparently passing to two foreign nationals, we become curious."

"But I told you!" said Toby. "We don't know these guys! We never saw them before! I only went to Jungle Norman's because of the . . ."

"Right, I know, the instant messages," said Turow. "Except you can't tell us who sent them."

"But it's *true*," said Toby. "Somebody IM'd me, and whoever it was is planning . . ."

"I know," said Turow. "He's gonna do something terrible at your school science fair. Except you don't know what."

"But . . ."

"Save it," said Turow. "You'll have plenty of time to try to explain. Days, in fact."

"But the science fair is *tonight*," said Toby.

"Looks like you're gonna miss it," said Turow.

"But . . ."

"*Save it*," snapped Turow. He pointed to the door. "Let's go, gentlemen."

The little weird foreign guy on the lower bunk said something to the big weird foreign guy in the upper bunk. The big guy said something back. The language they used made them sound as though they were just about to hawk up major loogies, but they never actually did. They both climbed out of their bunks. This was a major effort for the big guy, who seemed to be the main source of the odor, emitting powerful stink rays from his pants. When he finally had both feet on the floor, he turned to Turow and said something, sounding pretty angry. The little guy translated it.

"Fourth Vice President Drmtsi demands to speak immediately to a representative of the embassy of Krpshtskan," he said.

Turow nodded and said, "Mister . . . Vrsk, is it? Did I say that correctly?"

"Vrsk, yes."

"Here's the thing, Mr. Vrsk," continued Turow. "There isn't any Krpshtskan embassy here in the United States."

"Is not?" said Vrsk.

"Is not," said Turow. "Believe me, we checked. We also tried to call your country and speak to the authorities there, but we haven't been able to reach anybody."

Vrsk nodded. The phone system in Krpshtskan was unreliable because people kept using the telephone poles for firewood.

"Please tell Vice President Drmtsi we will keep trying," said Turow.

Vrsk translated this to Drmtsi, who said something back. Vrsk turned to Turow and said, "Fourth Vice President Drmtsi demands to know where is credit card."

"Tell him it's in a safe place," said Turow.

Again Vrsk translated. Drmtsi answered at length. Somewhat reluctantly, Vrsk turned to Turow and said, "Fourth Vice President Drmtsi says he requires card for TV shopping peoples show. Very good price coming on machine for to make fodge."

"Fodge?" said Turow.

"Yes, fodge," said Vrsk.

"I think he means fudge," said Micah.

"Yes," said Vrsk. "Fodge."

Agent Turow rubbed his tired, stubbled face with both hands. "Listen," he said. "Right now, you cannot watch TV, and you cannot have your personal belongings. Right now, you are going to be interrogated. I must insist that all of you come with me."

Vrsk translated this, and the four cell mates trooped reluctantly into the hall, where a half dozen largish agents

were waiting, apparently ready to help Turow if there was trouble. Toby, as casually as he could, stuck a hand into his back pocket; he felt the two backup coils of thin fiberoptic cable. He wiggled his toes: the insoles were still in place.

But he needed the phone and the hat. They'd been taken when he and the others had been brought into this building—wherever it was—the night before. The feds had stopped them at what looked like a reception counter and made them put their possessions into manila envelopes. Toby wondered where those envelopes were now, and how he could get to them.

Accompanied by their large escorts, the four cell mates trooped down the corridor. They stopped at another cell. The door opened and Tamara came out, accompanied by an agent whose ID badge said IMMIGRATION AND NATURALIZA-TION, and under that, LEFKON. Tamara looked exhausted, and her eyes were red from crying, but she managed a wan smile when she saw Toby and Micah.

"You know," she said, "I used to think the worst thing that could happen would be if I got detention."

Toby managed to smile back and was about to say something when Turow nudged him forward. The group continued down the corridor into a large room, which Toby realized was the reception area. As they passed the counter, Toby noticed that there was a small room behind the receptionist. On the door, which stood ajar, there was a red cross; apparently it was a first-aid station. Inside the room, Toby could see a supply cabinet, a sink, a cot, a chair, and a small desk. On the desk was a plastic box

containing a stack of manila envelopes. Toby's heart leaped; they looked like the envelopes the feds had used to hold the prisoners' possessions.

They were past the reception desk now, but Toby's thoughts were still focused on the first-aid room. If he could get in there, get his hat and phone . . .

"In here," said Turow, opening a door. The five prisoners trooped into what looked like a conference room. In the center was a long table surrounded by eight chairs. On a sideboard was a pitcher of orange juice, some plastic cups, and a plate of muffins.

"You'll wait here," said Turow. "We'll be back for you in a bit." He closed the door, and the room echoed with the click of a dead bolt sliding home.

Drmtsi and Vrsk headed straight for the food. Each man took a muffin and, while chewing it, stuffed several more into his pockets. Tamara, Micah, and Toby stood looking at each other.

"We gotta get out of here," said Micah.

Toby shook his head and pointed at the ceiling. Micah looked up.

"What?" he said.

Toby pantomimed a video camera.

"What are you doing?" said Micah.

Toby sighed.

"He's pantomiming a video camera," said Tamara.

"Why would he do that?" said Micah.

"Because they're *watching* us, you moron," said Tamara.

"Ah," said Micah. He winked at Tamara and Toby, then,

aiming his voice at the ceiling, said, too loudly, "Well, we certainly aren't planning to get out of here!"

Toby and Tamara rolled their eyes.

"What?" said Micah. "I don't really *mean* it. I'm just saying it for the . . ."

"Just shut up, okay?" said Toby.

"Okay," said Micah, looking hurt.

Toby sat down and drummed his fingers on the table, trying to force his tired brain to think. If he could get to the first-aid station behind the reception desk . . .

Toby sat up straight.

The first-aid station.

He looked toward Tamara and Micah, who had gone over to the side table with Vrsk and Drmtsi and were helping themselves to juice and muffins. Trying to keep his voice calm, Toby said, "Hey, Micah, Tamara—either of you guys have any gum?"

"Nope," said Micah.

"I don't chew gum," said Tamara.

Toby slumped in his chair. So much for his brilliant plan.

"Excuse me?"

Toby looked up: Vrsk was speaking to him.

"Did you say gom?" said Vrsk, through a mouthful of muffin.

"Gum, yes," said Toby.

"I have gom," said Vrsk.

Vrsk reached into his pocket and pulled out a small package. On it, in several languages, were the words "Air Zerkistan."

CHAPTER THIRTY-EIGHT

★

THE GYMNASIUM OF HUBBLE MIDDLE SCHOOL was humming. Literally. Motors were whirring, keyboards were clicking, lights were flickering, and the air itself seemed to buzz with tension as students worked frantically to get their science-fair projects ready before the deadline.

At four p.m. sharp, Mr. P would blow a whistle, then throw the master switch that cut off the power to the outlets. The gym would be cleared, closed, and locked. At six p.m., the students, along with parents, teachers, and school administrators, would gather outside on the ball field for what had become a major Hubble tradition and the much-anticipated highlight of the school year.

All eyes and ears would turn skyward, awaiting the dramatic arrival of the TranScent Corp. helicopter, which

would land near second base. Billionaire scientist/businessman/celebrity Lance Swingle would emerge from the chopper, waving to acknowledge the cheers of the crowd. After greeting the dignitaries, Swingle would lead the throng into the gym and take his place at the podium set up next to the master switch. There he would make what the official program described hopefully as "brief remarks," although they usually lasted quite a while, as Swingle loved to tell the story of how he overcame many obstacles and was able to succeed because of hard work and because of being, with all due modesty, a genius.

When Swingle was finally done, he would turn to the master switch, and, with a dramatic flourish, flip it up to the "on" position. Instantly, the science fair would come spectacularly to life. Then Swingle, accompanied by a clot of science teachers, would personally inspect the projects. With the inspection completed, they would confer, although this was really for show, as only one opinion counted. And then Swingle would, with great drama—he loved drama—announce the winner. The lucky student would come forward and, as cameras flashed, receive a check from Swingle.

This year the check would be worth $5,000, a fact that was on the mind of every student in the gym. Many of them were still fiddling with their projects when the big clock on the wall clicked off the last minute to four. A shrill blast echoed through the gym as Mr. P blew his whistle. A second later, he grabbed the master switch on the wall and flipped it down. The project lights went off; the motors

stopped whirring. Within ten minutes, all the students and teachers were gone. The doors were locked. The gym was empty.

Except for Prmkt.

Using his key, he entered through the side door of the gym. He carried a cheap vinyl athletic bag. It contained a coil of thick black cable, a flashlight, tape, rubber gloves, and tools. He walked down a long row of exhibit tables passing a variety of projects, including three, which were standing side-by-side, titled: DEATH BY PACKAGING, THE FLOATING FROG, and NUCLEAR MENTOS.

Prmkt paid no attention to these. His objective was a group of four projects, all submitted by idiot, spoiled ME students who had no idea what the projects really were. These projects really looked as though they'd been made by middle-schoolers—they had loose wires, paint smears, scratches, excess glue blobs, and misspelled words in the explanations. But this was camouflage to fool the judges, part of the service provided by the Science Nook.

In the quiet of the gym, Prmkt quickly examined the four projects. When he was done, he allowed himself a small smile. The Science Nook, as in previous years, had followed his plans exactly. Of course, in previous years, the projects were harmless. They were clever and technically sophisticated; that's why they won awards. But they posed no threat to anyone.

These four projects were different. These were the result of years of patient research and careful planning by Prmkt. He had designed the projects on two levels. On the

surface, they were scientific demonstrations that were educational, if a bit silly. But each project had far greater hidden capabilities, made possible by the technology supplied by the foolish ME parents, thinking they were helping their idiot spoiled children.

When the projects were linked together, as they would be shortly, their hidden capabilities would be networked and amplified, and they would become something altogether different: a hugely powerful, highly sophisticated weapon. It would be a weapon unlike any ever built—a weapon against which there was no defense; a weapon that would bring the mighty United States to its knees, groveling for mercy before Krpshtskan.

Prmkt smiled again, thinking about it, savoring the cleverness of his plan. He was confident now that it would work. He had been concerned when the student Toby Harbinger and his two friends had somehow become suspicious and tried to warn Principal Plotz-Gornett. He had been even more concerned when Grdankl the Strong had sent his idiot brother Drmtsi and Vrsk to the United States to "help."

But Prmkt had dealt with both of these threats, decisively and cleverly. He had, by planting the plasma in the boy's locker, managed to make the boy himself the object of the investigation, at the same time taking advantage of the fire-drill distraction to retrieve the project list from the principal's office and return it to the Science Nook. He had, even more cleverly, managed to send both the boy and his countrymen to Jungle Norman's, where they were

caught with the classified chip that had been planted by Prmkt, who had also called the FBI.

He had overcome all the obstacles. Nobody would stop him now; nobody was intelligent enough to even suspect what he was up to. He was sure that the Science Nook proprietor, Sternabite—clever as he was—had no concept of the true capabilities of the devices he had built. All Sternabite cared about was getting his money. As for the foolish ME parents and their idiot spoiled children, all that mattered for them was winning the stupid science fair and getting a check they didn't need.

But there would be no winner this year and no check. When the blowhard billionaire Lance Swingle threw the master switch to start the science fair, he would instead be starting Prmkt's machine. After that would come chaos.

Prmkt opened the athletic bag and began removing the tools and the roll of cable. He knew exactly what he needed to do; he had rehearsed this a thousand times in his mind. He uncoiled the cable, went to the four projects one by one, and carefully connected them together.

He began with the project submitted by Jason Niles. It was titled TERMITE FLATULENCE: POWER SOURCE OF TOMORROW. It looked a like a high-tech ant farm: a large metal box filled with dirt and rotting lumber, the front side of which was made of glass to show the termites inside busily eating tunnels through the wood. Atop the farm was a small, clear-plastic box containing a series of tubes and some crude-looking wiring—allegedly soldered by Jason—that connected various basic electrical components. Sitting

atop this was a single glowing five-watt lightbulb. According to the project explanation, the termites, as they digested the wood, produced methane gas, which was collected by the apparatus on top and converted, by a process called "oxidative coupling," into electricity, which powered the bulb.

This explanation was a lie. In fact, hidden behind the wood and dirt was the world's smallest neutron generator, a top-secret experimental prototype being developed by the military for use by troops in remote areas that lacked electricity. This generator was powering the lightbulb. But it could produce a *lot* more than five watts; it could power a small city.

Prmkt carefully connected the cable to Jason's project, then, routing it under the table, moved to the project submitted by Farrell "The Ferret" Plinkett, titled A PRACTICAL SOLUTION TO CELL-PHONE NOISE POLLUTION. It consisted of a lifelike female department-store dummy inside a crude box made of Plexiglas. The dummy's mouth had been replaced by a small speaker; wires ran from this speaker to a volume knob on the outside of the box. Next to the speaker was a decibel meter, and next to that was an older model cell phone, with some extra batteries taped to the back.

When the project was turned on, the speaker played a recording of a woman talking, with the volume controlled by the knob. If the volume was turned up past fifty decibels, the cell phone emitted a loud crack and a shower of sparks, charring the dummy's right ear, as a reminder that the dummy should keep its voice down.

The project explanation said that Farrell had built this "noise-suppression technology" using inexpensive capacitors that could easily be incorporated into new cell phones. But what was actually inside the cell phone in The Ferret's project was no ordinary capacitor. It was a bank of state-of-the-art supercapacitors made from an experimental process that used barium titanate nanoparticles in a polymer matrix. Each supercapacitor could hold extremely high voltage levels and discharge this energy extremely fast. Right now, the bank was getting its energy from the weak batteries strapped to the phone. Prmkt was connecting it to a far more powerful source.

He moved next to Harmonee Prescott's project, which was called THE HOTNESS BOX. It consisted of a black box with a dial labeled HOTNESS. The input to the black box was a video camera; the output was a computer screen. According to the project explanation, the box contained a programmable chip running a program written by Harmonee, which she had adapted from a program used to enhance digital photographs. Except that instead of just fixing the contrast and removing red-eye, Harmonee's program, according to the explanation, could make pictures of people's faces more attractive.

To demonstrate how it worked, the video camera was aimed at a picture of Ursula, the sea witch from *The Little Mermaid*.

With the HOTNESS knob set at zero, the image on the computer screen was identical to the picture. But as the HOTNESS knob was rotated from zero to ten, the output

223

image gradually changed, becoming more and more attractive, until finally, at maximum hotness, it looked remarkably like . . . Harmonee Prescott.

The project explanation said that the Hotness Box could make the same transformation with any image of a face, male or female, and could be used "by less-attractive people in a variety of applications, such as Facebook photos and dating Web sites."

It was an impressive demonstration. But the software running on the chip inside the black box was not written by Harmonee. It had been developed for the Central Intelligence and National Security agencies by Harmonee's father's company, PresTech. And it was capable of far more than altering a still photo. The software that turned the sea witch into a hot babe could radically alter the image and sound transmitted by any broadcast signal, TV or radio, in real time. It could make anybody look or sound like anybody, or anything, else. For example, if the leader of a hostile nation were to make a televised speech, the signal could be intercepted by U.S. spy satellites and almost instantaneously be processed and rebroadcast, with a far more powerful signal, so that the leader appeared to be saying something completely different. Or he could be made to appear tired or sick. For that matter, he could be made to look exactly like the sea witch.

Of course, this software, like the technology in the other projects, was supposed to be top secret, a fact that amused Prndki. He had been surprised at how easy it was to find out about these things. If you were smart—if you knew

where to look in scientific journals and, of course, on the Internet; if you befriended disgruntled or gossipy employees working for certain companies, certain agencies—it turned out that the "secrets" weren't so secret after all.

Prmkt then ran his cable to the final project, submitted by Haley Hess. It was titled THE ULTIMATE REMOTE CONTROL. This was the heart of Prmkt's weapon; this was his masterpiece.

In outward appearance it was unimpressive, consisting of what looked like an ordinary laptop computer and a foam-core poster board explaining the project. When the computer was turned on, it displayed a Google Earth map of North America; using the mouse, the user could zoom in on a specific location. In the science-fair demonstration, the user clicked a box that said RUN DEMONSTRATION. The computer then zoomed in on Haley Hess's house in Manor Estates—a large structure ablaze with lights in the gathering night. The user was instructed to position the mouse arrow over the house and click the left button; this highlighted the house. The user was then instructed to click the right button; suddenly the house lights all went off, leaving a dark hole in the middle of the neighborhood. Another right click turned the lights back on.

The explanation on the poster (written in Haley's neat handwriting with little circles for the dots over the *i*'s) said that the user really was, from the Hubble Middle gym, turning her house lights on and off over the Internet. This was made possible, the explanation said, by a device that Haley had designed and built herself, using an electrical

relay and a wireless router. There was a photograph on the poster showing a smiling Haley holding this device, which looked like a toaster oven with an antenna taped to the side. The explanation said that Haley's device had been installed on the main circuit breaker at Haley's house by a professional electrician, under Haley's supervision. There was also a photograph of this, showing Haley frowning thoughtfully at a man holding the device and peering at the circuit breaker.

The explanation stated that, with Haley's simple and inexpensive device, you could control your home electrical system, or even individual lights and appliances, from anywhere in the world, as long as you had access to a computer with an Internet connection.

But, as in the case of the other projects, Haley's remote control was quite deceptive. The device Haley was holding in the photo was, in fact, a toaster oven with an antenna taped to the side. The "electrician" allegedly installing the device in the other photo was a pizza-delivery man whom Haley had paid ten dollars to pose with the circuit breaker. The map demonstration was a fake, using a real Google Earth image but altering it to make it appear as if the lights were going on and off.

The key to the project was the laptop, which Haley's father had obtained for her. He worked for a company called DeathVolt, which did security consulting for power companies around the world; the laptop was designed to demonstrate to them why they needed it. It was a rugged, superfast computer capable of connecting to the Internet

via satellite from anywhere in the world. And it was running software developed by DeathVolt with the help of some extremely smart hackers who were paid very well for their time and knowledge.

This software probed the Internet sites of power companies, looking for ways past the firewalls into the business and administrative systems, which it almost always penetrated quickly. It then probed for weaknesses into the grid-control systems, which actually distributed the power. This took a bit longer, as these systems were supposed to be sealed off from the business side. But the seal was never perfect; the DeathVolt system found a way in. And once inside, a hacker could control the switches, the substations—the entire grid. With a few keyboard clicks, a hacker could utterly paralyze a vast area of the country.

Or worse.

Prmkt was almost done now; the four projects were networked via the thick cable. He ran the cable beneath the tables, where it blended in with the dozens of extension cords providing power to the projects. He routed his cable alongside these other wires and extension cords to the wall of the gym, where he guided it beneath the bleachers and through a hidden hole that he'd drilled earlier and that led into the utility room.

He now went to the utility room and unlocked the door. Once inside, he pulled his cable through and carefully laid it on the floor beneath a gray electrical box that was mounted to the wall. This was the main electrical breaker

box for the school; through it, the school was connected to the city's electrical grid and to the larger grids beyond. Next to the box was a small table on which Prmkt had set up some equipment, including his own laptop computer, which was packed with special software he had written. He put on a pair of rubber gloves, opened the breaker box, and went to work. When he was done, he looked at his watch. He'd set everything up in under forty-five minutes. Perfect.

He rose and left the utility room, locking it behind him. He went back to the darkened gym and took one last look around. For a moment he was tempted to do it himself— just walk over to the podium, throw the master power switch, and start his machine right now. Prmkt thought about it, but he didn't do it. One reason was that he wanted to wait until it was dark in more parts of the country. The other reason was that he liked the idea of having Lance Swingle throw the switch. Prmkt allowed himself another small smile at that thought. It was the windbag Swingle who had turned the science fair into a corrupt competition for spoiled kids and their foolish parents; let it be Swingle who would now unwittingly turn that same science fair into a weapon that would bring down the mighty and arrogant United States.

Prmkt looked at his watch: almost exactly an hour to go. He left through the side door. The gym was once again silent, except for the clock on the wall, where the big hand clicked forward every sixty seconds, signaling another minute gone.

CHAPTER THIRTY-NINE

THE BATTERED U-DRIVE-IT rental truck rattled into Milkwort Court and pulled to the curb in front of Toby's house. The Wookiee was behind the wheel; Vaderian, in the passenger seat, was dressed in his full Darth Vader outfit, including light saber, helmet, and voice distorter. He looked at the sky, which was getting dark. They watched the house for a few minutes, seeing no lights or signs of activity.

"Go check the back door," said Vaderian.

The Wookiee climbed out of the truck and walked around the side of the garage to the back of the house. A few minutes later, he returned to the truck, standing at Vaderian's window.

"Locked," he said.

"What?" said Vaderian.

"Locked," repeated the Wookiee.

"That little *weasel*," snarled Vaderian, pounding the truck seat. He took a breath, calming himself. "What about the house? Did you see anybody?"

"No," said the Wookiee. "It's dark inside."

"The little weasel said they'd be at the science fair," said Vaderian. He checked his watch, drummed his fingers on the dashboard, thinking, then said, "Try the kid's bedroom window, where he sneaked out."

The Wookiee returned a minute later. "It's unlocked," he said.

Vaderian nodded. "All right," he said. "We'll go in there."

They went to Toby's window, raised it, and climbed inside, the Wookiee helping Vaderian, whose cape made movement awkward. They opened Toby's bedroom door and listened for a long time. The house was silent. There was no sign of anyone.

"Nobody home," said Vaderian.

"I just want to sleep, okay?" said Toby's voice, causing both Vaderian and the Wookiee to jump and whirl around.

"Who said that?" said Vaderian.

"I just want to sleep, okay?" said Toby's voice.

"I think the bed," said the Wookiee, pointing at Toby's pillow.

"I just want to sleep, okay?" said Toby's voice.

"Yup," said the Wookiee. "The bed."

"I *hate* that little weasel," said Vaderian.

"I just want to sleep, okay?" said Toby's voice.

Vaderian, realizing he was losing a battle of wits with a pillow, closed his mouth. With a last glare toward the bed, he turned and slipped into the dark hallway. He drew his light saber and flicked the switch, filling the hall with a reddish glow. The two men moved carefully down the hall. They stopped at each door to listen; then Vaderian would quietly open the door and peer inside.

Near the kitchen, they encountered a locked door. Vaderian nodded to the Wookiee, who grasped the knob in his massive hand and twisted it hard. With a *clank* of snapping metal the doorknob gave way, and the door swung open.

They descended the stairs. The air was suddenly cooler and dryer. On the wall near the bottom of the stairs, they found a wall-mounted box with a row of indicator lights and a digital display showing temperature and humidity—a sophisticated environmental-control unit.

Vaderian started getting a good feeling about this.

He swung his light saber around. It was a furnished basement. At the far end he could make out a big-screen TV, an exercise bike, and . . .

An imperial stormtrooper uniform!

Vaderian jumped as he caught sight of it. It was mounted fully erect, like a museum piece, occupying the near corner and ghostly white in the cast of his light saber's glow. He walked over to it quickly and examined it with an expert's eye. He'd seen hundreds of reproductions, but this one was different; the more he studied it, the more

he wondered: *could it be?* For years he'd heard rumors of a few undocumented, authentic, *original* stormtrooper uniforms out there, somewhere. . . .

He tore his eyes away from the uniform and moved along the basement wall. The light-saber glow illuminated a box. Vaderian knelt, opened it, and found bundles of bubble wrap. He picked one off the top, unwrapped it, and gasped as he revealed the hilt of a light saber—not a later reproduction like the one he wore, but one that had the distinctive (to Vaderian's eyes) indications of an original handmade prop.

Could it possibly be?

"Is this the stuff we're after?" the Wookiee asked.

Vaderian glared at him. "This," he said, "is not *stuff*. This is . . . this is . . ." He waved a hand to indicate that there was no way he could explain the importance of this to an idiot like the Wookiee.

Valderian's heart beat faster as he rummaged through that box, and then another box next to it, and then another, finding more and more treasures, each more astonishing than the last, including what appeared to be the actual Chewbacca's ammunition bandolier. Flashing his light saber around the room, Vaderian saw more rare artifacts, large and small. In another corner he saw a sheet draped over a distinctive domed shape; peeking out the bottom were the unmistakable wheeled appendages of R2-D2. Under his black mask, Vaderian's face broke into a wide smile. He emitted a giggle, which the voice distorter transformed into a hideous sound.

This was it. Vaderian was certain. This was the mother lode. This was the fabled lost ark of Star Wars memorabilia. And soon it was all going to belong to him.

He stood and turned to the Wookiee, about to give orders for getting the collection upstairs and into the truck.

Then, a sound from upstairs. He froze. The front door had opened and shut. Voices: a man and woman. Footsteps crossing directly overhead. Vaderian and the Wookiee looked at the basement ceiling, the two of them rigidly still in the deathly glow of the light saber.

Vaderian considered their options. They could wait here in the basement until the people upstairs—the little weasel's parents, no doubt—had gone to sleep. But that could be hours. And even then, how could he and the Wookiee get the collection up the stairs and out the back door without being heard? Or what if the people upstairs noticed the broken doorknob on the basement door? What if they decided to come downstairs?

Vaderian pondered this, trying to figure out how he and the Wookiee would respond. One thing he knew for sure: now that he had found the mother lode, he wasn't about to let it out of his grasp.

Listening to the footsteps overhead, Vaderian tightened his grip on the light saber.

He would *not* let these people stop him.

Chapter Forty

TOBY, TAMARA, AND MICAH sat in uncomfortable plastic chairs on one side of the long wooden conference table. Drmtsi and Vrsk sat across from them, chomping their way through the plateful of muffins, which they had moved onto the table for easier access. The five of them had been sitting in silence for a while, pondering their situation and waiting for whatever was going to happen next. Toby was still holding the stick of Air Zerkistan chewing gum that Vrsk had given him; he planned to use it when the feds returned. Meanwhile, there was nothing to do but wait and watch the weird foreign guys eating the muffins.

Finally, tired of the silence, Toby spoke to the men across the table.

"Where are you guys from, anyway?" he said.

"We are from Krpshtskan," said Vrsk, pronouncing the name of the country in such a way that he sent a spray of muffin crumbs halfway across the table.

"Where's that?" said Toby, eyeing the crumbs warily.

"Is near Fazul," said Vrsk.

"Fazul?" said Toby.

"You know Fazul?" said Vrsk.

"No," said Toby.

"Is very famous hole there," said Vrsk. "Great Hole of Fazul. You never heard of this?"

"Sorry, no," said Toby. He glanced at the ceiling, where he was pretty sure there were cameras and microphones. He decided he no longer cared: he wanted to know who these guys were.

"So," he said. "What brings you here?"

"What?" said Vrsk.

"Why did you come to the United States?" said Toby.

Vrsk's eyes darted sideways toward Drmtsi before he answered. "We are tourists," he said. "We are here for touristism."

"Is that why you were at Jungle Norman's?" said Toby.

"Yes," said Vrsk. "We were touristing at Jungle of Norman."

"And you don't know anything about the thing that was in the gorilla's hat?"

Vrsk nearly choked on his muffin, then coughed for half a minute before he could speak. "No," he said finally. "We are never seeing this gorilla before. Is stranger gorilla to us."

"Really," said Toby.

"In our country," said Vrsk, "is no gorillas. Is mostly goats. But not singing."

Drmtsi, who had been watching this conversation with narrowed eyes, swallowed a mouthful of muffin and said to Vrsk in Krpsht, "What are you talking to this boy about?"

"He is asking why we are here. I told him we are tourists."

"Good," said Drmtsi. "But now stop talking to the boy, because I must tell you the plan to escape."

"Escape?" said Vrsk.

"Yes," said Drmtsi. "It is our duty to escape and help Prmkt destroy America. Also, I must order more merchandise from the television shopping people."

"But there are many guards here," said Vrsk. "Perhaps we should wait for—"

"No time to wait!" snapped Drmtsi. "Here is the plan. Do you have any more smerk?"

Vrsk felt his pants. "A little," he said.

"Good," said Drmtsi. "When the guards come back, I will watch them for the right moment. This moment is when the door is unlocked, and the guards are nearby to you. At this right moment I will give you a secret signal, like this."

Drmtsi clapped his hands twice, startling Toby, Micah, and Tamara.

"These guys," said Tamara, "are even weirder than they smell."

Drmtsi glanced at her, then continued speaking to Vrsk

in Krpsht. "When you hear this secret signal, you will take the smerk from your pants and hurl it into the eyes of the guards."

"Their *eyes?*" said Vrsk. "Are you sure?" There was an old expression in Krpshtskan that roughly translated to "Better to have an angry scorpion in your underwear than smerk in your eyes."

"Yes, I am sure," said Drmtsi. "When you throw the smerk, I will run out the door and escape."

"I see," said Vrsk. He frowned. "But how will *I* escape?"

Drmtsi reached for another muffin. "Maybe, after hurling the smerk, you can run out the door also," he said. "But if not, Prmkt and I will come get you after we destroy America."

"I see," said Vrsk.

"It is a good plan, yes?" said Drmtsi, chewing.

"Yes," Vrsk agreed, although not sincerely.

The hall outside echoed with the sound of approaching footsteps. All eyes turned to the door, which opened; in walked agents Turow, Iles, and Lefkon, who closed the door behind them. Toby quietly removed the Air Zerkistan gum from its wrapper, put it into his mouth, and began chewing. It was like chewing cardboard, only it didn't taste as good. Across the table, Drmtsi sat up, and watching the agents closely, prepared to give the attack signal to Vrsk when they got close enough.

But the agents didn't approach the two men. Instead they went to the head of the table. They looked tired, and they were. They'd been up all night monitoring their

suspects, first in their sleeping quarters, then in the conference room; both rooms, as Toby had suspected, were bugged. The agents had hoped to learn something, anything, about the relationship between the Krpshtskanis and the children. They had been disappointed. The children had said little, obviously aware of the cameras and microphones. The two men had spoken, but mostly to each other, and in a language nobody in the building understood; their conversation had been recorded and sent to government linguists with an urgent request for translation.

Meanwhile, there was intense pressure on Turow and the others from higher-ups in a half-dozen government agencies to find out who the Krpshtskanis were, what connection they had with these children, and—above all—how this motley group came to be in possession of what was supposed to be extremely classified technology.

Turow leaned on the table with both arms and glared. The agents had decided to use the Good Cop/Bad Cop interrogation technique. Lefkon was the Good Cop; Turow was the Bad Cop.

"All right," Turow said. "We need some answers, and if we don't start getting them *right now*, things are going to get very unpleasant for all of you."

Micah raised his hand.

"What?" said Turow.

"I need to go to the bathroom," said Micah.

"Tough," sneered Bad Cop Turow.

"But I—"

"I said NO!" bellowed Turow, slapping his hands hard on the table causing Micah to jerk backward so hard he almost tipped his chair over.

"Hey, easy," said Good Cop Lefkon, putting a restraining hand on Turow's arm. "If he has to go to the bathroom, let him go."

Turow glared at Lefkon as though he was about to slap *her*, although of course this was part of the act. For several dramatic seconds the room was silent as the two agents faced off. The silence was broken by Tamara.

"So, let me guess," she said. "You"—she pointed at Turow—"are the Bad Cop, and you"—she pointed at Lefkon—"are the Good Cop."

Turow sighed. Lefkon suppressed a giggle. They were both thinking the same thing: *These kids watch too much television.* Turow was pondering what he would say next when Vrsk said, "He is growing dark."

"What?" said Turow.

"Boy," said Vrsk, pointing at Toby. "He is dark."

Everyone looked. Tamara screamed. Toby's face had turned a startling deep purple. His eyeballs were rolled back, wide-open, showing only the whites. His body was rigid, vibrating; cords stood out in his neck.

"Toby, what's happening?" shouted Micah at his friend.

"He's having a seizure," said Iles, moving quickly to Toby. "Get some help!"

Lefkon ran from the room; Turow stood guard by the door. Drmtsi and Vrsk exchanged a look, but there was no opportunity to execute Drmtsi's escape plan. A moment

later Lefkon returned with the facility nurse, a man named Levine. He went to Toby, who was lying on his back on the floor, moaning. Toby's color was starting to return. He had quietly spat the gum into his hand.

"Son," said Levine, "can you hear me?"

"Yes," said Toby weakly.

"Can you tell me what happened?" said Levine.

"No," said Toby.

Levine examined Toby briefly, then said to Iles, "I'm going to move him to the station for observation." Iles, Turow, and Lefkon exchanged glances, then Iles said, "Okay. But you stay with him, and you keep the door locked."

Levine nodded and said, "I'll get a wheelchair."

In a few minutes, Toby was being wheeled down the hall to the first-aid station. He was feeling much better now; he always recovered quickly from the gum allergy. But he pretended he was still very weak. He felt a jolt of excitement as Levine wheeled him into the little room: the manila envelopes were still in the plastic box on the desk.

Levine helped Toby onto the cot, then took his pulse and blood pressure, and shone a light into his eyes. He asked a few questions, which Toby avoided answering by pretending to be tired and dazed. After a few minutes, Levine told Toby he'd be outside, and left the room. He closed the door; Toby heard the click of the dead bolt.

Toby lay on the cot for a minute, then rose, crept to the door, and looked through the envelopes. One had his name on it. He opened it; inside were his iPhone and his

240

hat. He reached into his back pocket and pulled out the two spare fiber-optic filaments. He uncoiled them and, glancing at the door every few seconds, attached them to the hat, then the iPhone, then the insoles in his shoes.

He stood up, hoping there was power left in the phone battery. He turned it on; the screen lit up. He pressed the magic-wand icon, then looked down at his legs. They weren't there.

Toby's eyes scanned the room, stopping at a wall-mounted phone. Toby went to it, lifted the handset, unplugged the cord, and tossed the handset under the cot. He turned off the light; the windowless room went dark. He positioned himself on the back wall of the room next to the cot facing the door. He took a deep breath and shouted, "Help!"

In seconds, Levine unlocked the door and swung it open. His eyes went to the cot, and in the dim light he saw that it was vacant. He stood in the doorway, scanning the small room. He did not see Toby, who stood just five feet away.

Toby tensed, praying that Levine would now look in the one remaining hiding place—behind the door.

Levine stepped into the room, swung the door partway closed, and looked behind it. As he did, Toby lunged past him through the doorway, grabbing the door and yanking it closed. Levine shouted as Toby spun and twisted the dead bolt. Levine attempted to turn the knob, but finding it locked, hurled himself against the door. He shouted and pounded.

Toby looked both ways down the corridor; it was empty. For now, nobody could hear Levine. Toby started running toward the conference room. Behind him, Levine stopped pounding; Toby figured he was now groping for the wall phone in the dark. It would take him a while to find the handset.

Toby sprinted down the corridor, considering his next move. His goal was to spring Micah and Tamara somehow, get out of this place somehow, get to the Science Fair, and somehow stop whatever was going to happen from happening. It was a lot of somehows. *One at a time*, he told himself.

As he approached a corridor intersection he slowed down to soften his footsteps. He turned right into the cross corridor; the conference room door where Tamara and Micah were being held was about twenty-five feet ahead on the left. There was a large man by the door, apparently standing guard. Toby looked past him all the way down the corridor. At the far end glowed a red EXIT sign.

Toby cupped his hands in front of his mouth and, in his deepest official-announcement voice, said, "ATTENTION ALL PERSONNEL."

The guard startled, spun, and looked right at Toby. He frowned, seeing nothing.

"THIS IS AN EMERGENCY," said Toby. "WE HAVE . . . UM . . . POISON GAS IN THE BUILDING. ALL PERSONNEL WILL PROCEED TO THE NEAREST EXIT IMMEDIATELY."

The guard, still frowning, took a few steps toward Toby,

his eyes searching the walls and ceiling for the source of the sound.

"THIS IS NOT A DRILL," said Toby. "THIS IS REALLY POISONOUS GAS. IT WILL EAT YOUR SKIN AND, UH, EXPLODE YOUR EYEBALLS."

Toby backed up quietly as the guard kept coming closer, approaching the corridor intersection. Toby slipped past him and hurried quietly to the conference room door. He carefully unlocked the dead bolt, constantly checking to his left, where the guard, still facing away from him, was searching for the source of the earlier announcement. Toby then quietly turned the knob, opened the door, and stepped inside. Tamara, Micah, and the weird foreign guys were still sitting at the table. All four heads had turned to face the door, which to them appeared to have opened and closed by itself.

"It's me," said Toby, causing everyone at the table to jump.

"Who said that?" said Micah.

"It's me! Toby!" said Toby. "I'm wearing the invisibility iPhone Sternabite made." He tried to press the invisible iPhone to make himself visible, but in his nervousness he couldn't find the right place on the screen. Frustrated, he reached across the table, grabbed the lone remaining muffin, and waved it in the air. "See?" he said. "I'm doing this."

"Whoa," said Tamara and Micah together.

Drmtsi and Vrsk stared at the floating muffin, their faces a mixture of awe and fear. Drmtsi said to Vrsk in Krpsht, "Ask them why this good-tasting bread item is floating in the air and speaking."

Vrsk, his eyes still on the muffin, said in English, "Why is bread item floating in air and speaking?"

"It's our friend," said Micah.

"What did boy say?" Drmtsi asked Vrsk.

"He said the bread item is his friend," replied Vrsk.

Vrsk stared at the floating, talking muffin. "The Americans must be giving us drugs," he said.

Finally Toby's fumbling fingers found the right spot on the iPhone screen. In an instant he became visible.

"Very powerful drugs," said Drmtsi to Vrsk.

"How does that—" began Tamara.

"No time," interrupted Toby. "Listen, there's a guard outside, down the hall to the right." Toby pointed. "I'm going to go out and try to get him around the corner. You peek out the door. As soon as he goes around the corner, you run the opposite way. There's an exit sign down there. I'll get past the guard and follow you."

"And *why* are we doing this?" said Tamara.

"Because we have to get to the science fair," said Toby. "We have to stop whatever's gonna happen."

"But if we escape," said Micah, "won't we get in trouble?"

"Micah," said Toby, "we're terrorism suspects. We're being held in a secret location. We can't *get* in any more trouble."

"Oh, you'll think of something," said Tamara.

"Listen," Toby said angrily, "I came back here to get you. If you don't want to . . ."

"Oh, shut up," said Tamara. "Of *course* we're coming."

"We are?" said Micah.

"Of course, we are," said Tamara, rising.

244

The three friends moved toward the door. Drmtsi said to Vrsk, in Krpsht, "What are these children doing?"

"I think they are escaping," said Vrsk.

"How?" said Drmtsi.

"They are walking out the door," said Vrsk.

"Ah," said Drmtsi, admiring the cleverness of this plan. He rose and said, "We are escaping also."

Toby turned the knob, quietly opened the door, and peered out into the hall. The guard was still at the intersection of the corridors, twenty-five feet to the right. Toby turned to Tamara, put his finger to his lips, then reached down and touched the wand icon on the iPhone.

Invisible now, he stepped into the corridor. Behind him, Tamara closed the door almost all the way, leaving it open just a crack so she could see what was happening. The guard had just finished looking around the intersection and was walking back toward the conference room. Toby ran past him, making no effort to soften his footsteps. The guard turned toward the sound, swiveling as Toby passed him. Toby stopped a few feet away, turned, cupped his hands, and shouted, "I THOUGHT I TOLD YOU PERSONNEL TO EXIT THE PREMISES."

The guard stepped forward, waving his hands at the air. He reached to his belt and unclipped a walkie-talkie. As he raised it to his mouth, Toby stepped forward, grabbed the antenna, and yanked. The walkie-talkie came free of the stunned guard's hand. Toby turned and ran with it.

"Hey!" shouted the guard, pursuing the floating walkie-talkie around the corner.

Behind him, Tamara quietly swung open the conference room door, turned left in the corridor, and sprinted toward the EXIT sign, followed by Micah, who was followed by Drmtsi, who was followed by Vrsk.

After fifty feet, they ran past another door, on the other side of which was the surveillance station. Inside this stuffy, dimly lit room was a wall-mounted bank of television monitors connected to the hidden cameras in the conference room. In front of the monitors was a long table with a speakerphone on it. Gathered around this table were agents Turow, Iles, and Lefkon, along with some other officials. None of them were looking at the monitors, which was why they hadn't noticed that the conference room was now empty. Instead, their attention was focused on the speakerphone, from which came the voice of a CIA linguist, who was heading the team trying to translate the recorded conversation between Drmtsi and Vrsk.

"I'm afraid it's a very obscure dialect," she was saying. "We've only been able to translate a fragment. We'll keep working, though."

"Well, tell us what you've got so far," said Turow. "We need something, *anything.*"

"To be honest," said the linguist, "all we have so far is 'cheese.'"

"'Cheese?'" said Turow. "As in, 'cheese'?"

"Cheese," said the linguist.

Turow rubbed his weary face with both weary hands. "Well, *that's* a big help," he said.

"We're doing the best we can," snapped the linguist.

"That's what I'm afraid of," said Turow, pressing the DISCONNECT button. He looked around at the others. "Cheese," he said.

"Maybe it's a code," said Lefkon.

Suddenly they heard shouting in the hall. All eyes went to the monitors, which showed an empty conference room. Lefkon yanked the door open; they all ran outside. To their left was the source of the shouts: the guard. He had chased his walkie-talkie around the corner and then down the corridor, where the invisible Toby had hurled it. He had then run back to the conference room, yanked the door open, and saw that it was empty. Meanwhile, Toby was racing down the corridor after his friends. He passed the surveillance-room door just as the agents opened it; in fact, Lefkon nearly ran into him as she burst from the room.

At the moment, the feds were all looking left toward the guard. He was standing at the doorway to the conference room.

"They're gone!" he shouted.

"Where?" shouted Turow.

"There!" shouted Lefkon, who had just spotted the running figures at the far end of the corridor.

"Call security!" shouted Turow, sprinting toward the figures. "Lock it down NOW!"

Lefkon ran into the conference room and grabbed the phone; the guard was shouting into his walkie-talkie. Moments later, a recorded voice boomed down the corridor, saying, "WE HAVE CODE MAGENTA SITUATION.

247

REPEAT, THIS IS A CODE MAGENTA SITUATION."

At the far end of the corridor, Tamara, Micah, Vrsk, and a red-faced, huffing Drmtsi reached a T-junction. To their right, they saw men running toward them; to their left was a door with a sign that said EMERGENCY EXIT ONLY—ALARM WILL SOUND. Tamara sprinted toward it and slammed into the bar. The door banged open, and an alarm began emitting a shrill *beep beep beep.* Tamara stopped and looked around. Night had fallen; she was in an alley in the rear of the building, and it was lit by the harsh glare of a security light. Along the wall next to the door was a large green Dumpster.

Micah burst through the door followed by Vrsk, who was followed by the flagging Drmtsi. Pounding down the corridor toward them were a half-dozen men.

"What now?" said Micah.

"I don't know," said Tamara. "Where's Toby?"

"Here!" said a voice next to them. "Close the door and give me a hand with the Dumpster!"

Micah slammed the door shut, then he and Tamara ran to the Dumpster and grunted, trying to move it in front of the door. It didn't budge.

"Help us!" shouted Tamara at Drmtsi and Vrsk. Vrsk said something to Drmtsi in Krpsht, and the two men ran behind the Dumpster and pushed. Slowly it began to roll on its creaking wheels. Just as it reached the doorway, the door slammed open, but the Dumpster kept it from opening more than a few inches.

"Push it toward the building!" shouted Toby. He and the others shifted positions and tried to push the Dumpster

against the door. But the men inside were also pushing, and they were stronger; the Dumpster was moving back, and the door was opening. The men were going to get out.

"You guys run!" said Toby. "I'll hold this as long as I can. They can't see me."

Tamara and Micah looked at each other, unsure about leaving Toby. Meanwhile Drmtsi was saying something to Vrsk.

"Looking out!" Vrsk shouted at the kids. "Is danger!"

Toby, Tamara, and Micah turned to the two men, who were reaching into their pants. The Dumpster, shoved by the men inside, creaked and shuddered as it was pushed toward them. The door was almost open enough for the men to slip through. Inside, somebody shouted "One . . . two . . ." as the men prepared for one last coordinated shove.

"THREE!" shouted the voice. As the men heaved into the door, Drmtsi and Vrsk pulled their hands out of their pants and hurled two globs of smerk through the opening. Instantly, the air was filled with a stench that smelled like a cross between a rotting buffalo and a sewer explosion, only worse. From inside, there were shouts of surprise, followed by yelps of terror.

"GAS ATTACK!" shouted a voice. "IT'S A GAS ATTACK!"

There were more shouts and the sound of pounding feet as the men fled back down the corridor.

"What was *that*?" said Micah to Vrsk.

"Is smerk," said Vrsk. "Cheese."

"Whoa," said Micah.

"Smerk?" said Drmtsi, preparing to reach back into his pants.

"No thanks!" said Micah and Tamara hastily.

Toby pressed his iPhone and made himself visible. "Come on," he said, trotting away from the building. "We gotta get to Hubble."

"Right," said Tamara, trotting behind followed by Micah. "But which way *is* Hubble?"

"I have no idea," said Toby. "But we can't stay here. They'll be coming back."

"Excuse me," said Vrsk, who was also trotting behind and followed by the huffing Drmtsi. "Did you say Hobble?"

Toby glanced back. "I said Hubble," he said.

"Yes," said Vrsk. "Hobble. Is this Hobble Middle School?"

Toby stopped short and turned around. "You know about Hubble Middle School?"

Vrsk nodded rapidly. "Yes," he said. "Is where we are going also."

"*Why?*" said Toby.

Vrsk exchanged a few rapid Krpsht words with Drmtsi, then turned back to Toby.

"Touristism," he said.

Toby was about to say something more when he heard shouts in the distance coming from the building they had just escaped.

"Let's go," he said, running away from the building toward the dark streets beyond, followed by his two old friends and his two new weird and smelly allies.

CHAPTER FORTY-ONE

★

ON THE HUBBLE MIDDLE SCHOOL ball field, nearly a thousand excited people—students, teachers, parents—watched the dark night sky, waiting.

"There it is!" shouted a boy. He pointed toward the south, where flashing lights showed on the horizon. A few moments later, the crowd heard the *whupwhupwhup* of big rotors slicing the air. As the TranScent Corp. helicopter swooped toward the school, teachers shouted at the excited throng to keep back from the roped-off landing area, which was brilliantly illuminated by four huge portable spotlights.

Soon, the chopper was over the ball field. It hovered for a few seconds, then settled gently onto second base, its downdraft kicking up a swirling dirt storm. The pilot shut

down the engines. As the rotors wound down, the chopper door opened and the folding stairway deployed. Cheers erupted from the crowd as Lance Swingle himself appeared in the doorway, waving as he descended the stairway. The handsome billionaire looked younger than his forty-three years, his radiantly white teeth gleaming in the spotlights, his dark hair tousled by the dwindling rotor breeze.

Swingle was greeted at the bottom of the stairs by Principal Plotz-Gornett and a dozen other school officials. Then, with Swingle triumphantly leading the way, the excited crowd thronged into the gymnasium and gathered around the platform set up for the opening ceremonies of the science fair.

Swingle was introduced by the president of the school board, who read brief opening remarks in which he compared Swingle's achievement of sending smells over the Internet with the work of Thomas Edison, Alexander Graham Bell, Albert Einstein, Leonardo da Vinci, Copernicus, Isaac Newton, and Bill Gates. Swingle smiled bashfully to indicate that he was unworthy of this praise, although in fact the opening remarks had been written by his vice president for public relations.

When the introduction was finished, Swingle strode to the microphone, acknowledging the crowd's cheers with sincerely faked modesty. He then launched into his "brief" remarks.

"Thirty-one years ago," he began, "an eighth-grade boy walked into this very same gymnasium. In many ways, he

looked like an ordinary young man; in fact"—here Swingle flashed a brilliant smile—"you might say he looked like a younger version of . . . me."

The crowd chuckled in recognition of the fact that the young man was, in fact, Lance Swingle. Principal Plotz-Gornett groaned inwardly and shifted on her feet; she knew from experience that it would take Swingle a good twenty minutes to get through the dull but supposedly uplifting story of how the young, ordinary-looking young man transformed himself, against great odds, into the wealthy, brilliant, handsome genius entrepreneur standing on the stage tonight.

Prmkt, listening from the edge of the crowd, was also calculating the time left before the insufferable windbag finished his speech and threw the master switch to power up the science fair. After listening for exactly five more minutes, Prmkt slipped away from the crowd. Passing between rows of silent exhibits, he walked quietly to the utility-room door, opened it, went inside, and gently closed and locked the door. He went to the laptop computer and tapped some keys, running a quick test; numbers flashed on the screen telling Prmkt that all was ready. He glanced at his watch and calculated that Swingle would throw the master switch in about ten minutes. Prmkt would then begin executing his plan.

The plan consisted of several stages. The first stage was designed to get the country's attention—to shake the smug Americans awake and show them that the safe and happy world they lived in was only a dream. Once he had

their attention, Prmkt would proceed to the next stages of his plan—showing the Americans what they had done and then delivering their punishment.

He looked at his watch. Less than ten minutes now. He rested his hands gently on the keyboard, feeling the power in the keys—keys that he would soon use to turn the American dream into the American nightmare.

CHAPTER FORTY-TWO

★

THE SIRENS DREW CLOSER. Toby, Micah, and Tamara, running as fast as their tired legs would carry them, made yet another random turn into yet another unfamiliar street. Ten yards behind them trotted Vrsk; behind him staggered the gasping and utterly exhausted Drmtsi.

Toby stopped and put his hands on his knees, gulping air. Micah and Tamara did the same. The *whoop whoop whoop* of the sirens grew louder.

"Maybe we should split up," said Tamara.

"Why?" asked Toby.

"I dunno," admitted Tamara. "But in the movies, when people are getting chased, they always split up."

"I wish *they'd* split up from us," said Micah, nodding at

Vrsk and Drmtsi, who had just staggered up.

"I wish I knew where we were," said Toby.

"There's some lights that way," said Micah, pointing toward the far end of the street. "Hey! There's a Starbucks!"

"Great," said Tamara. "That narrows our location down to . . . the planet Earth."

"No, it's good," said Toby.

"See?" said Micah. "It's good!" He turned to Toby. "Why is it good?"

"We can ask the Starbucks people where we are," said Toby, trotting toward the end of the street, followed by the others. In two minutes they were inside the Starbucks. Behind the counter, a young man and a young woman eyed them curiously, noting the filaments running from Toby's hat to his shoes, and the stained and stinky clothing of the two Krpshtskanis, who were pointing to the cappuccino machine and talking excitedly in Krpsht.

"May I help you?" said the woman.

"Yes," said Toby. "Where are we?"

The man and woman eyed each other. The woman said, "In a Starbucks."

"I know *that*," said Toby. "I mean, which one?"

"It doesn't have a special name," said the woman. "It's just a Starbucks like every other Starbucks."

"No, no, no," said Toby, exasperated. "I mean, where is it located? What's the address?"

But before the woman could answer, Vrsk, on orders from Drmtsi, broke in.

"Excuse my pardon," he said. "But are you selling this?" He pointed at the cappuccino machine behind the counter.

"You want a cappuccino?" asked the attendant.

"We are wanting this, yes," said Vrsk.

"What size?" said the man.

"What?" said Vrsk.

"We have tall, grande, venti," the man answered.

"Tall, grande, venti," repeated Vrsk.

"Tall is actually small," noted Micah.

"Tall is small?" said Vrsk.

"Yeah," said Micah. "I don't get it either."

"So, what size cappuccino?" said the man.

"Wait a minute!" said Toby. "We don't want a cappuccino, okay? We just want to—".

"Listen, *sir*," interrupted the attendant. "If this customer wants to buy a cappuccino, then we're going to—"

"Excuse my pardon," said Vrsk. "But we are to pay you with TV shopping–people's card? Is okay?"

"What?" said the man.

"TV shopping–people's card," said Vrsk. "We can use to purchase this machine?"

"The *machine*?" said the man. "You want to buy the *machine*?"

"Yes," said Vrsk. "The tall-small-grande-venti machine. We wish to purchase this."

The man and woman glanced at each other again. Outside, a police car shot past, siren whooping. The attendant followed it with his eyes, then studied the strange group in front of him.

"Who *are* you people?" he asked.

"We are touristing," said Vrsk.

Outside, there was a screech of tires. The police car had skidded to a stop about fifty yards down the street and began executing a hasty U-turn.

Behind the counter, the woman pulled out her cell phone.

"Let's get out of here," suggested Tamara. The three friends and two Krpshtskanis rushed out through the front door. To the right, the police car had turned and was heading back.

"This way!" shouted Toby, turning left and sprinting around the side of the Starbucks into a service alley. They crossed the alley and clambered over a low chain-link fence into a small darkened lot strewn with discarded tires and other junk. They stumbled through this lot onto another street, turned left and then right, trying to head away from the sound of the sirens.

But every minute there were more sirens.

After ten minutes of hard running, they stopped to catch their breath in a ragged, wheezing circle.

"Now what?" said Micah, gasping.

"I don't know," admitted Toby, feeling cold, tired, lost, and planless.

"Toby," Tamara said softly, "maybe we should just give up. Turn ourselves in."

Toby shook his head. "But then they win," he said. "Whoever they are, whoever got us into this, whatever they're going to do at the science fair—they *win*."

"Whoever they are," said Tamara, "they already *did* win. The science fair must've started by now. All we're doing running around out here is making things worse and maybe getting ourselves hurt. It's bad enough that we're in this much trouble—how would your parents feel if, on top of all of this, something happened to you? How would they feel, Toby?"

Toby bowed his head, thinking about his parents not knowing where he was, sitting at home . . .

His parents. At home.

"Oh, noooo!" he wailed.

"What?" said Tamara.

"My parents!" he said. "Those guys are coming to my house!"

"What guys?" said Micah.

"The Star Wars lunatics!" said Toby. "They're gonna rob my house tonight! I have to warn them!" He unclipped the iPhone from his belt, careful not to detach the filaments, then stabbed the ON button and moved the slider to unlock the phone.

"How do you know they're gonna rob your house?" said Micah.

Toby, tapping the phone touchscreen with trembling fingers, didn't answer. He finished dialing and held the phone to his ear, listening to the ringing tone, hoping he was in time.

Please, please answer. . . .

CHAPTER FORTY-THREE

IN THE HUBBLE GYM, Lance Swingle was finally reaching the climax of his speech. This was the part where he stressed that even though he, personally, because of his scientific genius, had made millions and millions of dollars, science was not about money. Here he paused and, with a winning and boyish grin that he practiced in front of a mirror, added, "But don't worry—the winner still gets the five thousand dollars."

The audience roared with laughter. Especially amused were Jason Niles, Harmonee Prescott, Haley Hess, and Farrel "The Ferret" Plinkett, who were standing near the front of the crowd with their parents and some other ME kids. They were absolutely sure that one of them would win, they had agreed, earlier that evening, that whoever

got first prize, they'd split the money four ways.

"But money," Swingle was saying, "is not the goal. Yes, I am a wealthy man. Yes, I travel the world, dine with heads of state, date actresses and top supermodels. Yes, I have eight homes, two helicopters, an NBA team, a three-hundred-foot yacht and a 737 jet with a customized interior including a sauna. But those things are not important to me."

In the crowd, The Ferret whispered, "Okay, then give me the supermodels."

"Shut up," hissed Harmonee Prescott.

"What is important to me," continued Swingle, "is that, through my role in making the Hubble Middle School science fair one of the most prestigious science fairs in the nation, I can encourage young people to advance the cause of science." He gestured toward the rows of projects in the gym before the crowd. "Who knows," he said, "what great new idea is sitting out there right now, waiting to be brought to life? It could be another TranScent, or perhaps something even more wonderful." Theatrically, Swingle reached out his hand, placing it on the master power switch, then said, "Let's find out, shall we?"

He paused for a moment of drama, then flipped the switch. The crowd cheered as the gym exploded with flashing lights and a cacophony of sounds—the *whir* of motors and gears, the *clunk* and *clink* of levers, the *snap* of sparks, the alarmed *ribbit* of a frog being suddenly levitated. Swingle stepped down from the stage and, followed by a flock of judges, headed for the exhibits to begin the judging.

In the utility room, Prmkt began tapping his keyboard.

CHAPTER FORTY-FOUR

THE PHONE WAS RINGING AGAIN. Toby's parents had ignored it the first three times, assuming it was reporters. Toby had been identified from the TV news broadcast of the Jungle Norman raid, and the press had been calling constantly, trying to get information. Except Toby's parents didn't have any information.

They had called the FBI over and over, but were told only that their son was being held on a matter of national security, and for the time being they could not see him. They had called the local police, who said they had no jurisdiction in a federal matter. They had called their congressman's and senators' offices and been told, essentially, nothing. They had just returned from a visit to a lawyer, who, after making a few phone calls, had told them that, for the moment, they had no effective legal options.

It was like a bad dream. Their *son*! A matter of *national security*!

The phone stopped ringing. It was quiet for five seconds and then started ringing again. Roger and Fawn, their faces haggard from worry and sleeplessness, looked at each other across the small round kitchen table where they were trying to eat dinner. Neither had much of an appetite, mainly because of Toby, but also because the dinner was meatless shish kebab, which was basically tofu on a stick.

"This is ridiculous," said Roger. "I'm gonna take it off the hook." He rose and went to the wall phone.

"What if it's not a reporter?" said Fawn. "Maybe you should check."

Roger looked at the phone for a second, sighed, and picked up the handset.

"Hello?" he said.

"Dad!" said Toby.

"Toby?" said Roger, and in an instant Fawn was on her feet.

"Yes, it's me," said Toby. "Listen—"

"Where are you?" said Roger.

"Ask him if he's all right," said Fawn.

"Are you all right?" said Roger.

"Please, Dad, just *listen*," said Toby. "There's these guys. They're gonna come to the house tonight."

"What guys? What are you talking about?"

"Two weird guys. One of them thinks he's Darth Vader. They want to steal your Star Wars stuff."

"*What*? Darth Vader? What are you *talking* about?"

"I can't explain it now," said Toby. "Just trust me. These guys are nuts, and they want your collection, so watch out, okay?"

"But—"

"I can't talk. I gotta get to the science fair. You and mom be careful. I'm sorry. I love you. Bye."

"Wait!" said Roger. But all he heard through the earpiece was the sound of a siren, which was cut off in mid-*whoop*. Toby had hung up.

"What is it?" said Fawn. "What did he say?"

Roger, frowning, hung up the handset. "He said some guys are coming to steal our Star Wars collection."

"But how would he know that? Where is he?"

"I don't know," said Roger. "But I heard a siren. And Toby said he was going to—"

THUMP.

Roger stopped.

"What was *that*?" said Fawn.

"I don't know," said Roger. "But it came from the basement."

CHAPTER FORTY-FIVE

★

TOBY, MICAH, TAMARA, and the Krpshtskanis were trapped. They'd been running away from the sound of sirens, going from street to alley to street, turning in so many directions they no longer knew which way they were headed. They had just emerged from an alley when they found themselves on a brightly lit, four-lane street with strip shopping centers on both sides.

Toby, leading the way, started running to his right, but before he'd taken ten steps, four police cruisers appeared at the end of the block, sirens whooping and lights flashing. The cars skidded to a stop in the intersection, blocking it; police in riot gear quickly emerged.

Toby turned to go the other way, only to see still more police cars screeching to a stop. Still more blue lights flashed at the end of the alley they'd just left.

"Now what?" panted Micah.

Toby looked around frantically: from several directions, at least two dozen shouting police officers were running toward them. The only escape path Toby saw was the parking lot across the street, which served a large grocery store.

"This way," he said, running toward the lot, followed by Micah and Tamara, who were followed by Vrsk with Drmtsi chugging in the rear. The pursuing police swerved to intercept them; some were shouting into two-way radios.

Ahead, Toby spotted a crowd that had gathered in front of the grocery store; he didn't know what it was about, but it gave him a flicker of hope. Maybe they could get into the crowd, where, hidden from the police, they could slip into the store and escape through the back.

As he reached the edge of the crowd, Toby saw why it had gathered: parked outside the main entrance to the supermarket was the Oscar Mayer Wienermobile.

About a hundred children and parents had gathered to look at the giant rolling hot dog, and get wiener whistles and other trinkets being handed out by the Wienermobile staff. Adding to the excitement was the presence of an animal-rights group, which was chanting and carrying signs to protest the Wienermobile and the practice of factory-farming animals. As Toby and the others drew close, an angry parent entered into a confrontation with one of the protesters—a person wearing a large, furry, pink pig costume and holding a sign that said PIGS ARE FRIENDS NOT FOOD.

Toby darted past the shouting match, heading for the supermarket entrance. But he stopped suddenly when he saw two police officers standing in the doorway, apparently stationed there because of the protest. One of the men was talking into his radio. His eyes scanned the crowd—and stopped at Toby. The man shouted something into his radio, then pointed; both officers began moving toward Toby and his group.

Toby whirled, looking for a way out; on every side, he saw police officers. He, Micah, Tamara, Vrsk, and Drmtsi stood in a small circle, watching as the officers approached them warily through the crowd—which was still focused on the parent-pig confrontation. Toby noticed that some of the officers had their hands on their pistols.

"Use your phone," said Tamara.

"What?" said Toby.

"Make yourself invisible," she said. "You can still get away. Maybe you can do something."

Toby looked down at the phone. Tamara was right: he could get away. His hand went to the magic-wand icon.

But he couldn't bring himself to touch it. He couldn't leave his friends here in a mess that he alone was responsible for. And even if he got away, what good could he do? He'd only make a bigger mess.

"Go on, do it!" said Tamara. "Do it! They're almost here!"

Toby shook his head.

"No," he said, his voice choking. "It's over."

He bowed his head, not wanting to see the police, not

wanting to look at his friends. He'd failed *everyone*. He stared at the ground, waiting: He heard the police shouting at him and the others to "GET DOWN! GET DOWN NOW!"

He started to kneel on the hard, cold, parking lot asphalt.

And then the world went dark.

CHAPTER FORTY-SIX

*B*EEP BEEP BEEP BEEP.

The harsh sound of an electronic alarm echoed through the master control room of the Mid-Atlantic Power Company's command center, a reinforced-concrete bunker 125 feet underground, where not even a bomb could do any harm. Two dozen technicians, suddenly jerked from their dull routines, sat up quickly to read the trouble messages flashing urgently across their computer screens.

A door banged open; a tall man with a football-flattened nose strode from the only enclosed office in the command center. This was Bernard Kosar; he was in charge and thus responsible for the entire Mid-Atlantic power grid. He hated alarms.

"Turn that off!" he shouted. Somebody hit a switch, and the beeping stopped. Kosar nervously slapped a football back and forth between his hands; he carried it everywhere, except the shower.

"What do we have?" Kosar said to the nearest technician, a woman named Laura Schweitzer, who really wanted to be a rock singer but had learned the hard way that being a power-company technician was steadier work. Although she often hummed at her computer station.

"It's down," she told Kosar.

"*What's* down?" he said. *Slap, slap* went the football.

Schweitzer waved an arm and said, "Everything."

"That's impossible," snapped Kosar. Technically, he was right: the power grid was designed with many safeguards and backup systems. Parts of the grid—even large areas—might go down. But only very rarely, and never for long.

Technically.

"Look at the tree," said Schweitzer, pointing. Kosar's gaze went up to a map high on the wall, dotted with over a thousand lights. This was the Master Grid Status Indicator Board. It was more commonly known as the Christmas Tree, because normally most, if not all, of the lights were green, indicating that electricity was flowing everywhere in the Mid-Atlantic region. Sometimes, during lightning storms or bad winter weather, parts of the Christmas Tree—little patches here and there—might glow red. Even then, it was mostly green.

Not now.

Now, every light—*every single light*—was red.

The entire grid was down. This meant that Maryland, Virginia, and much of West Virginia and Delaware had no electricity. It also meant that all of Washington, D.C., was dark, except for buildings that—like the command center—had emergency generators.

As Kosar stared at the Christmas Tree, a chilling thought came into his mind: *nuclear attack*.

"Anything from the military?" he asked, keeping his voice calm.

"Nope," said Schweitzer.

Kosar exhaled. "Weather?" he said.

"Nope," said Schweitzer.

Phones were ringing all over the command center. Technicians were answering them, speaking urgently while tapping their keyboards.

Kosar raised his voice, addressing the room: "Can someone tell me what's happening?"

A young man two desks over looked up. His name was Robert Joseph, and he was the command center's sharpest computer jockey. He was also Laura's boyfriend; they thought nobody knew this, but everyone did.

"What?" said Kosar.

"We've been hacked," said Joseph, pointing at the screen.

"So un-hack us," said Kosar. He felt a bit of relief; Mid-Atlantic Power's computer network, like most big corporate and government networks, was often attacked

by hackers. They rarely succeeded, and even if they did penetrate the system, the problem was usually corrected quickly.

"We're trying," said Joseph, his eyes back on his screen. "But whoever they are, they're good. They got the whole net, and they're shutting us out."

"What do you mean?" said Kosar, frowning.

"I mean, right now, it doesn't respond to anything we do," said Joseph. He quickly tapped some keys, hit ENTER, and pointed at the screen. "Nothing," he said.

"Is *anybody* getting anything?" Kosar asked, looking around the room. All the technicians shook their heads. Every phone in the room was ringing now. Behind him, Kosar heard his office hotline phone ringing; that would be somebody very important and very unhappy.

Kosar ran a hand through his wiry hair. "ALL RIGHT, PEOPLE," he shouted. "WE NEED TO FIX THIS *RIGHT NOW*." This was unnecessary; the technicians were all working furiously on keyboards and phones. Kosar again looked up at the Christmas Tree, a mass of red dots. For every tiny dot, he knew, there were more than ten thousand people—people who had just been jolted out of their comfortable, brightly lit, electrically powered cocoons; people who were now confused, frightened, and vulnerable.

Kosar turned away and walked toward his office to answer the insistent ring of his hotline. But his mind was still on all those helpless people without electricity.

Bad things happened to people in the dark.

CHAPTER FORTY-SEVEN

WHEN THE LIGHTS WENT OUT, Toby's parents had been in the kitchen, arguing in whispers about the *thump* they'd heard in the basement. Fawn Harbinger wanted to call the police in case it was an intruder. Roger was balking.

"We'll look stupid if the police come and there's nobody down there," he said.

"I'd rather look stupid than get shot by a burglar," Fawn replied.

"There's no burglar down there," he said.

"Then what went thump?"

"I don't know. Maybe the plumbing."

"If it's the plumbing," said Fawn, "why are you whispering?"

Roger didn't have a good answer for that. The truth was, he'd been a little spooked by the *thump*. But, being a guy, he was reluctant to admit this even to himself, let alone his wife. And he definitely didn't want the police to see the basement filled with rare Star Wars memorabilia. He didn't want word of the collection to get out.

"I'm gonna go look," he whispered. He went to a drawer next to the sink and began rummaging through it.

"What are you looking for?" asked Fawn.

"Just something . . . just in case," he said, pulling out the largest kitchen implement he could find in the drawer. It was a set of barbecue tongs. The Harbingers used them in the summer when they barbecued tofu.

"You're going to *tong* the burglar?" said Fawn.

"Maybe I am," said Roger, who at this point was feeling pretty stupid but, still being a guy, could not see a way to back down. Gripping the tongs, he started toward the basement door. He was relieved when Fawn grabbed his arm and stopped him.

"Please, Roger," she said. "I really don't want you to go down there. I'm going to call the police and tell them it was totally my idea."

Roger sighed. "All right," he said.

"Thank you," said Fawn. She went to the wall phone and picked up the handset.

Then the lights went out.

For a moment they stood in darkness. Then Roger said, "Maybe it's a circuit breaker." He hoped it wasn't, because the circuit breakers were in the basement.

"I don't think so," said Fawn, peering out the window. "The whole neighborhood is dark."

Roger looked out. The neighborhood was ink black. "Call the power company," he said.

"I can't," said Fawn. "The phone's dead." All the phones in the Harbinger house were cordless and required electricity to work.

Roger unclipped the cell phone at his waist. He looked at the screen: NO SIGNAL.

"The cell isn't working, either," he said. "Weird."

In the distance, a siren wailed.

"What should we do?" said Fawn.

"I'll get a flashlight," said Roger. He put the tongs on the counter and began to feel his way through the darkness toward the drawer where they kept things like flashlights, Scotch tape, mystery keys, foreign money, random pieces of string, and half-used tubes of Krazy Glue.

"No," said Fawn. "I mean what are we going to do about the noise in the basement?"

Roger didn't answer that. He found the drawer, opened it, and groped around until he found a flashlight. He flicked the switch; nothing. He found a second flashlight; nothing.

"What good is it to have flashlights," he said, "if the batteries are dead?"

In the distance, another siren wailed.

"I think we should get out of the house," said Fawn.

"Are you *crazy*?" said Roger. "It's pitch black out there."

"It's also pitch black in here," Fawn pointed out. "And

there might be somebody in the basement."

"Don't be ridiculous," said Roger. He began groping the counter for the barbecue tongs.

"What was that?" hissed Fawn.

"What was what?" whispered Roger.

"I heard a voice," said Fawn. "Listen."

The voice was the Wookiee's. He was getting antsy waiting in the basement, listening to the footsteps in the kitchen directly above. He also didn't like hearing sirens.

"I'm leaving," he said.

"Shh!" said Vaderian, pointing at the ceiling.

"I don't care," said the Wookiee. "I'm outta here."

"But the collection," whispered Vaderian, waving his light saber at the Star Wars memorabilia. "We have to—"

"No," said the Wookiee. "This junk ain't worth going to jail for." He started toward the stairs.

"No!" said Vaderian, and as he did, he realized he'd said it much too loudly.

"See?" hissed Fawn. "There *is* someone down there. We're leaving." She started toward the door. Roger was right behind her. But then he grabbed her arm.

"Wait," he said.

"What?"

"The truck," he said. "Outside, when we got home. Remember?" They'd noticed the U-Drive-It truck when they came home.

"So what?" she said, trying to yank her arm free. "Let go!"

"Toby said they're after the collection," he said, recalling the strange phone call. "I didn't believe him at the time, but what if that's what the truck is about? What if that's why there are noises coming from the basement?"

Fawn hesitated, thinking about the memorabilia, all the effort they'd put into collecting it, maintaining it. . . .

"We *can't* let them take the collection," Roger whispered. "We *can't*."

"But . . . how can we stop them?" she said. "We can't call the police."

"Maybe we can trap them down there," said Roger. "Until the power comes back."

"How?" said Fawn.

"I have an idea," said Roger, groping his way back to the flashlight drawer.

"A thousand dollars extra," said the Wookiee.

"Yes," said Vaderian.

"Cash," said the Wookiee.

"Yes, cash," said Vaderian.

"For one load of stuff," said the Wookiee.

"As much as you can carry in one load, yes," said Vaderian. He was already gathering together the items he intended for them to take. His plan, formulated out of desperation, was that he and the Wookiee would load themselves with memorabilia and charge up the stairs. Whoever was up there—the parents of the little weasel, he assumed—might not like it. But whoever they were, they would back off when they saw the Wookiee. Everyone did.

They'd bully their way out of the house, put the memorabilia in the truck, and be gone. Vaderian deeply regretted
that he'd have to leave some items behind. But he'd take
what he could get.

In two minutes he'd loaded up the Wookiee. The big
man's arms strained under the weight of four large items,
including the stormtrooper uniform, and a half-dozen
smaller ones. Vaderian carried only one item, but it was
the ultimate prize: R2-D2 himself. He thrust his glowing
light saber into his belt and reverently picked up the robot.

"Let's go," he said. With the Wookiee going first, feeling
his way with his feet, they started slowly up the stairs.

Fawn was in the ink black hallway, her ear to the basement
door.

"Hurry!" she whispered. "They're coming up!"

She felt Roger behind her, coming from the kitchen.

"How many were there?" she said.

"I found two," he said. "Here, take this one." He thrust
something into her hand. "I think I got the cap loose.
Ready?"

"Ready," she said.

"Now!" shouted Roger.

He yanked the door open. Fawn screamed at the sight of
the two figures on the stairs lit by a ghastly reddish light,
one huge and hairy, one black-clad, with that hideous yet
familiar helmet. . . .

"Do it!" said Roger, his voice snapping Fawn out of her
shock and into action. As they'd agreed, she took the lower

part of the door, and he took the upper. Squeezing the tubes as if their lives depended on it, they squirted two long lines of Krazy Glue along the door frame.

Roger finished first. The figures on the stairs, momentarily stunned by the sudden opening of the door, had started up again.

"Hurry!" Roger shouted.

"Done!" answered Fawn.

Together they slammed the door shut. Roger grabbed the knob and pushed with all his strength, pressing the door against the glue. From the other side, he heard the steps coming closer. In those desperate fearful seconds, he had only one thought in his mind:

Please let this be the quick-drying kind.

Chapter Forty-eight

Toby was crouching under the Wienermobile. Next to him were Micah and Tamara; Drmtsi and Vrsk were behind them.

All around was chaos. It had started the instant the lights went out and blackness enveloped the supermarket parking lot. People started shouting; children started crying. The crowd began surging in random directions; people were knocked over, including whoever was in the pig suit. Somebody grabbed a woman's purse; she screamed. Then there were more screams.

The police switched on their flashlights and waved them around, looking for the escapees and shouting at everyone to "STAY CALM, STAY CALM." But nobody was calm, and soon the police had a small riot on their hands.

As the police struggled with the crowd, Toby and

the others—already on their knees, as ordered by the approaching police—had crawled under the Wienermobile, mainly to avoid being trampled. They could see little of what was going on around them except for running feet occasionally illuminated by darting flashlight beams.

After a few minutes the police began to get better organized. Peeking out from under the left side of the Wienermobile, Toby saw that the police had formed a rough perimeter, waving their flashlights and shouting at the crowd to "MOVE! MOVE!" They were herding everyone to an open area behind the Wienermobile, where people were being funneled toward a half-dozen officers who were shining their flashlights into each person's face, one by one.

"They're still looking for us," Toby said. He looked out at the edge of the parking lot.

He crawled to the right-hand side of the Wienermobile, the side next to the supermarket. It was deserted and dark.

"Stay here," Toby whispered to Micah and Tamara.

"Where are you going?" said Tamara.

"To see how we can get out of here," said Toby. He crawled out from under the Wienermobile, stood up, and slid forward along the side of the big hot dog. When he got to the front, he saw that the police—there were a lot of them now—had established a perimeter all around the edge of the parking lot, clearly intended to keep anybody from sneaking away.

Toby stood there, drumming his fingers, trying to think of a way past the line of police. Then he looked at what he was drumming on.

The Wienermobile.

He went to the passenger door and, holding the door closed with one hand, pulled on the latch with the other. It was unlocked. He took a breath; he'd have to do the next part fast and hope that the confusion behind the Wienermobile, and all the flashlights shining around, would keep the police from noticing the cab light go on.

He yanked the door open, jumped inside, and closed the door. The light had been on for maybe three seconds. Toby listened for a few seconds but didn't hear anyone approaching. In the dark cab, he felt for the steering wheel, then the ignition switch. No key. He felt for the visor, which was where his parents sometimes hid their car keys. Nothing.

He dropped to his knees and felt under the driver's seat. His hand touched something.

Keys.

Toby reached up and found the dome light switch; he slid it to the off position. Then, clutching the keys—which were attached to a wiener-shaped holder—he got back out of the cab. There was still a lot of shouting going on in the parking lot behind the Wienermobile. Toby crouched.

"Tamara," he whispered.

"What?" said Tamara.

"Can you drive this thing?" Tamara's family spent summers at a cabin in Maine; she'd told Toby that her dad sometimes let her drive their car on the dirt roads up there.

"What?"

"I have the keys."

"You want to take the *Wienermobile*?" said Micah.

282

"Yes," said Toby.

"Cool," said Micah.

"I can't drive this!" said Tamara. "It's *huge*."

"Excusing," said Vrsk.

"What?" snapped Toby.

"I can drive," said Vrsk.

"You can?"

"Yes," said Vrsk. Back in Krpshtskan, one of his duties was to be backup driver for the 1961 Checker taxi that served as the presidential limousine. Vrsk figured that qualified him to pilot the giant sausage vehicle.

Toby nodded. "All right," he said.

In a minute they were all in the cab of the Wienermobile, with Vrsk in the driver's seat, Toby next to him, and Micah and Tamara with Drmtsi in an open area behind. The smell of smerk hung heavy in the air. Toby put the key into the ignition.

"Okay," he said.

"Okay," said Vrsk, none too confidently. He turned the key. The engine started. Vrsk started fiddling with his feet.

"Where is clotch?" he said.

"Where is what?" said Toby.

"Clotch. Is not a clotch here."

"I think he means the clutch," said Tamara.

"What's a clutch?" said Micah.

"It's a pedal on old cars," said Tamara. To Vrsk, she said, "There is no clutch."

"No clotch?" said Vrsk.

"No clotch," said Tamara.

Micah, peering out a side window, said, "I think somebody's coming."

"Forget the clotch," said Toby. "Just go!"

Vrsk stomped on the gas. The engine roared. Nothing else happened.

"The cops are coming!" said Micah.

"You have to put it in gear!" said Tamara.

"What?" said Vrsk, over the roar of the engine.

"THE GEARSHIFT!" shouted Tamara. She leaned forward, grabbed the shift lever, and yanked it down. With a squeal of tires, the giant frankfurter-shaped vehicle lunged forward, sending Tamara, Micah, and Drmtsi tumbling backward. Toby saw police running outside toward the Wienermobile from all directions, shouting. Vrsk was rigid, gripping the wheel with a look of pure terror on his face. The Wienermobile, gaining speed, was heading straight toward a half-dozen police officers waving flashlights and shouting.

"DON'T HIT THEM!" shouted Toby.

"I AM NOT WANTING TO!" shouted Vrsk.

"THEN TURN THE STEERING WHEEL!" shouted Toby.

Vrsk looked down at the steering wheel, as though realizing for the first time he was holding it. He yanked it hard to the left, sending Toby slamming into the passenger door and the three in the back tumbling sideways. The giant hot dog, now going fifty miles per hour, skidded and squealed into a sharp left turn, leaning so far over that Toby thought it might flip. Outside, the police scattered as the Wienermobile shot past them, sideswiped a cruiser, went off a curb, and landed

in the street. Vrsk spun the wheel right, fighting for control as the fishtailing Wienermobile roared forward into the utter darkness of the blacked-out neighborhood.

"I CANNOT SEE!" shouted Vrsk.

"TURN ON THE LIGHTS!" shouted Toby.

"HOW?" shouted Vrsk. The lights in the Krpshtskani presidential limousine were never used, the last bulb having burned out in 1989.

Toby pushed away from the door and reached across the cab, praying that the light switch on the Wienermobile was in the same place as on his parents' car. It was; he found it and turned the switch. The lights came on just in time for Vrsk to see that they were about to ram a Dunkin' Donuts. He yanked the wheel to the right again, sending everyone sprawling left. He managed to miss the building as he made a skidding turn onto a cross street. For the moment, the road ahead was clear, although in the distance Toby could hear sirens wailing. *Many* sirens.

Behind him, Micah, Tamara, and Drmtsi, having been hurled around by Vrsk's violent maneuvers, were struggling to get up. Tamara looked out the windshield.

"Where are we?" she said.

"I have no idea," said Toby.

"So," she said, "we're wanted as terrorists, we've stolen the Wienermobile, police are chasing us, *and* we're lost."

"Yeah," said Toby.

"I honestly don't see how things can get any worse," said Tamara.

Micah said, "I think I'm gonna throw up."

CHAPTER FORTY-NINE

In THE UTILITY ROOM next to the Hubble Middle School gym, Prmkt was hunched over the computer screen, watching the futile efforts of the power-company computer people to regain control over their system. Prmkt smiled: they weren't even close.

Through the utility-room door, he could hear the sounds of scared people—students, teachers, parents—as they groped their way around the science-fair projects in the dark gym. A voice was shouting for everyone to stay calm.

"There's nothing to worry about!" the voice was saying.

Yes, there is, thought Prmkt.

He touched the control pad, opening a window on his computer screen. He tapped some keys; the window was

now showing the CNN satellite feed. Superimposed on the screen were the words MASSIVE BLACKOUT. A frowning announcer was talking.

". . . Millions of people are affected," he said. "There is still no word from Mid-Atlantic Power about what caused the blackout, or when power will be restored. We have been told by the FAA that planes in the affected area are being diverted to airports outside the blackout area, which as we said earlier covers much of the Mid-Atlantic region. We've also been told that telephone service has been severely disrupted, which is making it difficult to get any information; in fact, at the moment we are not in touch with our CNN Washington bureau. Already there has been speculation that, since so many major government facilities are affected, this could be an act of terrorism. But I repeat that at the moment we have no information that would confirm this. We are continuing to . . ."

Prmkt clicked off the sound. His hands went to the keyboard again.

He would show them what terror felt like.

CHAPTER FIFTY

"**WE'RE BACK UP!**" shouted a voice in the Mid-Atlantic Power command center.

Bernard Kosar slammed his phone down and ran from his office, so excited that he left the football on his desk.

He looked up at the Christmas Tree and felt a surge of relief: the red lights had turned green. The power was on again.

Kosar turned to Robert Joseph, the computer genius, and said, "What happened?"

Joseph shrugged and answered, "I have no idea."

"What?" said Kosar.

Joseph pointed at his computer screen. "We didn't get it back. They gave it back. Whoever they are."

Kosar felt a knot in his stomach. "Are you saying

they could take it down again?" he asked.

Joseph nodded glumly. "Yup," he said.

Kosar ran both hands through his wiry hair. "All right, listen up, people!" he said. "We need to . . ."

"Excuse me, Bernie," said the technician/singer Laura Schweitzer.

"What?" Kosar said, annoyed at the interruption.

"I think you'll want to see this," she said, pointing at her screen.

Kosar leaned over. The screen showed a map of the eastern United States. The top half of the map was covered with dozens of symbols flashing red.

"Does that mean what I think it means?" he said.

Schweitzer nodded. "I'm afraid it does. Now the whole Northeast is down. New York, Boston, Philly—all down."

Kosar straightened up. "All right, people!" he said. "We have to find out WHO IS DOING THIS, and we have to STOP THEM, and we have to do it NOW." There was no need for this speech; everybody in the room was already busy.

Kosar's direct-line phone was ringing again. On the way to answer it, he picked up his football.

CHAPTER FIFTY-ONE

★

"**H**EY," SAID TOBY, looking out the Wienermobile windshield, "the lights are back on."

Tamara, in the backseat with Micah and Drmtsi, looked out. "Good," she said. "Maybe now we can figure out where we are."

"Can we stop?" said Micah. "Because I am *really* carsick."

"If you throw up," said Tamara, "I will kill you."

"Thanks for your concern," said Micah.

Vrsk had taken a number of sharp, random turns since they had driven away from the supermarket; at the moment, there didn't seem to be any police cars behind them. But in the distance, the sound of sirens seemed to be coming from all directions.

"We can't stop yet," said Toby. "If we stop, the cops'll catch us."

"Maybe we should lose the Wienermobile," said

Tamara. "It's a little obvious, don't you think? People tend to notice a giant hot dog."

"Yeah," said Toby. "But it's all we have right now. When we get near the school we can ditch it. But right now we need to figure out where we are."

"There's a Starbucks," said Micah.

"*That's* a big help," said Toby.

From the backseat, Drmtsi, who was feeling a bit queasy himself, said to Vrsk, in Krpsht, "Are we there yet?"

"I will ask the boy," answered Vrsk. He asked Toby in English, "How far is to school?"

"I don't know," said Toby. "We're trying to figure out where we are."

"There's another Starbucks," observed Micah.

"What did the boy say?" Drmtsi asked Vrsk.

"He said we will be there soon," answered Vrsk, who was busy driving and didn't want to be answering questions from Drmtsi.

"Can I ask you something?" Toby said to Vrsk.

"Yes," said Vrsk.

"Who are you really?"

Vrsk kept his eyes on the road. "I told you, we are tour—"

"You're not tourists," interrupted Toby.

Vrsk said nothing.

"Why do you want to go to the school?" asked Toby.

Nothing.

"What do you know about the science fair?"

Nothing.

"There's another Starbucks," said Micah.

"Micah," snapped Toby, "will you stop pointing out every single . . . wait a minute. I *know* that Starbucks. That's the one near my house!" He frowned, then said to Vrsk, "Turn left here."

"What're you doing?" said Tamara.

Toby turned around to look at her. "We're going to stop by my house just for a second."

"*What?* I thought we were going to the science fair!"

"We are," said Toby. "But we're right near my house. I just want to stop by, in case the Star Wars guys are there."

"What if they are?" said Tamara. "What're *we* going to do about it?"

"I could throw up on them," said Micah.

"Turn right here," said Toby to Vrsk.

From the backseat, Drmtsi said to Vrsk, "Where are we going now?"

"We are going to the boy's house to stop there on the way to the school," Vrsk answered.

"Why?" said Drmtsi.

"I am not certain, but I think the boy said that people from Star Wars are coming to his house."

"Excellent!" said Drmtsi. It did not surprise him that, in this amazing and rich country, show-business celebrities would be abundant. In English, he declared: "May this Force is with you!"

Toby, Tamara, and Micah looked at him.

"These guys are *weird*," whispered Tamara.

"Turn left," said Toby to Vrsk. "We're almost there."

"Good," said Micah, suppressing a burp. "Because I'm almost there, too."

CHAPTER FIFTY-TWO

★

Now that the power was back, the anxiety level in the Hubble gym had ratcheted down a few notches—from panicky to merely nervous. The big room roared with the sound of a thousand excited voices; rumors swirled everywhere as the crowd, half of whom held mobile phones pressed to their ears, tried to work out what, exactly, had happened.

So far they'd learned little, other than that the blackout had hit a large area around Washington and that there was no official explanation yet. Somebody had just picked up a rumor that the Northeast, including New York City, had also been hit by a blackout; hearing this, parents exchanged worried looks and a few whispered the feared word . . . *terrorism*. This particular buzz was spreading quickly across the gym when the PA system came to life.

"Attention! May I have everybody's attention, please!"

As always, The Hornet's commanding voice quickly quieted the room. All eyes turned toward the small stage, where The Hornet stood with Lance Swingle, her prim, pursed lips close to the microphone.

"As I'm sure you all know by now," said The Hornet, "the blackout we experienced here at Hubble was widespread. I am sure the authorities are taking whatever steps are needed to deal with any, ah, problems that may have arisen. But for the time being, the police have ordered all nonemergency traffic to stay off the roads. So since we're temporarily confined here anyway, and since Mr. Swingle has very graciously agreed to remain with us, we are going to continue with the science fair."

The crowd applauded. Swingle waved and smiled, as if he were absolutely thrilled. He was not. The second the lights had gone out, he had grabbed his nearest lackey and said he wanted to get out of there *immediately*. The lackey had run out to the ball field to inform the helicopter pilot, who had informed the lackey that the Federal Aviation Administration was not allowing any civilian aircraft to take off, even one owned by a billionaire. This was the only reason Swingle remained in the gym.

After acknowledging the applause, Swingle shouldered The Hornet off the microphone and said, "We're not going to let a little blackout worry us, are we?"

"Nooo," answered the crowd, somewhat unconvinced.

"Of course we're not!" said Swingle. "So let's have a look at these projects!"

With that, he joined The Hornet and a gaggle of teachers.

"Ready?" he said to The Hornet.

The Hornet frowned and looked around. "Where's Mr. Pzyrbovich?" she asked.

"He was here a few minutes ago," answered one of the teachers.

Swingle looked pointedly at his watch. The Hornet looked around some more, but saw no sign of Mr. P. She did not look pleased.

"We'll just have to do this without him," she said.

"Good idea," said Swingle, leading the way, as the group set out once again to judge the science fair.

A few feet away, inside the utility room just off the gym, Prmkt was watching his computer screen. He had four windows open. Two were showing him the efforts—still futile—of the power companies to regain control over their systems. One was showing the statuses of various communications satellites. The fourth window was showing CNN. There were several people on the screen, all frowning deeply; one was described on the screen as a TERRORISM EXPERT. They were saying that the president of the United States would soon be addressing the nation.

Prmkt smiled at that. He began tapping the keys again.

He would give the president something more to talk about.

CHAPTER FIFTY-THREE

NOBODY HAD EVER SEEN ANYTHING LIKE IT anywhere, ever. Somebody, somehow, was turning the power off, and then back on, over huge sections of North America, like a child flicking switches in a living room. A few minutes earlier the power had been returned to the Northeast, but at that same moment the Midwest, including Chicago, had gone dark. Then the Midwest came back and California went down. Right now Texas was dark.

Every available technician in North America was working frantically to find answers. But as yet nobody had a clue who or what was causing the blackouts or where the next one would strike.

The U.S. military was now on high alert all over the world—a world becoming more tense by the second as the

chaos spread across America. Financial markets were severely disrupted as critical computer systems lost power, threatening huge amounts of data. Backups were holding; but for how long? Planes were making emergency landings everywhere as the FAA, not knowing which airports would be affected next, struggled to halt commercial air travel. Telecommunications, including the Internet and e-mail, had become highly erratic and unreliable, as had radio and TV transmissions. Many cities were paralyzed by horrendous traffic jams; tens of thousands of drivers were abandoning their cars on freeways and trying to get home on foot.

This disruption had already—in less than an hour—cost the country billions of dollars. But that was a pittance compared to the devastating price to be paid if the mysterious blackouts were not stopped soon. Americans depended on electrical technology for every element of their lives—their economy, their government, their food, their shelter, their communication, their transportation, their medical care—*everything*. Without that technology, American society would plunge into a primitive, desperate, fearful, and dangerous state from which the country might never recover.

Panic was spreading, particularly in the big cities. There already were reports of supermarkets being looted by mobs of people who feared that the food would soon run out. Gunshots had been reported in some areas. Rumors swirled everywhere about who, or what, was causing the blackouts. Most of the rumors involved terrorists, but

there were many other theories, including some that blamed extraterrestrial beings.

Americans were scared. They felt their comfortable world crumbling around them. They wanted the blackouts to stop, and they wanted somebody to assure them that everything would be all right again. The person they most wanted to hear these assurances from was the president, who was scheduled to address the nation "in a matter of minutes." The networks had been saying that for the last half hour.

The problem was that, at the moment, the president didn't know any more about the blackouts than anybody else did. The president was very angry about this. He was running for re-election, and he did NOT want to tell the nation he didn't know what was happening. He wanted to tell the nation he had everything under control. So he was putting extreme pressure on his people to get him some answers RIGHT NOW. His people were, in turn, putting extreme pressure on power-industry officials, who were putting extreme pressure on their staffs.

This was why Bernard Kosar was currently holding a phone to each of his ears. In each ear was the shouting voice of a high-level executive of Mid-Atlantic Power. Kosar had tried to explain that his people were already working as hard as they could, but this didn't stop the executives from shouting; they had been shouted at by the people above them, and they felt a need to shout at the people below.

Kosar heard a tap on his doorframe and looked up to see

Robert Joseph gesturing to indicate he wanted to tell Kosar something. Kosar put the two phones down on his desk.

"What?" he said to Joseph.

"It's coming from around here," Joseph said.

"What is?'

"The hack," said Joseph. "It's coming from Maryland."

Kosar waved his arms. "For everything? The whole country?"

"I think so," said Joseph.

Kosar was on his feet. "How do you know that?"

Joseph started to answer, but he was using computer terms so technical that to Kosar it might as well have been Chinese. Worse, actually, because Kosar spoke a little Chinese. He waved an arm to make Joseph stop.

"Okay, never mind," he said. "Where, exactly, are they in Maryland?"

"I don't know yet," said Joseph.

"Find out," said Kosar.

Joseph started to say something, but then he saw the look in Kosar's eyes.

"Okay," he said and left.

Kosar picked up the phones. The executives were still shouting. He gently put the phones back down, a few inches apart. He'd let the executives shout at each other, while the nerdy kid in the other room tried to save the world.

CHAPTER FIFTY-FOUR

BAM BAM BAMBAMBAMBAMBAM

The men in the basement were trying to break down
the door. They'd been pounding on it with their fists, but
the door proved to be too solid. Now, however, they'd
found something heavier to bludgeon it with—a chair,
maybe, or a baseball bat. They were hitting the door hard;
from what Toby's parents had seen, one of them was huge.

Roger stood by the door, watching it warily as it shook
with each blow. Fawn was at the kitchen telephone; she'd
just dialed 911 yet again. She hung up in frustration.

"It's still busy!" she said. "How can 911 be busy?"

"It's the blackout," said Roger.

BAMBAMBAMBAMBAM

"Roger," said Fawn, "they're going to knock it down. We should go."

"You go," he said. "I'm staying. I'm not letting them take the collection."

She went to him, put a hand on his arm. "Roger," she said softly, "it's just some old movie props."

He turned from the door, took her hands in his, and looked into her eyes. "Fawn," he said, "do you remember how we met? *Do* you?"

She nodded, but he answered anyway: "We met in a movie theater, Fawn. We met because we were the only two people who went to every single showing of *The Empire Strikes Back*. Every single one, for *three days*, until the movie theater called the police. People said we were crazy, but we didn't care, because we knew we were part of something great, something that would last.

"And it did last, Fawn. We were right, and those people were wrong, just like they were wrong when we quit our jobs and spent all our time and money scavenging for those props. That collection is worth a fortune today, Fawn."

BAMBAMBAMBAMBAM

"What does it matter what it's worth?" said Fawn. "You'll never sell it."

"That's right," said Roger. "I won't sell it because it's part of me—part of *us*. Star Wars brought us together, Fawn. It gave us a purpose when we didn't have one. It taught us that there is good and evil in the universe, and if good doesn't stand up to evil and fight back, then evil will win."

He pointed at the door. "And right now, somebody dressed as Darth Vader, the very embodiment of evil, is trying to take our collection."

"But the big one looks like Chewbacca," said Fawn. "Isn't he supposed to be good?"

"Maybe he switched sides," said Roger.

BAMBAMBAMBAMBAMBAMBAM—CRACK

The door was giving way.

"You go," said Roger. "Maybe you can find help. I'm going to stay and fight."

"With *what*?" said Fawn. "You don't have a weapon."

"I do too have a weapon," said Roger. He turned and strode down the hall to their bedroom, with Fawn following. He went to the closet and reached up to the top shelf.

"Are you *insane*?" she said. "It's a *movie prop*!"

Roger brought down a custom-made case and set it on the bed. He flipped the latches and opened the lid.

BAM BAM BAM BAM BAM

"It may be a movie prop to you," he said. "To me, it is the weapon Luke Skywalker used in the greatest duel of all— the duel with Vader in the freezing chamber on Cloud City." He pulled out a battered-looking light saber.

"But Luke lost that duel," said Fawn. "Vader cut off his *hand*."

"Yes, but Luke lived to fight again," said Roger.

"I think you're better off with the barbecue tongs," said Fawn.

Ignoring her, Roger put the light saber on the bed and went back into the closet, emerging a moment later with a

black Jedi Knight uniform on a hanger. He quickly stripped down to his underwear and shrugged into the black top.

BAMBAMBAMBAMBAM

"You're wearing *that*?" said Fawn.

"I want him to know what he's fighting," said Roger.

"A lunatic?" said Fawn.

"He's fighting the Force," said Roger. "The *good* side of the Force. And there is no power in the universe more powerful. Help me with my pants." Roger had put on a few pounds since the last time he had been a Jedi Knight. The black pants were stuck midway up his thighs.

*BAMBAMBAMBAMBAM***CRACK CRACK CRACK**

"Roger!" said Fawn, "they're breaking through the door!"

There was no time now for pants. Roger grabbed the light saber and, hindered by his halfway-up pants, waddled into the hallway to do battle with evil.

CHAPTER FIFTY-FIVE

LANCE SWINGLE—TRAILED BY THE HORNET, a gaggle of science teachers, and a crowd of spectators—walked slowly through the Hubble Middle gymnasium, pretending to be interested in the science fair. What he was really interested in was getting out of there. The mysterious blackouts had made him very nervous; he'd told his lackeys to let him know as soon as the TranScent helicopter could take off.

Meanwhile, though, he was looking with fake fascination at science-fair projects. He had just reached the one submitted by Brad Pitt Wemplemeyer, who stood next to it, beaming with pride. His project consisted of a fifty-five-gallon drum containing a brown liquid. Suspended

over this, hanging from a wire, was a large, multicolored disc, about the size of a small car tire. Next to the project was a sign that said THE POWER OF SURFACE TENSION.

Swingle stopped, looking at the disc.

"What is that thing?" he said.

"It's a giant Mentos," said BPW.

"A what?" said Swingle.

"A Mentos," said BPW. "The candy. Actually I made it by gluing a whole bunch of regular Mentos together. It took, like, a week."

Swingle leaned closer to the disc and saw that it was, in fact, made of thousands of Mentos.

"And why did you do that?" he asked Brad.

"To see what happens when you drop it in Diet Coke," said Brad, pointing at the drum.

"You filled a fifty-five-gallon drum with *Diet Coke*?" said Swingle.

"Yeah," said Brad. "We had to get it from the beverage distributor. My dad says this project better win the prize, because he spent my college tuition on Diet Coke."

"Perhaps we should move on," said The Hornet, glaring at BPW.

"Not yet," said Swingle. To BPW he said, "I have to know. What, exactly, will happen when you drop that thing into the Diet Coke?"

"I'm not totally sure," said Brad. "For the actual experiment, I'm going to move it outside. They won't let me do it in here. You want to see it happen?"

"Not really," said Swingle.

There was a loud *Ribbit!* and a sudden motion next to Brad's project. The group turned to see a large frog inside a glass globe rise several inches off a metal plate. It hovered in the air, looking nervous even by frog standards.

"What is THAT?" said Swingle.

"It's Fester," said BPW. "He's a frog."

"I *see* it's a frog," said Swingle. "But what . . . what . . ."

"It's Mucus's project," said Brad.

"*Mucus*?" said Swingle.

"Micah Porter," said BPW. "It works on magnets or something. Micah has it on a timer. He's not here because he got kicked out of school for . . ."

"That's *enough*, Mr. Wemplemeyer," snapped The Hornet.

"Okay," said BPW. "But I think Fester's getting hungry."

"Why don't we move on?" said The Hornet.

"Why don't we?" said Swingle.

Ribbit! said Fester the floating frog. But nobody was listening.

The judges came next to a row of impressive-looking projects, all submitted by ME kids. The Hornet perked up, as did the teachers with her; one of these projects, they were sure, would be Swingle's choice for first prize. This was also the opinion of the group of ME kids and their parents—including Harmonee, Haley, Jason, and The Ferret, all of whom were smiling with varying degrees of smugness.

But The Ferret's smugness turned to fear when Swingle pointed at his project and said, "This looks interesting.

Can someone tell me what it's about?"

"Go ahead, Farrel," Harmonee said to The Ferret, her smiling face radiating sweetness. "Explain your project to Mr. Swingle." The other ME kids snickered, knowing that The Ferret could no more explain his project than he could produce frozen yogurt from his ear.

"Is this your project, young man?" said Swingle.

"Um," said The Ferret, adding, "um."

"Yes?" said Swingle.

"Um," said The Ferret.

"He means yes," said Harmonee, batting her eyelashes at Swingle.

"Well, then," said Swingle to The Ferret, "tell me what it does."

But before The Ferret could totally humiliate himself, one of Swingle's lackeys tapped him on the shoulder and whispered something into his ear. He, in turn, conferred quietly for a minute with The Hornet. She nodded grimly and turned to face the crowd.

"Apparently," she said, " the situation with the black-outs is becoming, ah, a bit more of a problem."

A man in the crowd, with a cell phone to his ear, said in a loud voice, "There's rioting in Los Angeles."

"Miami, too," said another voice. "And Cleveland."

The crowd was buzzing now.

"Quiet, please!" shouted The Hornet. The crowd quieted, stunned; The Hornet *never* shouted.

"We cannot have panic," said The Hornet. "We *will not* have panic. Now Mr. Swingle has informed me that the

president is going to address the nation about this situation, and I'm sure he will tell us what steps are being taken to bring everything under control. I'm going to ask everybody to move to the north end of the gymnasium, and I'm going to ask Coach Furman to bring a television monitor so we can watch the president's address."

The crowd, buzzing again, began moving. Swingle grabbed his lackey by the arm and snapped, "Get me out of here. I don't care how you do it, but *get me out of here.*" The lackey trotted off through the crowd, leaving Swingle, momentarily alone, standing by the ME kids' projects. His eyes happened to fall on a thick cable running from one of the projects; he noticed the same type of cable running from another project, and another. For a moment he wondered about that. But then he decided it was not his concern.

He started walking toward the end of the gym, having decided that, until his idiot staff could get him out of here, he would hear what the president had to say about what was causing these strange blackouts. He took a few steps. Then something made him stop, turn, and take another look at the ME projects. Something bothered him about them—the elaborate technology, the thick cable. . . .

He stared at the projects for a few more seconds.

Nah, he decided. *Not my concern.*

He turned and started walking again.

CHAPTER FIFTY-SIX

Roger Harbinger, Jedi Knight, stood in the hallway, gripping his light saber with his right hand while using his left to pull up his Jedi pants. His eyes were fixed on the basement door.

BAM CRACK CRACK CRACK

The door was being splintered into kindling. It now had a big hole, through which Roger could see the legs of a chair. The men in the basement were breaking out.

CRASH

The last pieces of the door clattered into the hallway, followed by the chair. Roger, hardly breathing, gripped his light saber tighter and focused on the now-empty doorway. He felt a drop of sweat run down his forehead and sting his eye.

He twitched as the Wookiee's enormous hairy head appeared in the opening. The head swiveled and looked directly at Roger. Then the Wookie looked back over his shoulder and said, "He has a light saber."

From the stairwell, Roger heard a voice he knew well from hours spent in the tenth row of the movie theater—a deep voice taking loud hissing breaths between each phrase.

"Step aside!" spoke the voice of Darth Vader. "I shall deal with him."

The Wookiee stepped aside. Roger heard the tromp of heavy bootsteps climbing the stairs. Finally, the gleaming plastic of the black-helmeted head appeared. Vaderian stepped into the hallway, adjusted his cape, and faced Roger.

"So," he said, "we meet at last."

He flicked the switch on his light saber. Nothing happened.

"I said *no more discount batteries*!" Vaderian hissed at the Wookiee.

"The batteries are good," said the Wookiee. "Jiggle the switch."

Vaderian jiggled the switch, and the light saber came to life. Again Vaderian faced Roger.

"So," he said, raising his saber, "we meet at last."

"So we do," said Roger, wishing he could come up with something more dramatic. He also wished his light saber lit up, but it was a real prop, and in *Star Wars* the glow was added as a special effect.

Vaderian, waving his light saber, stepped forward. Roger stepped back. In moments they were in the living room, circling. The Wookiee stood in the hallway entrance, watching.

Vaderian slashed his light saber toward Roger. Vaderian's saber hummed as it sliced the air. The hum was digitally recorded and triggered by motion sensors in the handle of the light saber, which Vaderian had purchased on the Internet.

Roger, still tugging at his pants with his left hand, dodged out of the way and thrust his saber at Vader. Vader blocked it with his own saber. The two sabers made a loud *clunk* as they hit each other. Each man winced, secretly afraid that his saber would break.

Now they were circling again. The Wookiee was watching intently.

Then all three heard it: "*AIIIEEEEEEEEEE!!!*"

The piercing shriek came from the end of the hallway. Roger and Vaderian turned to see what had caused it. The Wookiee started to turn, but before he got his head around, Fawn Harbinger had leaped on his back. She was wearing one of her Princess Leia costumes, specifically the metal bikini Leia wore when she was held captive by Jabba the Hutt.

Fawn had considered wearing her white-robe costume, but she felt it would be too confining for fighting. Also, she was proud that she could still fit into the bikini.

"LEAVE MY HUSBAND ALONE!" she shouted, pounding a fist on the Wookiee's head.

"Get off me, lady!" shouted the Wookiee. "OWW!" he added, as Fawn grabbed a handful of his thick hair and yanked on it. Her other arm was now wrapped around the Wookiee's head, covering his eyes. Temporarily blinded and shouting in pain, he staggered, spinning, back to the hall, with Fawn still screeching and clinging to his back like a crazed bikini-clad monkey.

"Fawn!" shouted Roger. He lunged after his wife but found his path blocked by Vaderian, breath hissing in his voice-changing box.

"Get out of my way, Vader!" said Roger.

"Make me, Jedi!" snarled Vaderian.

Roger swung his light saber, but Vaderian was ready. With a quick and practiced move, he parried Roger's blow and then struck one of his own, hitting Roger's light saber just above his hand. Roger lost his grip; the light saber clattered across the living room.

Roger was now unarmed. He stepped back as Vaderian swung at him, the humming blade just missing his face. He heard screeching and thumping from the hallway, but couldn't see what was happening because of the advancing black-caped bulk of Vaderian.

Roger looked to his left and saw his light saber on the floor, ten feet away. He took a step toward it, but Vaderian cut him off.

"Why don't you use the Force to get your light saber, Jedi?" said Vaderian. Then he chuckled a chuckle that he had been waiting his entire adult life to deliver.

Roger looked at the light saber. He remembered the

scene from *The Empire Strikes Back* when Luke, left hanging upside down by an ice creature on the Planet Hoth, stretches his hand out and summons the light saber to him.

If only . . .

Roger jerked his head away as the humming blade flashed past again. He took another step back; he was almost to the wall. In desperation, he reached his hand out toward his light saber. Vaderian chuckled. Roger could tell he had practiced chuckling. Another step back, and Roger felt the wall behind him. There was nowhere to go now. Vaderian drew back for a final blow. . . .

And then Roger's light saber moved. Roger gasped; Vaderian turned to look. Both men stared in astonishment as the light saber rose, traveled across the floor, and settled gently into Roger's outstretched hand.

"Here you go, Dad," said Toby's voice.

Roger gripped the light saber with both hands, allowing his pants to fall to his knees. He swung the saber with all his strength. Vaderian raised his saber to block it.

CLUNK

Both men opened their eyes and saw that Vaderian's light saber had shattered into pieces; the batteries—six C cells—were rolling across the floor. Vaderian held only the handle now. Roger drew his saber back, preparing to strike again. But Vaderian was already at the door, yanking it open and barging out, followed closely by the Wookiee, howling in pain and chased by Fawn, who was holding a clump of hair in each hand. As the Wookiee ran out the

door, she stopped and shouted, "AND DON'T COME BACK, HAIRBALL!"

As Vaderian and the Wookiee fled, they barely avoided barreling into Drmtsi, Vrsk, Tamara, and Micah. The four had been ordered by Toby to remain outside while he entered the house, invisible, through his bedroom window. They'd been standing on the front walkway, listening to the battle rage inside; now they jumped aside as Vaderian and the Wookiee barreled past.

For a moment, all four of them could only stare at the two weird figures. It was Drmtsi who first found words, calling out in English as Vaderian and the Wookiee disappeared into the night: "May this Force is being with you!"

CHAPTER FIFTY-SEVEN

PRMKT'S QUICK, ACCURATE FINGERS danced over the computer keyboard. His eyes were focused on the screen window displaying the status of a Hughes communications satellite. The satellite hosted several dozen network relays that fed ground-based cable systems.

Prmkt intercepted a feed being relayed to the satellite from a location not far from Hubble. His fingers flashed for a few more seconds. The feed was now routed *through* his laptop, then *back* to the satellite for rebroadcast.

He watched the window on his screen, which now displayed a test pattern. He checked his watch. Any second now . . . *there*.

On the screen, the test pattern had been replaced by the

image of a man sitting at a large desk, a pair of flags behind him. Prmkt studied the man's face. He looked tired; Prmkt thought he detected a hint of anxiety in his eyes.

Prmkt nodded. He enjoyed knowing that he was the cause of this man's anxiety. And soon he would be the cause of more.

Much more.

CHAPTER FIFTY-EIGHT

★

TOBY HAD SPENT SEVERAL MINUTES talking very fast, trying to explain to his parents how he and his fellow prisoners had managed to (a) escape from federal custody, and (b) show up in the middle of a robbery with the Wienermobile *and*, by the way, an invisibility device. Toby had then tried to explain why they needed to get to the science fair *right away*, because of Sternabite's warning that something very bad was going to happen.

His parents were still stunned from their battle with Vaderian and the Wookiee and still wearing their Star Wars costumes. They did not want to go anywhere. They were more interested in explaining to Toby why—if he ever got out of prison—he was going to be grounded for the next, approximately, three thousand years.

"But the science fair!" Toby cried. "We have to—"

"If there's a problem with the science fair," interrupted Roger, "the police will handle it."

"But the police *won't* handle it!" Toby shouted. "They don't believe us. *Nobody* believes us. Please, we have to get to the school!"

"No, Toby," said Roger. "We're not going to discuss—"

He was interrupted by the sudden blare of the TV set, which Drmtsi had managed to turn on, hoping to find the shopping network. On the screen, in big letters, were the words BLACKOUT PANIC SPREADS. The announcer was saying: ". . . expecting the president to address the nation at any moment now about the rapidly deteriorating situation as city after city is descending into anarchy. We have still not received any hard information about what is causing these blackouts and communications disruptions, although as we said moments ago there has been a report—so far unsubstantiated—that whatever is causing this problem is originating from Maryland, possibly in the Washington, D.C., area. But again, we have no . . ."

"Did you hear that?" said Toby. "It's got to be the science fair!"

"You don't know that," said Fawn. "It could just be a coincidence."

"No!" said Toby. "Sternabite said the ME kids had collected all this, like, top secret technology!"

Roger and Fawn exchanged a look. Vrsk said something in Krpsht to Drmtsi.

"Dad," said Toby, "what if I'm right?"

"*That* would be a first," said Micah. "Ouch," he added, when Tamara punched him.

"Really, Dad," said Toby, "what if I *am* right, and something terrible happens, and we didn't try to stop it? Don't you always tell me that no matter what, you have to try to do the right thing?"

Roger exchanged a look with Fawn—Fawn, who had jumped on the Wookiee to save him; he turned back to Toby, took a breath, and exhaled.

"All right," he said.

"We have to hurry!" said Toby, already at the door.

They rode in the Wienermobile, because there wasn't enough room for all of them in the Harbingers' car. They took side streets in an effort to avoid the police. Vrsk drove, with Toby in the front passenger seat giving directions; the others were crowded into the back.

"What exactly are we going to do when we get there?" asked Micah.

"We're going to find the ME kids' projects," said Toby.

"And then what?" said Tamara.

"I don't know," admitted Toby. "Unplug them?"

"Good thing we have a plan," said Tamara.

"What's that smell?" said Fawn, wrinkling her nose.

"It's some kind of cheese," said Toby.

"They keep it in their pants," added Micah.

"Their *pants*?" said Fawn.

"It is traditional Krpshtskani cheese," said Vrsk, who'd

been following the discussion. "Also is for scaring wolfs. Is called smerk."

Hearing that word, Drmtsi, who was sitting next to Fawn and admiring the way she looked in her Star Wars bikini, reached into his pants and said, "Smerk?"

"No!" said Fawn, recoiling.

"UH-oh," said Toby.

"What?" said Roger.

Toby pointed at the sideview mirror. "Police!"

They heard the *whoop* of a siren.

"He wants us to pull over," said Toby.

WHOOP WHOOP WHOOP

"So," said Micah, "are we gonna pull over?"

"We're almost to the school," said Toby, looking out the window. He turned to Vrsk and said, "Can this hot dog go any faster?"

"We will find out," said Vrsk, as he stomped on the accelerator.

CHAPTER FIFTY-NINE

★

SWINGLE LOOKED AROUND the crowded gym, seeing anxiety on the faces of the people waiting for the president to speak. Swingle *hated* this situation—hated waiting, hated crowds, hated the feeling of not being in control. He made up his mind. He wasn't staying here with these losers.

He was getting out.

He slipped away from his lackeys and, keeping his face down, pushed through the crowd to the exit. He strode quickly across the ball field to the TranScent helicopter sitting in the darkness. He yanked open the door, startling the pilot, a young man named Jake Ungerman, who had dreamed his whole life of being a helicopter pilot. He loved his job and took great pride in it.

"Mr. Swingle!" he said. "Is something . . ."

"We're leaving," snapped Swingle, climbing into the chopper. "Now."

"Uh, sir, we can't right now. The FAA . . ."

"I don't care what the FAA says," said Swingle. "Start the engine!"

"Sir," said Ungerman. "I'd lose my license."

Swingle leaned forward and grabbed Ungerman's shirt. "You listen to me, kid," he said. "I can get you your license back if you lose it. But if you don't take off right now, I will make sure you lose it *forever*. You'll never fly again. You won't be allowed to fly a *kite*. Do you understand me?"

Ungerman nodded glumly.

"Good," said Swingle. "Then start the engine."

Ungerman began flipping switches. "What about your staff?" he asked.

"Forget them," said Swingle. "Go."

The big rotor began to turn. Swingle buckled himself into his seat. He looked out the window toward the gym, which was full of scared people worrying about what was going to happen, waiting to be told what to do. *Bunch of sheep*, Swingle thought. He was very pleased with the way he'd handled the situation. He had *taken charge*. That's why, he, Lance Swingle, was a winner. As the rotors spun faster, he took one last look out the window at the school and the gym full of losers. He smiled a thin, self-satisfied smile, the smile of a man in control of his own destiny.

If he had looked out the window on the other side, he would have seen an indication that his destiny was not, after all, entirely in his own hands: a four-ton frankfurter, coming fast.

CHAPTER SIXTY

"**YOU'RE GOING OFF THE ROAD!**" shouted Toby.

"I KNOW THIS!" answered Vrsk.

The hurtling Wienermobile, followed by the whooping police car, had barely made the turn into the Hubble Middle School driveway. The giant hot dog fishtailed wildly as Vrsk fought to regain control. He did not totally succeed. The driveway curved gently left, but the Wienermobile kept going straight, lurching into the air as the wheels hit the curb. The impact shoved the terrified occupants forward, and Vrsk's foot slammed down hard on the accelerator. The Wienermobile shot forward onto the ball field.

WHOOP WHOOP WHOOP

The police car vaulted the curb right behind them. Directly ahead was the chain-link fencing of the baseball backstop.

"STOP STOP STOP STOP!" shouted Toby, whose voice was joined by a chorus of desperate shouts and screams from the people in the back of the Wienermobile. None of this had any effect on Vrsk, who was totally focused on trying to get the steering under control, and thus had pretty much forgotten about his right foot, which remained on the accelerator as the Wienermobile crashed into and through the backstop, bouncing wildly as it hurtled over fencing and fence post. The police car hit the fallen backstop next and lost control, spinning in a full circle, then another, then rolling over several times before ending up on its side, still whooping.

Meanwhile the Wienermobile hit the pitcher's mound at a good sixty miles per hour. The sudden impact sent the occupants sprawling, including Vrsk, who now lost all control. Toby was the first to get his head up and see, directly ahead, a helicopter.

A HELICOPTER?!?

"LOOK OUT!" shouted Toby, but at that point even if Vrsk had the skills of a NASCAR driver—which he definitely did not—he could not have prevented the collision. As the occupants screamed and covered their faces, the Wienermobile slammed into the back of the TranScent helicopter. The entire tail section was sheared off cleanly, and it tumbled wildly toward first base, with the tail rotor still spinning. The cockpit and cabin rolled over several times and wound up at third base.

Meanwhile, the Wienermobile hurtled into the out-field, where Vrsk was finally able to slam on the brakes and bring the vehicle to a fishtailing stop. The windshield was shattered; the front end was badly smashed. Smoke poured from the engine and billowed around the Wienermobile, which looked like a bratwurst left on the grill too long.

Toby felt himself for injuries; he seemed to be okay. He looked at Vrsk, who was still gripping the wheel, staring ahead, breathing hard. A medley of groans sounded in the backseat as Micah, Tamara, Drmtsi, and Toby's parents disentangled their limbs and sat up, blinking.

"Well," said Toby. "We're here."

CHAPTER SIXTY-ONE

"THIRTY SECONDS, MR. PRESIDENT."

The president, sitting at his desk in the Oval Office, nodded slightly, his eyes on the teleprompter. He looked grim and felt grimmer. Trouble was erupting all over the United States; as the blackouts continued to wreak havoc, the national mood had quickly gone from worry to fear to full-blown panic. The president understood now that he was facing his ultimate test as a leader: this was the crisis that would define his presidency and his place in history. In a few moments, the nation—no, the world—would be watching him, expecting reassurance, answers—*leadership*.

But the president had no answers. He had shouted at people; he had bullied; he had pressured; he had begged.

He had committed the vast resources of the mightiest nation on earth to an intense effort to stop the blackouts, or at the very least, explain them. So far, that effort had produced, essentially, nothing. The consensus of the experts was that the blackouts were being caused by some very sophisticated technology. But as for the specific kind of technology and who was using it—the experts had no clue.

So the president was about to face the world armed with nothing more than a vague speech about the need to remain calm and a promise that all would soon be well.

The president didn't believe that all would soon be well.

"Five seconds, Mr. President."

The president took a breath. The red light on the camera came on.

"Good evening," the president said. "As you know, large areas of the United States have been affected by a series of power outages, which have also affected communications in many areas. Tonight I want to talk to you about what action we in the federal government, along with the public utilities, are taking to correct these problems. I also want to talk about how we, as a nation, can work together to minimize the disruption until this situation passes. And you have my word: it *will* pass."

The president paused and smiled his most confident-looking smile.

I hope they're buying this, he thought.

Prmkt, seeing the president's smile on his computer screen, responded with a smile of his own.

His fingers went to the keyboard.

It was time to show America who was *really* in charge.

In the Hubble gymnasium, only yards away from Prmkt's makeshift headquarters in the utility room, the science fair crowd was gathered around a large-screen television, watching the president. The volume was cranked up; nobody had heard the Wienermobile-helicopter collision on the ball field two minutes earlier.

By the second sentence of the president's speech, the crowd had already begun to relax a little. The president was a good speaker, and he had a sincere-looking face. When he smiled his confident smile, people in the crowd, relieved to be reassured by their leader, smiled gratefully back at him.

And then something began to happen to the president's face.

"What on *Earth*?"

The White House communications director grabbed his phone. He was in his office, watching the president's speech on network TV. He could have been in the Oval Office, just down the hall, but he preferred to see the president exactly as the American people saw him.

At the moment, he couldn't believe his eyes.

He stabbed the speed-dial for the broadcast control room. Two seconds later a voice said, "Yes?"

"What's wrong?" the communications director asked.

"What do you mean?" said the voice.

"Something's wrong with the broadcast!" said the communications director, pointing the remote control at the screen and switching rapidly from channel to channel. "Look at the president's face!"

The voice said, "I'm looking at the president's face right now, on our monitors and on the satellite feed. It looks fine."

"WELL, LOOK AT IT ON THE NETWORKS, YOU MORON!" said the communications director.

There was a pause, and then the voice came back.

It said: "Oh. My. God."

The crowd in the Hubble gym—along with millions of people around the nation and the world—stared at the screen with a mixture of fascination, puzzlement, and fear. As the president's face began to change, he still sounded like the president; he was giving a very reassuring speech about the need to remain calm while steps were being taken to *blah blah blah.*

But the president no longer *looked* like the president. As he spoke, his face was morphing into another face entirely—the hair getting longer, the skin getting softer. . . . And although the president's new face was unfamiliar to the rest of the world, it was recognized instantly in the Hubble gym.

"Hey!" shouted a voice. "The president turned into Harmonee Prescott!"

Prmkt said a very bad Krpsht word. After doing everything else perfectly, he'd forgotten to change the settings on the

Hotness Box. His fingers flashed furiously over the keyboard. Meanwhile, on millions of television screens around the world, the president's deep and manly voice continued to come from Harmonee Prescott's heavily glossed lips.

The White House communications director was on his feet now, shouting into the phone: "How can somebody hijack a satellite? GET THE SATELLITE BACK!"

He paused a moment, listening, then said, "No! We can't stop the speech! That would look even worse! You have to . . . what?" He looked back toward the TV. "It is?"

On the TV screen, the president—or, more accurately, the girl whose mouth the president was speaking through—had started to change once again, morphing back to an older face, a masculine face. A wave of relief swept through the communications director, who was already starting to formulate an explanation to give to the media about what had just happened. *Technical difficulties . . . solar flare interference with satellite radio transmissions . . .*

"Okay," he said into the phone. "When we get his face back, we'll have him wrap it up as quickly as—" He stopped speaking, now staring at the screen, his throat tightening as if tied into a knot. When he managed to say something again, his normally deep, controlled voice came out close to a shriek.

"THAT . . . IS . . . NOT . . . THE . . . PRESIDENT'S . . . FACE!"

Chapter Sixty-two

★

Among the few Americans not watching the president on television were federal agents Lefkon, Iles, and Turow. They were sitting in the conference room that, a short time earlier, had held their high-priority, top secret prisoners. Now it held only them.

They were still trying to comprehend how these prisoners had managed to escape their top secret facility and then elude a massive manhunt. At the moment, the federal government's attention was focused on the blackouts. But Lefkon, Iles, and Turow knew that once the immediate crisis was over, they would need to explain how they managed to be outwitted by two bumbling foreigners and three teenagers. *Teenagers!* The three agents could already see

their careers swirling down the toilet. Their only hope was to find the escaped prisoners *right now*.

The problem was, they had no idea where to look for them.

"I still don't understand," Turow was saying, "how you lose track of a thirty-foot-long hot dog."

"It's more like twenty-five feet," said Iles.

"Oh, well, THAT explains it," said Turow, giving Iles a you-moron look. "No wonder we can't find them! They're in a twenty-five–footer! It's practically invisible!"

"You don't have to be sarcastic," said Iles.

"Well, if you would . . ." Turow began, but he was cut off by the ringing of the phone on the wall. Lefkon reached it first. She listened for a few moments, then said, "They *what?*" She listened another minute, then said, "Okay, get everybody we have over there. Hold them until we get there. Do *not* let them get away."

She hung up and turned to Turow and Iles, who were watching her intently.

"They're at their school," she said. "A patrol car picked up the Wienermobile and chased it there. It crashed into a helicopter. The patrol car crashed, too, but the officers saw three kids and some adults running into the school gymnasium."

"How did they crash into a helicopter and manage to survive?" said Iles.

"Who knows?" said Turow, already out the door. "And who cares? Let's get over there."

Only minutes later, the three of them were in a

government car with Turow at the wheel, violating many traffic laws.

"You know, it's funny," Lefkon said.

"What is?" asked Iles.

"Well, the one kid, Toby," she said, "kept insisting that something really bad was going to happen at his school science fair tonight."

"So?" said Turow, running a red light.

"And now he's gone to all this trouble to escape, and where does he go? He doesn't go home. He doesn't run away. He goes to his school science fair." She turned to Iles.

"What's your point?" said Iles.

"Well," said Lefkon, "this might sound a little crazy, but what if he's right? What if the science fair has something to do with all this weird stuff going on?"

"You mean the blackouts?" said Turow.

"Yes," said Lefkon. "They're saying on the news that whatever's causing the blackout might be in this area."

Turow looked at her, then back at the road.

"Yeah, you're right," he said. "That's definitely crazy."

CHAPTER SIXTY-THREE

TOBY REACHED THE DOOR FIRST. He peeked inside and saw hundreds of people crowded at one end of the gym watching a TV screen set up on a stand. That was good news; as long as the crowd's attention was on the TV, it would not be on the science-fair projects.

Toby turned around. Behind him, just outside the door, were Micah and Tamara; behind them were Toby's mom and dad, who were still—Toby was beginning to regret this—wearing their Star Wars costumes. Behind them were Drmtsi and Vrsk, who had been talking to each other quietly in Krpsht.

"All right," Toby said to Micah, Tamara, and his parents. "We need to find the ME kids' projects and disable them."

"How do we do that?" said Roger.

"I don't know," said Toby. "Unplug them, or just break them, if we have to. Just as long as they don't work."

"I need to check on Fester first," said Micah. "I bet he's starving."

"Micah," said Toby, "we're trying to save the country, okay? This isn't the time to feed your frog."

"It'll only be a minute," said Micah, trotting off.

"Good to have priorities," said Tamara.

"Come on," said Toby. "Let's find the ME kids' projects."

He and Tamara took the first aisle; his parents, trailed by Drmtsi and Vrsk, took the second. Toby had hoped it would be an easy search, but there were dozens and dozens of projects, many of them elaborate, emitting a confusing profusion of lights and sounds. He and Tamara had to stop and check each one, looking for the student's name. Toby glanced back toward the crowd at the end of the gym; people seemed to be getting quite agitated about whatever was happening on the TV screen. That was fine with Toby; he was grateful for the distraction. He turned to look at the next project.

Then he froze, as a voice boomed behind him:

"THERE THEY ARE! STOP THEM!"

Toby whirled around and saw, standing in the gym doorway, the furious figure of Lance Swingle. His hair was messed up, his jacket was torn, and his nose was bleeding. He was pointing at them.

"GET THEM!" he bellowed. "THEY WRECKED MY HELICOPTER!"

In the crowd, heads turned. One of the heads belonged to Jason Niles, who yelled, "Hey! It's Hardbonger!" More heads turned.

"GET THEM!" yelled Swingle again.

Some people—including Jason Niles and Coach Furman—separated from the crowd and started heading toward Toby and the others.

"What do we do now?" said Tamara.

"Now," said Toby, "we run."

Chapter Sixty-four

★

THE PRESIDENT, now that his emergency broadcast to the nation had been hijacked, was no longer sitting at his desk in the Oval Office. He was a few doors down, in the office of the communications director, who was on the phone. Also in the room was the president's chief of staff, talking on another phone and furiously scribbling notes.

The president was watching a bank of six television monitors. Each was tuned to a different network, but all showed the same picture: a man sitting at the president's desk in the Oval Office, wearing the president's suit, the same suit the president was wearing now. But the head sticking out of the suit was not the president's. It was, instead, the head of a large man with a puffy red face, a thick beard, a low forehead, and small, close-together eyes peeking around an enormous red nose.

The man on the screen wasn't talking. He was simply staring into the camera, as he had been doing for several minutes now—ever since the satellite had been hijacked. The president was glaring back at the man wearing his suit. The president was very, *very* unhappy.

The chief of staff hung up the phone.

"Well?" snapped the president.

"Okay," said the chief of staff, glancing down at his notes. "The State Department says this guy"—he pointed at the screen—"is Grdankl the Strong."

"Who the *what*?" said the president.

"Grdankl the Strong," said the chief of staff. "He's the president of Krpshtskan."

The president frowned and said, "Is that the one with the hole?"

"No, that's Fazul," said the chief of staff. "Krpshtskan is next door."

The president glared at the screen again. "And can anybody explain," he asked, "how on earth the president of Krap . . . Karp . . . Kapa . . ."

"Krpshtskan," said the chief of staff.

". . . of this dirtbag little nation is being broadcast to the entire world while sitting in my office, *wearing my suit*?" said the president, his voice straining.

"At the moment, sir, no," the chief of staff admitted. "But—"

"Well, can we at least shut the satellite down?" said the president, aiming his glare at the communications director.

338

"Apparently we . . . *cannot* . . . sir," he answered.

The president took another breath, trying to calm himself. "So," he said, "you're telling me that in the biggest crisis of my presidency, in the most powerful nation on earth, we can do nothing about the fact that I can't communicate to the American people BECAUSE *MY* HEAD, ON *MY* BODY, HAS BEEN REPLACED BY THE HEAD OF A FOURTH-WORLD DICTATOR WITH A NOSE THAT LOOKS LIKE A TOMATO?"

The chief of staff and the communications director looked at each other but said nothing. Neither wanted to inform the president that, minutes earlier, he had had the head of an attractive teenage girl. Now both men cringed as the president prepared to bellow something. But before he could start, he was interrupted by a new voice.

Grdankl the Strong had begun to speak.

All three men turned to the bank of TV screens. "Turn it up!" said the president. The communications director increased the volume, and the room was filled with the harsh sounds of the Krpsht language.

"What's he saying?" snapped the president.

"I'll find out," said the chief of staff, reaching for a phone.

"Wait," said the president. "I'm hearing English."

A new voice was coming from the speaker, talking over Grdankl's voice. The new voice spoke English with a thick accent, apparently translating Grdankl's words.

"People of the United States of American," the voice said. "I am Grdankl the Strong, president of Krpshtskan,

son of Bmepl the Brave, grandson of Kminkt the Good at Remembering Names. I will tell you now why my country, Krpshtskan, will destroy your country."

The president turned to the communications director and snapped, "Is this being broadcast everywhere?" The communications director nodded. The president rubbed his face with both hands.

"In Krpshtskan," said the Grdankl translator, "we have a saying. We say, if you steal the goat of a Krpsht, you are stealing a goat from *all* Krpshts. And you, United States of American, you have stolen a Krpsht goat."

"We stole their *goat*?" said the communications director.

"Shut up," said the president.

"Five years ago," said the translator, "a young Krpsht man came to your country with a big hope in his heart. You told him, 'Welcome! We are liking you very much!' But these were lies, United States of American. You were laughing at him. Big funny ha-ha American joke. But this joke was not funny to this young man. You stole the goat of his hope. And now, for this, you will be destroyed. But first you will see one last time a brave son of Krpshtskan. Enjoy this, people of American. It is the last thing you will see."

On the screen, the president body/Grdankl head disappeared. It was replaced by a brightly lit stage. On it was a smiling young man with long, floppy hair.

"Who is *that*?" said the president.

Both the chief of staff and the communications director shrugged.

An unseen piano began to play. The melody sounded familiar to the three men, but none of them could quite place it.

Then the young man began to sing:

"Spring was never waiting for us girl . . . "

The chief of staff snapped his fingers. "That's 'MacArthur Park,'" he said.

"The one about the cake?" said the president. "In the rain?"

"Yeah," said the chief of staff.

The president, his eyes on the screen, said, "What was it he said? The Grdankl guy? That this is the last thing we're going to see?"

"Yeah," said the chief of staff.

"All right," said the president. Beads of sweat had formed on his brow and upper lip. "We need to find out *right now* who this kid is, what the heck we supposedly did to him, and how to communicate with Mr. Tomato Nose. We are putting an end to this now."

"Right," said the chief of staff, grabbing a phone.

The president turned to the communications director. "And *you*," he said, "need to find out how long this song is."

CHAPTER SIXTY-FIVE

THREE MINUTES AND TWENTY-SEVEN SECONDS. That was the precise length of the version of "MacArthur Park" that Prmkt was now broadcasting to the world from the utility room next to the Hubble Middle School gym.

Prmkt looked at his watch. The song had been going for thirty seconds. Just under three minutes to go. When the song ended, he would start the final sequence.

Some kind of commotion had erupted in the gym; Prmkt could hear muffled shouts through the utility-room door. He thought about checking to see what it was, but decided he should focus on the task at hand.

He glanced at his watch again. Just over two minutes left.

Prmkt flexed his fingers over the keyboard, getting ready.

CHAPTER SIXTY-SIX

"**G**AH YAFOO OUMA MOUF," said Tamara.

"What?" whispered Toby.

"I said get your foot out of my mouth," said Tamara, giving Toby's sneaker a shove.

"Sorry!" said Toby, shifting position.

The two of them were crouched under one of the science-fair exhibit tables, hidden from view by the cloth that was draped over each of the tables. They'd been here for several minutes, listening to running feet tromp past and to the shouts of their pursuers, directed by Lance Swingle. They heard other voices, as well, coming from the crowd gathered around the TV set. People were reacting with alarm to something, but Toby and Tamara couldn't tell what it was.

Toby pulled the drape aside and peeked out. He and Tamara were almost at the end of one of the rows of tables. At the far end, he saw Jason Niles and Coach Furman, one on each side, methodically going from table to table, lifting the drapes and looking underneath. Toby ducked back.

"They're looking under the tables," he said.

"What do we do?" said Tamara.

"I dunno," said Toby. "Maybe we could crawl under the tables until we get to the ME projects—but I don't even know which way that is."

"Okay," said Tamara. "So get out and look for them."

"They'll see me," said Toby.

"Not if you're invisible," said Tamara.

"The iPhone!" said Toby, reaching down to turn it on. "I forgot!"

"Duh," said Tamara.

"Uh-oh," said Toby, looking at the phone's screen.

"What?" said Tamara.

"The battery's low."

"Then you better get going," said Tamara.

"What about you?" said Toby.

"Don't yew worry 'bout me, podner," said Tamara. "Ah'll hold 'em off long as ah kin."

"What accent is that supposed to be?" said Toby.

"Cowboy," said Tamara.

"Needs work," said Toby.

"I'll practice in jail," said Tamara. "Get going."

"Okay," said Toby. He reached for the drape, then said, "Seriously, what are you going to do?"

"I've got a bold and daring plan," said Tamara.

"Which is?"

"I'm going to scream like a girl."

Toby, despite the seriousness of the situation, smiled. He looked for a moment at Tamara—his oldest and, now that he thought about it, his closest friend, who had stuck with him right to the end of this basically insane effort. He realized this was probably the time to say something meaningful.

"What are you waiting for?" she said.

"I'm, uh . . . I just . . ."

"You're not going to say something meaningful, are you?" she said.

"'Course not," said Toby.

"Good," she said. As she said it, she touched his hand for part of a second, and they both blushed.

"Okay," said Toby. His finger hovered over the magic wand on the iPhone screen. He noticed the sunglasses icon next to it. Back before everything had gone horribly wrong, Sternabite had said to use the sunglasses icon to summon him. *Probably too late now*, Toby thought, but he touched the sunglasses anyway. Then he touched the wand, and he disappeared.

"See you," he said, ducking out through the drape.

"Good luck," said Tamara from under the table.

Toby stood up and looked around. Jason and Coach Furman were getting closer; they'd reach Tamara's table in a minute. In the next aisle over, Swingle was looking under tables and directing his lackeys to do the same. Beyond

them, at the end of the gym, Toby saw the crowd gathered around the TV; over the buzz of the crowd Toby heard a wavery voice singing about a cake in the rain.

Weird.

Toby trotted away from the searchers to the back of the gym. His plan was to do a methodical search for the ME kids' projects. He went to the end row, rounded the corner, and . . .

"Micah!"

Micah spun to look but saw nobody.

"Toby?" he said.

"Yeah," said Toby. He made himself visible as he trotted up to Micah, who was standing next to his project, which was between Tamara's and Brad Pitt Wemplemeyer's projects.

"Listen," said Toby, "have you seen . . ."

"Fester's okay," said Micah, holding up his frog.

"Great," said Toby. "Listen, have you . . ."

"I had him on a timer," said Micah, pointing to his project. "He was going up and down, up and down, like, a *foot*. It must've been awful. I'm gonna turn it off." He reached for the knob that controlled the power to the fusion reactor Sternabite had lent him. Toby grabbed his arm.

"Micah, *listen*," said Toby. "I need to find the ME kids' projects! Do you know where they are?"

"Yeah," said Micah. "I was going to tell you as soon as I got Fester . . ."

"WHERE ARE THEY?" shouted Toby, grabbing Micah's shirt.

"Right there!" said Micah, pointing at the tables to the right of his.

"Why didn't you *tell* me?" said Toby, letting go of Micah's shirt. He looked around for something he could use to trash the ME kids' projects. His eyes fell on Tamara's project, on the table to the left of Micah's. It was labeled PACKAGING—THE DEADLY KILLER IN YOUR HOME. On the backboard were vivid photographs showing a shard of plastic packaging being used to decapitate a Rollerblade Barbie doll. Displayed on the table was the headless Barbie herself, wearing tiny pink Rollerblades with flint wheels that sparked when they were rolled. Alongside Rollerblade Barbie was her head, still looking blond and perky, next to the shard used to sever it. The shard, Toby decided, might be just the thing for slashing the electrical cables in the ME kids' projects. He was about to grab it when Micah tugged at his arm.

"Uh, Toby . . ." said Micah.

"What?" snapped Toby.

"They see you," said Micah.

"Who does?"

"THERE HE IS!" shouted Lance Swingle.

"Them," said Micah.

Toby looked toward the far end of the row. Swingle stood there, pointing at him; two burly lackeys were already running his way. Toby whirled and looked away. Jason and Coach Furman were coming. Toby was trapped in the middle of the row. He reached for the iPhone and stabbed the magic wand. He looked down and watched with relief as his legs disappeared.

And then they reappeared.

He looked at the phone. The screen was black.

The battery was dead.

"GET HIM!" screamed Swingle.

Swingle's men had arrived; so had Jason and Coach Furman. Toby and Micah were surrounded. Swingle's men moved in.

"Stay back!' shouted Toby, reaching his right hand behind him. "I have a knife!"

One of Swingle's men reached into his sport jacket. Toby felt around desperately on the table. Finally his hand closed on something. "I'm warning you!" he said. "If you come near me, I WILL cut you!" Then, with a dramatic flourish, he whipped his arm around and waved his weapon.

Unfortunately, it was the headless Rollerblade Barbie.

"Whoops," said Micah.

"Is that a *doll*, Hardbonger?" said Jason.

"No!" said Toby, quickly stuffing it into his back pocket.

The large man pulled his hand from his jacket; he was now pointing a large gun at Toby. "Raise your hands," he said.

Toby raised his hands.

"You, too," said the man to Micah.

"I have a frog in my hands," said Micah.

"Then raise the frog, too," said the man.

Micah raised his hands, and Fester.

"Now *don't move*," said the man with the gun.

"We're not moving," said Toby.

"I think I'm gonna wet my pants," said Micah.

"Well, do it without moving," said Toby.

CHAPTER SIXTY-SEVEN

THE PRESIDENT WATCHED as the floppy-haired young man on the TV screen headed into the home stretch of "MacArthur Park," straining hard and failing to reach the high notes. The president turned to his two aides, both on the phone, both frantically taking notes.

"He's finishing," the president said. "Somebody tell me something."

"Okay," said the communications director, reading from his notes. "Here's what we've got: this kid is from *America's Next Superstar*, the TV show, five years ago."

"*Five years* ago?" said the president.

"Right," said the communications director. "The song ends"—he listened to a voice on the phone—"pretty soon."

"I know the song," said the president. "But who *is* this kid? Why do we care?"

"His name is Gmygmy," said the chief of staff.

"What?" said the president.

"G-m-y-g-m-y," said the chief of staff, looking at his notes. "Americans pronounce it basically like 'Jimmy-Jimmy.'"

"But *who* is he?" asked the president.

"He's the son of the president of Krpshtskan."

"What?"

"He's the oldest son of Grdankl the Strong," said the chief of staff. "Five years ago, he came to the U.S. to compete on *America's Next Superstar*. He got pretty far into the competition, but it seems people were voting for him mainly as a joke. But he didn't know it. He bought into it. Thought he was going to win. When he got voted off the show he broke down on camera, cried like a baby, had a nervous breakdown right on TV. It was a huge scandal in Krpshtskan—son of the president and all. It's a culture where a man *never* cries. Big loss of face for the family."

The president looked at the TV screen. Gmygmy was finishing "MacArthur Park," trying, with no success, to hit a final high note, sounding like a seriously injured cat. The camera flashed to the three judges, one of whom was plugging his ears with his fingers.

"So you're telling me," the president said, "that this lunatic Grdankl wants to destroy the United States because *his son got voted off a TV show?"*

"It looks that way, sir."

"It gets great ratings," said the director of communications. "My daughter and wife—"

"Shut up," said the president.

"Yes, sir," said the director of communications.

"Sir," said the chief of staff, his ear pressed to the phone, "there's something else."

"What is it?" said the president.

The chief of staff listened over the phone for another few seconds, then said, "Grdankl the Strong has another son. Named . . . ah . . . Pr . . . P-something. I can't pronounce it."

"So?" said the president.

"He's here."

"*Here?*" said the president. "As in?"

"INS places him as being employed at a middle school in the Maryland suburbs. Which . . ." The chief of staff was listening to the phone again.

"Which *what?*" the president said impatiently.

"Which is in the same general area the FBI thinks the power-grid attack is coming from," said the chief of staff. Again, he listened to the phone. His eyebrows arched. "*Seriously?*" he said.

"WHAT?" said the president.

"Seems the local cops up there just chased two suspect Krpsht nationals to the same middle school in . . . well . . . in a *Wienermobile*," said the chief of staff.

"The police were driving a *Wienermobile?*" said the president, rubbing his hair.

"No, sir. The Krpshts were. Apparently they stole it from a supermarket in—"

"Never mind how they got it," snapped the president. "Are they in custody?"

"Um, no, sir."

"WHY THE HECK NOT?"

"The police car . . . crashed, sir. Wrecked."

"I want EVERY AVAILABLE AGENT at that school *NOW*," shouted the president.

"Yes, sir. We're on it. Everybody's responding and converging on the school," said the chief of staff. "FBI, Homeland, police, everybody we've got."

The president looked at the screen. It showed a freeze-frame close-up of Gmygmy's smiling, floppy-hair-framed face. From the speakers came an odd moaning noise, like a walrus giving birth. On the screen, below the smiling frozen image of Gmygmy, appeared the words REPUBLIC OF KRPSHTSKAN NATIONAL ANTHEM.

The president glared at the screen. "A *TV show*," he said, spitting out the words. "I am going make those people so sorry they ever—"

"Sir," said the chief of staff, his ear still to the phone.

"What?" said the president.

"The grid's going down again."

"Where?" said the president.

The chief of staff waved an arm.

"Everywhere," he said.

Chapter Sixty-eight

PRMKT'S FINGERS DANCED on the keyboard, issuing command after command in rapid sequence. One by one, he was taking down the major regions of the North American power grid. Soon all of America—except for Hubble Middle School, which Prmkt would keep online—would lose its electricity. More than three hundred million people—already terrified—would be plunged into full-on panic, in the dark.

But that would be just the beginning. Because when the grid was down, and America was most vulnerable, Prmkt would issue his last sequence of commands. He would summon the full power of the science-fair projects he had networked, and then, in one lightning strike, he would unleash the final punishment, the attack from which the United States would never recover.

He would unleash the Pulse.

CHAPTER SIXTY-NINE

TOBY'S ARMS WERE GETTING TIRED. He and Micah had stood for several minutes with their hands up, watched closely by Swingle's big bodyguard with the big gun. Behind this man stood Swingle with two more lackeys. A third lackey was just trotting up to meet them.

"The cops are here," he told Swingle. "They're rounding up the rest of them."

"Good," said Swingle, glaring at Toby.

"Listen," said Toby. "You got us, okay? Can you tell the Hulk here to put down the gun?"

"Not a chance," said Swingle.

"What are you afraid of?" said Toby. "The frog?"

"Listen, *punk*," said Swingle, stepping forward. But before he could say any more, a commotion erupted to the

right. Toby looked that way and saw Tamara being dragged toward them by Coach Furman and Jason Niles.

"Unhand me!" she was shouting. "I am a lady!"

"Unhand?" said Micah.

"Lady?" said Toby.

As Jason and Coach Furman dragged Tamara up from one direction, a large group appeared at the other end of the row of tables. The group was headed by The Hornet, who was followed by agents Turow, Iles, and Lefkon, who were followed by a dozen police officers, some with guns drawn. Toby saw why: they had captured Drmtsi and Vrsk, who were being hustled forward, along with . . .

Oh, no. Toby groaned as he saw, in the middle of the cluster, his mom and dad in their Star Wars costumes.

As The Hornet walked up, she gave Toby a glare that he could feel all the way down his back. Then she turned to Swingle and, gesturing to the three feds, said, "These are agents of the federal government. They're going to take these students into custody."

"Good," said Swingle. "I want them prosecuted to the fullest extent of the law. Not only did they destroy my helicopter, but they nearly killed me!"

"This isn't about your helicopter," said Turow. "Or you."

"By the way," said Iles. "Your pilot? The one you left unconscious in the cockpit? Paramedics say he's going to be okay. In case you were worried."

Swingle reddened.

"Later on," said Turow, "we'll talk about why you were trying to take off against an FAA directive."

Swingle started to say something, but Turow, ignoring him, turned to Toby.

"For a supposedly smart kid," Turow said, "you are unbelievably stupid."

"Please," said Toby. "Listen. I—"

Turow held up his hand. "I'll listen when you and the rest of the Wienermobile gang"—he waved at the prisoners—"are locked up again."

"My parents had nothing to do with this," said Toby.

Turow glanced at Roger and Fawn.

"Mr. and Mrs. Han Solo?" he said. "They're your parents?"

"It's a Luke Skywalker costume," said Roger.

"Yes," sighed Toby. "They're my parents."

Turow shook his head. "Should have guessed," he said. "Anyway, they aided the escape, so they're coming with us."

"Please," said Toby. "Let me do one thing first, okay? Please?"

"What?" said Turow.

"Let me unplug those projects," said Toby, pointing at the ME kids' section.

"Hey!" said Jason. "Those aren't yours!"

"They're not yours, either," said Toby. "You didn't build them."

"You shut up!" said Jason, stepping toward Toby.

"Hold it!" said Turow, shoving Jason back. To Toby, he said, "You're not unplugging anything. You're coming with us." He took Toby's arm. Toby shook free.

"No! Listen!" said Toby. "The blackouts! They're coming from here! He's using those projects to cause the blackouts!"

"You're *nuts*," said Jason.

"Toby," said agent Lefkon, "*who* is using the projects?"

"I don't know," said Toby. "But he's here!"

"See?" said Jason. "Nuts."

Turow looked toward the ME projects, then back at Toby. "All I see," he said, "is some stuff on some tables. Let's go."

"No!" said Toby. "You have to believe me!"

"Why?" said Turow.

"Because he's right," said a new voice.

"And who are *you*?" said Turow.

A tall, thin figure with wild hair and dark glasses stepped forward.

"My name," he said, "is Neal Sternabite."

Lance Swingle's face went from red to white. "You!" he said.

"Yes," said Sternabite. "Me."

CHAPTER SEVENTY

THE PRESIDENT, at the insistence of his staff, had been hustled down to the Situation Room in the basement deep under the West Wing of the White House, where he would be safer in case of an attack. He was now standing with his top civilian and military advisors, looking at a large video screen displaying a map of the United States. Overlaid on the map of the States were lines showing the ten major regions of the U.S. power grid.

The regions that still had power were white; the ones that had lost power were dark gray. At the moment, there were only three areas left with power: Texas, the Southeast, and the Mid-Atlantic states. As the president watched, Texas went gray. The president said a bad word, then spun toward his chief of staff, who was, as always, on the phone.

"Well?" said the president.

"FBI is at the school, and they have apprehended some suspects," said the chief of staff.

"Have they found the guy who's doing this?" said the president, pointing at the screen.

"Not yet, sir," said the chief of staff, wincing.

"WELL TELL THEM TO FIND HIM NOW!" said the president.

On the screen, the Southeast went gray.

CHAPTER SEVENTY-ONE

Turow looked at Sternabite, then at Swingle.

"You know this guy?" he said.

"Yes," said Swingle. "And I wouldn't believe anything he says. He's insane."

"Nice to see you, too, Lance," said Sternabite.

"Okay, whoever you are," said Turow, "I don't have time for you now. We're dealing with a matter of urgent national security."

"It'll get a lot more urgent if you don't listen to that boy," said Sternabite.

"Is that a threat?" said Turow.

"No," said Sternabite. "It's a fact. The blackouts are being controlled from here, from this science fair."

"Okay," said Turow. "Who *are* you?"

"My name is Neal Sternabite. I'm a scientist."

Swingle snorted loudly. Turow ignored him.

"Mr. Sternabite," he said, "if you know something about the blackouts, I'm going to ask you to come with us. You can explain your theory when we get back to headquarters."

"It's not a theory," said Sternabite. "And we don't have time to go anywhere. Do you know what an EMP is?"

"No," said Turow. "And *I* don't have time to—"

"It's an electromagnetic pulse," said Sternabite. "It's usually created by a nuclear detonation, but there are other ways. That's what's going on here." Sternabite pointed toward the ME kids' projects. "He's going to shut the power down again, and then he's going to discharge a capacitor bank into the grid. The grid will act as a giant antenna. He's going to fry all the electronics in Washington, D.C., and probably for hundreds of miles around. You understand what that means?"

"No," said Turow. "And I—"

"It means the government goes down," said Sternabite. "And it doesn't come back up. Even when they get the power restored, if they can, most of the federal government computers are lost, along with a major chunk—a *huge* chunk—of data. All erased. The government is crippled. Its brain and central nervous system are gone. There are no records, no communications, no money coming in or going out. You, for example, no longer get paid—you and millions like you. Federal authority breaks down everywhere. These blackouts? The riots? The panic? It's *nothing*

compared with what's going to happen next. The economy goes, civil society collapses, and the United States stumbles back to the Stone Age."

"How do you know this . . . this EMP is going to happen?" said Turow.

"Because I built these kids' projects," said Sternabite.

"Wait a minute," said Turow. "Why would you *build* them, if you want to *stop* them?"

"Because I didn't realize what he was going to do with them," said Sternabite.

"What *who* was going to do?" said Turow.

Sternabite looked at Toby, who shook his head.

"I don't know," said Sternabite.

"I told you," said Swingle, smirking. "He's insane."

Turow looked at Iles and Lefkon, then turned back to Sternabite.

"You're coming with us," he said.

"No, *listen*," said Sternabite. He took a step toward the ME kids' projects. "Just give me two minutes and I'll—"

"Hold it," said Iles, grabbing Sternabite's arm.

Turow said, "You're not touching anything." He turned to the waiting police officers. "All right," he said. "Let's get these people out of here. And don't let any of them touch anything."

As two officers approached him, Sternabite looked around desperately. His eyes fell on Micah, who was standing next to Toby and still holding Fester.

"You," he said. "Kid. Did your frog levitate?"

"What?" said Micah.

"Your *frog*," said Sternabite, his voice rising. "Did it float?"

"What's he talking about?" said Turow.

"He's lost his mind," sneered Swingle.

"*Did it float?*" repeated Sternabite.

"Um, yeah," said Micah. To Toby, he whispered, "Why's he asking about Fester?"

Toby was wondering the same thing.

"Because I was thinking," said Sternabite, as the officers grabbed his arms, "you'd get better results if you *increased the power*."

"Huh?" said Micah. "But you said to keep it at ten percent. You said if—"

"*I know what I said,*" hissed Sternabite. The officers were pulling him away, along with Toby's parents, Vrsk, and Drmtsi. Two more had taken hold of Tamara; four more were coming toward Micah and Toby.

"You need more power!" shouted Sternabite. "Now!"

"What is he *talking* about?" said Micah.

Suddenly, Toby understood. As the officers reached him he reached for the controls to Micah's project. The power knob was set at ten percent.

"STOP HIM!" shouted Turow. "DON'T LET HIM TOUCH THAT!"

An officer grabbed Toby's right arm, but his left was still free. He grabbed the knob and cranked it all the way to one hundred.

Suddenly, Toby, Micah, the four police officers, and Fester the frog were lifted off the ground, tumbling in the

air above Micah's project. Micah yelped as he lost his grip on Fester, who floated upward to the gym ceiling.

"Fester!" shouted Micah, watching helplessly as the levitating frog landed upside down on a heating duct, then wriggled through a vent. Toby and the other humans stopped rising about ten feet above the table, where they waved their arms and legs with no effect other than to accidentally punch and kick each other. Toby heard shouts below, the loudest being Turow yelling, "'GRAB THEM! GRAB THEM!" Three more officers lunged forward, only to be swept up in the super-powerful magnetic field. There were now nine bodies thrashing in the air while the FBI agents and the remaining earthbound officers stood by uncertainly.

In the confusion, Sternabite broke away from Turow and walked quickly toward the ME projects.

"HE'S GETTING AWAY!" shrieked Swingle, pointing at Sternabite.

"Stop him!" shouted Turow. Before Sternabite could reach the projects, one officer tackled him to the gym floor, and a second landed on top of them. As they struggled on the floor, Turow turned his attention back to the shouting people suspended in the air above Micah's project.

"Any ideas?" he said to Lefkon and Iles.

"Maybe we could unplug it?" said Lefkon.

"Right!" said Turow. "The plug must be under the table." He studied the situation for a moment, then dropped down onto his belly. "Hold my feet," he said to

Iles. Then, with Iles gripping his shoes, Turow inched forward toward the table. He pulled the drape aside and looked underneath. Micah's project, he saw, was not plugged into the school electrical system; it was plugged into a small, humming device that looked strangely like a Slurpee machine. The device had an on/off switch. Wincing, Turow reached out and turned it off.

THUD CRASH CRASH THUD OWW OOOH CRASH THUD

Nine bodies slammed down onto the table, which slammed down onto Turow. Iles, Lefkon, and the remaining officers lunged forward to help. Moaning bodies were sprawled everywhere. Nobody noticed that when Micah's table collapsed, it knocked the lid off the fifty-five–gallon drum full of Diet Coke that formed part of Brad Pitt Wemplemeyer's project. And nobody noticed that, in the struggle to help his fallen comrades, one of the police officers was now bumping into the metal stand that held the giant nuclear Mentos, which was s-l-o-w-l-y falling over into the barrel . . .

FWOOOOOOSH

What happened next was undoubtedly the greatest demonstration of unleashing the power of surface tension in the history of science fairs, although none of the participants actually saw it. Instead, they found themselves engulfed in a wave of brown foam that billowed upward and outward from the fifty-five-gallon drum in a spectacular Diet Coke volcano. Toby felt himself being swept across the floor, unable to see anything except foam, and barely able to breathe. He slammed into a wall and

managed to get to his feet, then felt himself being dragged sideways. He clutched the wall, trying to find something to hold on to. He came to an opening—a doorway?—and tried to duck into it, but the foam surge was pulling him past.

Then somebody grabbed his arm. He felt himself being yanked into the opening. It was, in fact, a doorway. Like Toby, the person holding his arm was covered with foam; his only distinguishing characteristic was his sunglasses.

Sternabite.

"Okay, kid," he said. "Now it's up to us."

CHAPTER SEVENTY-TWO

As the president and his top staff watched glumly, the last bright section on the electronic map of the power grid—the Middle Atlantic region—went gray.

The president shot a questioning look at his secretary of Homeland Security, who was on the phone. The secretary nodded and said, "Washington's dark again, sir. Telecommunications are totally down everywhere, nationwide."

The president said a bad word. Nobody disagreed.

"What about the school?" barked the president. "What's *taking* them so long?"

"Uh, sir," said the chief of staff, also on the phone. "About the school. There's been a, um, setback."

"What?" said the president.

"Our FBI people have, um, lost contact with some of the suspects."

"Lost *contact*? How?"

"There was some kind of . . . eruption."

"You mean explosion?"

"No, sir. They're calling it an eruption, a massive quantity of foam."

"Chemical weapons?"

"Uh, no, sir. They're saying it smells like, um . . ."

"It smells like *what*?"

"Coke, sir."

"Coke? As in . . . *Coca-Cola*?"

"They say it also could be Pepsi, sir," said the chief of staff. "They're not sure."

The president stared at his chief of staff for five full seconds. "Are you saying," he said, "that our people have been DRIVEN OFF BY A SOFT DRINK??"

One of the military men snorted. The president silenced him with a glare.

"Um, apparently, yes," said the chief of staff. "The school building has been evacuated."

"WELL TELL THEM TO PUT ON GAS MASKS OR SOMETHING AND GET BACK IN THERE!" said the president.

"Yes, sir," said the chief of staff, back on the phone.

The president looked at the map of the country, now totally gray. Then he looked at the circle of people gathered around him.

"*Coke?*" he said.

Nobody had an answer.

CHAPTER SEVENTY-THREE

Prmkt **CHECKED HIS SCREEN.** The power grid, except for Hubble Middle, was completely shut down. This left the country's huge power-transmission network free of electrical charge, ready for the Pulse. He checked the capacitor bank, which stored the electrical voltage he would use; it was fully charged and ready to go. The Pulse would travel through the empty grid and every wire plugged into the grid. It would attack any magnetic medium—including computer chips and hard drives; the data stored on them would be erased or permanently corrupted. Anything that used these media would instantly become junk. Computers would be useless, as would telephones, televisions, elevators, microwave ovens, refrigerators, even some toasters.

One more command to enter. Prmkt typed it slowly, carefully. He checked to make sure it was correct. He put his finger on the ENTER key, took a breath, and thought for a moment about Gmygmy.

Then he pushed ENTER.

Nothing happened.

Prmkt cursed in Krpsht. Swiftly he retyped the command and again pressed ENTER.

Nothing.

Prmkt clicked on a diagnostics program and ran it. In a few seconds, he saw the problem—a cable had come unplugged from Farrell Plinkett's project. Prmkt had heard shouts and the sounds of a struggle outside; apparently, the cable had been knocked loose in the commotion.

Prmkt didn't panic; he never did. This was a setback, but a minor one, easily corrected. Plinkett's project had been set up close to the utility door. Prmkt would simply slip out, reattach the cable, return to the utility room, and proceed with the Pulse.

He went to the door, unlocked it, and carefully opened it a crack. A spray of brown foam shot through the opening. Prmkt quickly shut the door and staggered back, sputtering and frantically wiping the foam from his face. His first fear—that it was a chemical attack—dissolved when he realized that the foam was a cola-flavored soft drink. He didn't know *why* the gym was suddenly filled with cola foam, and he didn't much care: all he knew was that he had to get to the cable.

Prmkt stood for a moment with his hand on the door-

knob, visualizing the layout of the science-fair projects outside. Then he took a breath, opened the door, and stepped through the surge of incoming foam. He closed the door behind him, electing not to lock it, so he'd be able to get back in quickly. He dropped to his hands and knees. He found that, even though he was engulfed in foam, if he kept his head down, he could create enough of a pocket so that he could breathe foam-free air.

Slowly, surrounded by the swirling, blinding foam, Prmkt began crawling across the gym floor.

CHAPTER SEVENTY-FOUR

Toby WAITED ANXIOUSLY in the small air pocket formed by the doorway, cut off from the world by the wall of Diet Coke fizz. A dim, brown-colored light filtered through the foam from the gym lights, which, somehow, were still burning.

Toby wiped off the face of his watch: Sternabite had been gone for five minutes now. He'd told Toby to stay in the doorway, while he'd crawled off through the foam to try to disable the ME kids' projects. Toby had offered to go with him, but Sternabite had said no.

"You don't know what to look for," he said. "You might touch the wrong thing and kill yourself."

Toby looked at the foam, still thick, still surging. He wondered how Sternabite could breathe in that stuff. *If he* could breathe.

He jumped as he felt something touch his leg. With relief he saw that it was Sternabite, returning from his mission. He got to his feet, sputtering and dripping foam from head to toe. He still had his sunglasses on.

"From now on," Sternabite said, "I am drinking Mountain Dew."

"Did you find the projects?" said Toby.

"I found one," said Sternabite. "I pulled out a cable. I wanted to do more, but the foam is really thick by the floor; I was starting to drown out there. For now we're okay. He can't launch the EMP without that cable. Now we need to find him."

"How do we do that?" said Toby.

"He has to be nearby," said Sternabite. "He could be in a classroom or in a room right off the gym, like this one." He tapped the door they were standing next to, which they had already determined opened to a small supply closet.

"So what do we do?"

"We start with the gym," said Sternabite. "We go along the walls—the foam's not as bad there—and we open every door we come to. If we don't find him, we start looking in the rest of the school."

"How do we know what he looks like?"

"We don't," said Sternabite. "But he'll have a computer, and it'll be near some gear that's hardwired into the school electrical system. He won't be able to move it. We'll know when we see him."

"But then what do we do?"

"We point him out to these moron FBI agents who want

to arrest everybody in the world except the guy causing the problem."

"Okay," said Toby.

"I'll go this way," said Sternabite, pointing to the left. "You go that way. Stay against the wall. If you see the guy, run in my direction and *yell*."

"Okay," said Toby.

"Good luck," said Sternabite. He stepped into the foam and was gone.

"You, too," said Toby, to the foam. He took a breath, stepped out of the doorway, and felt the foam surround him. He turned and pressed his face against the wall, then began sidestepping along it, keeping his head turned to give himself a breathing space. He counted his steps, figuring that might help him find his way back.

He'd gone twenty-seven steps when he came to another doorway. He stepped into it and tried the knob. The door opened. He stepped inside and found himself in a room considerably larger than the supply closet. It was lit by fluorescent lights, with plumbing, air-conditioning, and electrical conduits running along the walls and ceiling. Toby's eyes quickly scanned the room; there was nobody else there.

Stepping inside, he closed the door behind him. His eyes fell on a workbench at the far end of the room. He took a few quick steps toward it.

The workbench held some electronic gear and a laptop computer.

The laptop's screen was glowing.

Cables ran between the gear and some kind of electrical box on the wall.

This is it.

Toby turned to run back and alert Sternabite.

Then he heard it: *click*.

The door was about to open.

CHAPTER SEVENTY-FIVE

TOBY LOOKED FRANTICALLY around the utility room.
In the gloomy far corner stood a large tank with pipes
running to it. Toby, on tiptoe, hurried over to the tank and
squeezed behind it just as the door swung open. This was
followed by the sound of the door closing, a key sliding
into a keyhole, and the disturbing finality of a *click* as the
door was locked from the inside. Then he heard footsteps
come across the room. Toby crouched low to the floor and
peered around the tank. From here, hidden in shadows, he
could see the workbench and computer.

A figure appeared. It was a man, but his features were
obscured by a head-to-toe coating of brown foam. He
turned away from Toby and began brushing himself off.
Toby considered making a break for the door. If he could

get outside, he could find Sternabite, maybe the FBI agents. But he'd have to unsqueeze himself from behind the tank, then run right past where the man was standing; even if he reached the door, he couldn't unlock it without the key. So he stayed crouched where he was, watching, waiting to see the face of the man who had caused so much trouble and was about to cause so much more.

The man looked vaguely familiar from the back: his build, his hair, the shape of his head. Toby was pretty sure he'd seen him before. But where? He frowned, studying the man, who was still brushing himself off, the foam spattering onto the concrete floor. The man said something harsh in a foreign language—apparently a curse word. It reminded Toby of how the two weird smelly foreign guys talked.

Then the man turned, his face finally coming into view. Toby cupped his hand over his mouth, stifling a gasp as he recognized the man—a man he'd seen around Hubble Middle School hundreds of times.

Janitor Dude.

Toby shook his head in disbelief. *Could it possibly be?* He thought he must be mistaken—J.D. had come into the utility room for some other reason, like escaping the foam.

But then why did he lock the door?

As Toby watched, J.D. stepped to the computer and tapped a key, bringing the screen to life. That did it. Toby realized there was no mistake. The school janitor—the guy everybody saw as a complete loser—was about to cripple the United States government. And there was nobody to stop him.

Except Toby.

He was looking around for something to use as a weapon. To his right he saw nothing. To his left, a few feet away, a thick pipe ran from floor to ceiling. Scattered on the floor around the pipe were some filthy rags and a bunch of old paint cans. There was nothing else. Toby decided a paint can would have to do. As quietly as he could, he slipped from behind the water tank, took a step, then another, and then slowly reached down for the wire handle of the nearest paint can.

He never touched it. There was a sound, and before Toby could turn toward it, he felt his head slam into the concrete-block wall. The next thing he knew he was on his back, with J.D. leaning over him. J.D.'s face was the same, but the look in his eyes was profoundly different. It was no longer slack and listless; now this total loser appeared utterly focused and intense.

And scary.

"I thought I got rid of you," said J.D., his deep voice calm, cold.

Toby said nothing; he could barely think, let alone talk. The left side of his head throbbed viciously. He felt blood seeping from his scalp.

"How did you know to come here?" said J.D.

Toby shook his head. That was a mistake; a wave of pain surged through his body.

"Doesn't matter," said J.D. "You're too late anyway."

Quickly, J.D. snatched a fat roll of duct tape from the workbench. He took Toby by the shoulders and yanked

him up to a sitting position. Toby moaned as another wave of pain engulfed him. J.D. dragged him backward, pushed him up against the thick pipe, and yanked his arms around the pole and behind his back. Toby heard tape being ripped off the roll, then felt his wrists being wrapped very tightly with the sticky tape.

"That will hold you long enough," said J.D. He started toward the workbench and the computer. Toby yanked on the tape, but it was too tight. He wasn't going anywhere anytime soon.

J.D. had just reached the workbench when the doorknob rattled. He whirled around.

"HELP!" shouted Toby.

"Quiet!" snarled J.D., taking a step toward Toby, realizing he should have gagged him as well.

"Hello?" Toby recognized Sternabite's voice coming from the other side of the locked door.

"HE'S IN HERE!" shouted Toby, though his last word was garbled as J.D., moving swiftly, reached him and roughly wrapped duct tape around his head, covering his mouth.

"Make another sound," he hissed into Toby's ear, "and I will bash your skull in."

He turned back toward the workbench. The doorknob rattled as Sternabite tried it again. But the door was locked.

Sternabite had heard the fear in Toby's voice. He gave the doorknob one last try, then reached into his pocket and

pulled out a small box. He flipped it open. The thing inside looked, sort of, like a large spider: it was black, with eight metallic legs. Sternabite called it Charlotte.

Charlotte was a robot. Mostly, anyway. Sternabite had taken the two main nerve clusters from an actual spider—its "brain"—and implanted them in a computer microchip, which controlled Charlotte's mechanical body. His theory was that the spider "brain"—which had amazing capabilities—could work together with the computer chip to form a new, enhanced creature that could be used to peform many tasks, including surveillance and counterespionage.

Unfortunately, Charlotte still had some bugs. Her spider brain and her computer brain didn't always agree, so her behavior could be erratic. But Sternabite had brought her along anyway, on the hunch that she might come in handy. That hunch had been right: he needed her now.

"Charlotte," said Sternabite. "Wake up."

Two glowing red eye spots appeared, and Charlotte, with a *whir*, came to life, rising up on her eight legs. Sternabite moved the box next to the doorknob.

"Charlotte," he said, "open."

Charlotte scuttled onto the doorknob and slid a jointed leg into the keyhole. Locks were child's play for Charlotte; in a second, the door was unlocked. Sternabite plucked Charlotte off the doorknob and tucked her into his pocket as he opened the door and stepped inside.

The first thing he saw was Toby on the floor in the corner, hands behind his back, mouth gagged, his head bloody. Sternabite started toward him.

MMMPHH! said Toby, pointing with his head. Sternabite looked and saw a man standing with his back to a workbench on which sat a laptop computer. The man was facing Sternabite. In his right hand he held a thick, black wand. A stun baton. He raised it, showing it to Sternabite.

"Eight hundred thousand volts," he said. "If I touch you with this . . ."

"I know what it will do," said Sternabite.

"Yes," said the man, with a hint of a smile. "I imagine you would know."

Sternabite took a casual step forward. "So you're the one who sent me those project plans," he said. "Mr. . . ."

"My name is Prmkt," said the man. "Although the students here call me Janitor Dude. They think I'm a loser. This makes them easier to use."

"You used *me* pretty well, too," said Sternabite, taking another step forward.

"Yes," said Prmkt. "I was afraid you'd catch on sooner or later. I respect you. You're a very intelligent man."

"As are you, obviously," said Sternabite, taking another step. "It's a brilliant plan, using these kids, their parents . . ."

"I am intelligent enough to know what you are trying to do right now," said Prmkt, thrusting the baton at Sternabite. "If you come any closer . . ."

"Charlotte," said Sternabite.

Prmkt frowned.

"Attack," said Sternabite.

It happened faster than Prmkt's eyes—or any human eyes—could follow. Charlotte shot from Sternabite's

pocket and scuttled in a whirring blur to his forehead, from which she launched herself at Prmkt. She could jump thirty feet, so she easily shot across the five feet separating the two men. She hit Prmkt, as she was programmed to do, directly between his eyes, clinging to his face with needle-sharp legs. Prmkt reached up with both hands to claw at her and, in the process dropped the stun baton, which clattered to the floor and rolled under the workbench.

Sternabite ran toward the bench, but Prmkt sensed the movement and managed to get in front of him. Sternabite ran into him, and the three of them—including Charlotte—fell to the floor. The two men wrestled for position, each trying to get to the baton and to keep the other at bay. Sternabite quickly noticed two things: one was that Prmkt was stronger than he was. The other was that Charlotte was no longer clinging to Prmkt's face. In fact, Sternabite didn't see her at all.

"Charlotte!" he gasped. "Attack!"

Nothing.

Where was she?

In fact, Charlotte *was* attacking; she had simply chosen a new target. Her sophisticated robot sensors had detected an intruder, and her spider brain, overruling her computer brain, had decided that the new intruder was far more worthy of her attention. And so at the moment, as her creator struggled on the floor below, Charlotte was climbing up the wall. Stalking.

* * *

In the corner, Toby struggled to break free from the duct tape. He'd made no progress; Prmkt had bound him too tightly. As the two men rolled around on the floor in front of him, grunting, Toby felt around behind himself, looking for something, anything, that might help. His fingers brushed against an oily rag. He shifted position so he could grab it. As he did, he felt a sharp pain in his butt, caused by . . .

Rollerblade Barbie.

Frantically, Toby twisted his body until, with painful effort, he was able to pull the doll out of his pocket. Turning his head as far as he could in an effort to see behind his back, he pressed the doll's roller wheels against the oily rag and then spun the flint wheel with his thumb. He saw a flash of sparks. He spun the wheel again.

He smelled it, then saw it: gray smoke. Then he felt the heat.

Great, he thought. *I just set myself on fire.*

He bit his lip to keep from screaming as the rag caught fire, and flames singed his arms. But he also felt the tape weakening. He leaned forward and yanked with all his might—once, then again, then . . .

Yes. The burning tape parted. Toby lunged forward on the floor. Behind him, the burning rag ignited others. Flames shot up, and an acrid, billowing smoke began to fill the utility room.

"Stop him!" shouted Sternabite. He'd lost the wrestling match; Prmkt had knocked him aside and was crawling toward the stun baton. Toby staggered to his feet and

jumped onto Prmkt's back, but the man was too strong for the boy. He flung Toby off, sending him crashing to the floor. In a second, Prmkt was on his feet. He had the baton in hand and was backing away toward the computer.

"No!" gasped Sternabite. He made a last desperate lunge toward Prmkt, who raised the baton and squeezed the trigger. Sternabite screamed, twitched violently, and fell to the floor with a sickening thud, unconscious. Prmkt whirled and aimed the stick at Toby, who was pulling himself up, coughing in the dense, choking smoke.

"Stay back!" shouted Prmkt, thrusting the baton at Toby. He took another step toward the workbench.

Toby looked down at Sternabite's limp body, then, through the thickening smoke, at Prmkt. He moved closer.

"I said stay back!" shouted Prmkt. He thrust the baton at Toby again and pulled the trigger. Toby heard a *ZZZZZZZT* as it brushed his shirt. He jumped back.

One more step and Prmkt would reach the computer. He switched the baton to his left hand, to keep it between himself and Toby. Then he turned and reached his right hand out toward the ENTER key.

And then they both heard it, from directly above: *RIBBIT!*

Prmkt looked up, an unfortunate move for him, because he caught the full, moist force of Fester—not a lightweight frog—who had fallen directly on his face after wriggling through the vent from the heating duct above. Prmkt yelped and swiped at the frog with his right hand, still keeping Toby at bay with the baton. Another *RIBBIT,*

and Fester leaped off, which again was unfortunate for Prmkt, because a millisecond later Fester was replaced by Charlotte, who was in hot pursuit of Fester. Charlotte landed hard on Prmkt's face with all eight of her sharp talons in Full Penetration Mode.

Prmkt screamed and reached for his face with both hands, including, of course, the one holding the baton. Toby saw his chance and lunged, managing to get hold of Prmkt's left arm. Prmkt roared with rage and swung the baton down. His target was Toby, but with his vision mostly blocked by Charlotte, his aim was way off.

It was only at the last possible second, as he simultaneously knocked Charlotte loose and pulled the trigger, that Prmkt saw where he was sending the 800,000 volts.

Directly into the computer.

There was a loud crackling sound as a brilliant flash of light shot from the end of the baton and across the keyboard. Sparks flew everywhere, and then smoke curled and rose from the laptop, joining the already-thick smoke filling the utility room. The screen flashed white and went black.

And then it started to rain.

Actually, it was the fire sprinklers, which had been triggered by the smoke. For a moment, as the water cascaded down on them, neither Prmkt nor Toby moved. Toby stared at Prmkt, who was still holding the baton. Prmkt stared at the smoking ruins of his plan to destroy America.

Then Prmkt turned toward Toby. Slowly, he raised the stun baton. Toby flinched, closing his eyes, waiting for the awful shock. . . .

Clunk

No shock came. Toby opened his eyes.

Prmkt had dropped the baton. In a daze of defeat, he turned away from Toby and slumped to the floor, his back against the wall. He sat there, unmoving, his eyes utterly blank, as sprinkler water cascaded down his face. Like the Janitor Dude of old.

Toby heard a groan. It was Sternabite, regaining consciousness. Toby went over and knelt next to him.

"Are you okay?" he said.

"No," said Sternabite. He raised his head a little, blinking, looking around the room through the smoke and the drizzling water. His eyes fell on Prmkt, slumped against the wall. Then he looked up at Toby.

"What happened?" he asked.

Toby smiled.

"I think we won," he said.

CHAPTER SEVENTY-SIX

OF ALL THE THINGS that happened over the next month, the coolest, for Toby, was meeting the president. This happened at a ceremony in the White House Rose Garden honoring the group the news media had dubbed the "Hubble Heroes": Toby, Tamara, Micah, and—to the president's annoyance—Fester.

"I am NOT going to honor a frog," the president had declared when his chief of staff briefed him on the ceremony.

"But, sir," said the chief of staff, "the frog played a critical role in taking out the Krpsht agent. And it was almost killed by the robot attack spider. The Porter boy has been nursing it back to health, and he won't come to the ceremony without it."

"But it's a *frog*," said the president.

"It's a *hero* frog, sir."

The president sighed. He knew he didn't really have a choice; at the moment, the Hubble Heroes were a lot more popular than he was. They were huge, their names in every newscast, their faces on the cover of every magazine. Oprah had them on speed dial, and at least three movies were already in the works. They had been offered millions for endorsements, most notably from the manufacturers of Diet Coke and Mentos.

"All right," said the president. "The frog can come. But I'm not touching it."

"I doubt the Porter boy would let you anyway, sir. He's concerned about infection."

The president shot his chief of staff a glare, then said, "What about whatshisname? The science genius?"

"Sternabite, sir. He declined the invitation to the ceremony."

"*Declined?* Why? Is he still worried about legal problems?"

When the science-fair plot details became public, there had been some discussion of prosecuting Sternabite for illegally obtaining classified technology. But in light of his heroic efforts to stop Prmkt once he realized what was happening—not to mention his immense popularity as a Hubble Hero—the president had decided to grant Sternabite a pardon for any crimes he may have committed.

"No, sir, it's not that," said the chief of staff. "It's a

privacy issue. Sternabite has been besieged by offers from companies and investors who want to give him money for his inventions."

"Doesn't he want to be rich?"

"Apparently not, sir. He threw both Bill Gates and Steve Jobs out of his store. He used some kind of owl on them."

"Owl?"

"Owl, sir. Anyway, he's gone into seclusion now, and says he won't be attending the ceremony. At least, not in person."

"What does *that* mean?"

"I don't know, sir, but those were his exact words. 'At least, not in person.'"

As it turned out, Sternabite showed up as a hologram. One moment he wasn't there, and the next moment he was standing next to the president and looking totally lifelike, except that when two freaked-out Secret Service agents tried to tackle him, they passed right through him.

Eventually, after everyone calmed down, the president proceeded with the ceremony, noting that the Hubble Heroes deserved the nation's thanks for thwarting the terrorist plot "against overwhelming odds." (He did not mention that one of the biggest obstacles confronting the Hubble Heroes had been federal agents trying to arrest them.) The president also noted that the "misguided threat from the Republic of Krpshtskan had been swiftly and permanently eradicated."

This was definitely true. The Republic of Krpshtskan had formally surrendered to the United States before the

Diet Coke had finished fizzing in the gym. Grdankl the Strong had agreed to turn over to the Americans all of the Krpsht army's weaponry, which consisted of a few dozen nonfunctioning rifles and a cannon from World War II that had rabbits living in it. Grdankl had also agreed to resign. For the first time in Kprshtskan's history, free elections were held, under American supervision, with more than a dozen candidates vying for the job. The winner, by a landslide, was: Grdankl the Strong. He immediately requested, and received, a multibillion-dollar aid package from Kprshtskan's new ally, the United States; within weeks, construction had begun on more than a dozen Starbucks.

As for Prmkt, he had been taken into federal custody and interrogated extensively by the FBI, the CIA, the NSA, and other agencies. He was totally cooperative, and, after much analysis, the experts concluded that he was a brilliant if unbalanced man who, out of love for his shamed brother, had managed to concoct and execute his intricate plot with no American help, other than from some clueless spoiled rich kids and their hyperambitious parents.

Clearly, Prmkt had to pay for his crimes: the question was, how? After much discussion at the highest levels, it was decided to punish Prmkt by making him a full-time employee of the federal government. Specifically, he would work for Homeland Security, where he would head the Anti-Hacking Task Force. The feds wanted him to wear an electronic monitoring bracelet on his ankle, but within fifteen minutes after they attached it to him, he had reprogrammed it so that it appeared, to the tracking computer,

to be sending signals from Mount Everest. In the end, the feds decided that they either had to put Prmkt in jail or trust him, and by that point it was clear that he was way too valuable to put in jail.

Vrsk and Drmtsi were also a bit of a headache for the American government. On the one hand, they had entered the country with the intent of aiding and abetting Prmkt. On the other hand, they had not actually done anything useful for him; in fact, they had, in their own way, helped the Hubble Heroes as well as the American retail economy. They had also both declared their desire to remain in America and become citizens.

The government decided to let them stay as long as they could support themselves. This they did by forming what turned out to be a very successful business venture with Toby's parents—a new health-food-product television channel. From here they sold a "dietary additive," based on a secret Krpsht recipe that allegedly offered near-miraculous health benefits to anybody who was able to actually choke it down. This product was called "smerk."

As for Gmygmy—whose humiliation was the cause of Prmkt's elaborate scheme—his career received a huge boost when the video of his hideous rendition of "MacArthur Park" on *America's Next Superstar*, broadcast incessantly as part of the news coverage, became a camp hit.

Cable-TV host Greta Van Susteren tracked Gmygmy down. He had spent the past five years traveling around the country, pursuing his hopeless dream of stardom, but mostly working as a waiter. When Van Susteren found

him, he had worked his way up to a small part in a dinner-theater production of *Cats* in Sandusky, Ohio. Her interview with him got such strong ratings that he was offered a good-paying gig in Las Vegas, opening for Barry Manilow.

On the other hand, Lance Swingle's fortunes declined rapidly after the science fair. Word quickly got around that he had acted like a coward during the blackouts, and that he'd ordered his thugs to stop the Hubble Heroes. Even worse, his company, TranScent, whose core business was transmitting fragrances over the Internet, started to have major technical problems. No matter what fragrance a sender scanned into the fragrance digitizer—lilac, rose, watermelon, strawberry, cinnamon, etc.—the decoder at the other end emitted a smell like a musk ox passing gas. Swingle was sure that Sternabite was responsible, and he ordered TranScent's lawyers to sue him. All of them quit when their BlackBerrys mysteriously exploded.

D. Arthur Vaderian, disheartened by his defeat at the hands of Luke Skywalker and Princess Leia, abandoned his Star Wars hobby altogether and became a successful political consultant.

As for Toby, life was good. Mostly, anyway. There were a few not-so-good parts: for example, his parents were very, *very* unhappy when he confessed to them about selling their Han Solo blaster pistol to buy a computer. They made him sell it and give them the money, and they grounded him for two months, a record. Toby accepted this punishment without complaint, because (a) he knew he deserved it, and (b) Sternabite let him keep the invisibility iPhone

so he could get out of the house if he really needed to.

Life at school was definitely better for Toby. The Hornet called him into her office and apologized to him—The Hornet! Apologized! To *him*!—for not believing him.

The Hornet also ordered Mr. Neckstrom to apologize to Toby. She would have forced Mr. Pyzrbovich to do the same, but he was no longer at Hubble Middle. It turned out that on the night of the blackouts, he had panicked and gone home without telling anybody. The Hornet, who did not tolerate this kind of disciplinary breach, had insisted that he be transferred.

Speaking of discipline: the ME kids, of course, got into big trouble with the school, and their parents got into even bigger trouble with their companies and the federal government. All of the ME projects were disqualified from the science fair. There was no way to judge the rest of the projects, since most of them were destroyed by the nuclear Mentos, so the judges—consisting of The Hornet and the science teachers—decided to give four special achievement awards. Three of them went to Tamara, Micah, and Brad Pitt Wemplemeyer, since theirs were the three projects that, combined, had helped to save the country. The fourth special achievement award went to Toby. He protested that he didn't deserve it, because in all the craziness, he never got around to actually doing a science-fair project. The judges disagreed; in their citation, they said that Toby had done "important scientific research concerning the effects, on combustible materials, of sparking Rollerblade wheels."

393

Winning the award was cool; all the other attention was pretty cool, too. But for Toby, the best part was going to the White House and being honored by the president. Toby could hardly believe it was happening as he stood in the Rose Garden with Tamara, Micah, and, in hologram form, Sternabite, listening to the president of the United States thank them for saving the country.

"Without your efforts," the president was saying, "this nation could have suffered an attack from which it quite likely would not have recovered. You, the Hubble Heroes, saved America from a vicious act of terrorism—the greatest threat that we, as a nation, face today."

Next to Toby, hologram Sternabite snorted.

"What's so funny?" whispered Toby.

"The line about terrorism being the greatest threat we face," Sternabite whispered back.

"You mean it isn't?" whispered Toby.

"Not even close," whispered Sternabite.

Toby turned to stare at Sternabite. "What do you mean?" he whispered.

Sternabite was about to answer, but then he and Toby saw that the president, annoyed by their conversation, was glaring at them.

"Don't worry," whispered Sternabite. "We have a couple of months to deal with it."

"Deal with what?" said Toby.

"If you don't mind?" said the president.

"Deal with *what*?" repeated Toby.

But Sternabite, in a flicker of light, was gone.

God's grace. His gentle urging to spend time in His presence becomes an irresistible practice that transforms the soul."

Janet Perez Eckles, author of
bestselling *Simply Salsa*

"When I wept through Day One, I knew *The 30-Day Praise Challenge* would change my life. Get ready! You're about to pick up the greatest weapon in a Christ-follower's arsenal: praise."

Jane Rubietta, international speaker
and award-winning author

"This book came at a great time for me. I recently realized the majority of my prayers were asking God for things. Becky showed me how to add praise. This book will help you start a lifetime habit of praise."

Bruce Johnson, president of SIM USA

"You'll find a refreshing and joyful encounter with God on every page of Becky Harling's life-changing book."

Linda Evans Shepherd, author of
When You Don't Know What to Pray

"As you rest in God's presence, offer Him thanks and praise, and listen to the worship songs Becky suggests, you'll find your soul filled once again. Bless you, Becky, for providing a simple yet beautiful resource for finding faith and perspective once again."

Susie Larson, national radio
host, speaker, and author of
Your Beautiful Purpose

"*The 30-Day Praise Challenge* is an anointed book that I highly recommend. I laughed, I cried, and I drew closer to the Lord because of the praise challenge experience."

Yvonne Ortega, author of *Moving
from Broken to Beautiful*

"Over the years, we have seen Becky live out the principles she is teaching. Her book provides a clear and compelling pathway toward transformation that uplifts the goodness of God and brings personal victory."

Dr. Jerry and Dee Sheveland,
Converge Worldwide

the **30**day
praise
challenge

becky harling

David C Cook®
transforming lives together

THE 30-DAY PRAISE CHALLENGE
Published by David C Cook
4050 Lee Vance View
Colorado Springs, CO 80918 U.S.A.

David C Cook Distribution Canada
55 Woodslee Avenue, Paris, Ontario, Canada N3L 3E5

David C Cook U.K., Kingsway Communications
Eastbourne, East Sussex BN23 6NT, England

The graphic circle C logo is a registered trademark of David C Cook.

The website addresses recommended throughout this book are
offered as a resource to you. These websites are not intended
in any way to be or imply an endorsement on the part of
David C Cook, nor do we vouch for their content.

LCCN 2013936242
ISBN 978-0-7814-0895-0
eISBN 978-1-4347-0599-0

© 2013 Becky Harling

The Team: John Blase, Liz Heaney, Nick Lee,
Tonya Osterhouse, Karen Athen
Cover Design: Amy Konyndyk
Cover Photo: istockphoto.com

Printed in the United States of America
First Edition 2013

2 3 4 5 6 7 8 9 10

082813

To
Jesus Christ, my Redeemer,
Healer, Savior, and Friend.
I live to praise You!

contents

foreword

Why should you take Becky's 30-day praise challenge? I know why. Let me tell you. Because Becky has *a lot* to teach you. You see, I had a front-row seat watching Becky struggle with cancer and a double mastectomy at age forty-two. I wept with her as she walked through healing from sexual abuse. I watched and marveled that through it all, this amazing woman praised God. Becky's vibrant praise and worship lifted her heart and mind above the horrible circumstances that swirled about her. Praise literally lifted Becky from the painful prison of her circumstances.

So I say, "Take this praise challenge!"

When I took the 30-day praise challenge, a truth from each day spoke to me. No pain or trouble was left out. And I believe each praise day will minister to you as well.

I also think that one day you'll turn the page and God will have an aha moment for you—maybe a name or quality of your great God will make you feel softly loved; or you'll have a moment of realization that Becky understands how difficult your life is right now, and it will feel good to be understood.

When I took the 30-day praise challenge, I loved the way each of the thirty days of praise had four unique parts:

> *The Invitation*—A personal love message from Abba inviting you to come to Him
> *Listen*—A list of praise songs for you to listen to as you praise God
> *Pray*—A praise prayer that can help guide you
> *Journal*—A place for you to record your personal response

I can promise you that this praise challenge:

> will draw you closer to God
> will make your faith grow

will fill you with hope

will envelop you with the Father's love

Whether you are facing cancer, don't have a job, are on a pain-filled healing journey, or are just stuck in a rut that makes life seem unbearable, Becky says you can praise your way out. It's true; I've watched Becky do just that! And the 30-day praise challenge declares that you can discover your way out of pain and panic through praise! So take the challenge. You'll be glad you did!

Linda Dillow, author of
What's It Like to Be Married to Me?
and *Calm My Anxious Heart*

Part One

the challenge

give praise a chance

For the past twelve years I have participated in a practice that has radically changed my life. I began right after I was diagnosed with breast cancer. Scared and stressed out at the thought of a double mastectomy, worried about my kids and whether I would be alive to finish raising them, anxious and paralyzed over the thought of a year full of treatments, I decided to fast, pray, and beg God for healing and peace of mind. When I told my mentor about my plan, she had another idea. She challenged me to spend twenty minutes a day for a week in pure praise. At the time I remember thinking, *Why in the world would I do that? Won't it be hypocritical to praise God if I'm not feeling thankful?* After wrestling with her suggestion, I decided I had nothing to lose. I may as well give praise a chance.

Tackling that challenge was the beginning of an extraordinary adventure. As I devoted twenty minutes of every day to praising God, I developed a strong sense of His presence. Praise awakened my heart to His voice. Many mornings before my alarm went off, He woke me up with an invitation that went like this: *Wake up, My child. Come and be with Me. Praise Me and enjoy My presence.* I came to realize that God was excited to have me come and spend time with Him. He longed for intimacy with me. That thought alone boggled my mind.

As I continued the practice of private praise, God's presence became more tangible, and I began to change into a more positive, confident, and secure woman. The transformation I have experienced is undeniable. Praise changed me from being fearful, frantic, and insecure to being a calm person filled with passion and purpose.

Before taking the praise challenge, I found it difficult to feel God's love for me. After I took the challenge, I found myself experiencing His love beyond anything I imagined. Before, I sometimes felt abandoned by God. Afterward, His presence in my life became more concrete and I found it easier to trust Him. I am more convinced than ever that

establishing intentional time for private praise is critical to transformation in the life of the believer.

I am guessing that you picked up this book because you are longing for a deeper encounter with God. Maybe life has dealt you an unfair blow and you feel afraid. It could be that you are wrestling with some significant doubts about God, and someone recommended that you read this book. Perhaps your heart is crying for a fresh awakening to the Holy Spirit's voice and power. That longing comes from God; He is prompting it. Praising Him was His idea in the first place. God invites us to praise Him, not just because praise gives God His due, but also because of what it does in us and for us. Praise restores our faith, fills us with joy, calms our fears, and inspires us to love and obey God. If you long for those changes in your life, I invite you to take the praise challenge:

Spend 20 minutes intentionally praising God for 30 consecutive days.

In Part 2 of this book, "30 Days of Praise," you'll find help for doing just that. Each day begins with an invitation to praise God for some characteristic of His deity. Written as

if they are from God Himself, these Scripture-based invitations are designed to help you hear God's voice. Each day also includes guidance for how to praise God, suggestions for music to listen to in order to prompt your praise, and a journal idea to help you process your praise journey.

In addition, each day has a prayer of praise. Because we worship a triune God, these prayers may be directed to one or more members of the Trinity. The Bible teaches that God exists eternally in three distinct persons: God the Father, God the Son (Jesus Christ), and God the Holy Spirit. As you praise each person of the Trinity, your faith will grow and you will be drawn into deeper intimacy with each member of the Godhead.

In Part 3, "Taking It Further," you will find ideas and tips for how to enhance your praise journey. You will learn how to praise God through His names, through the Psalms, through the book of Revelation, and through a declaration of faith. In addition, you will gain insight into how to praise when you are grieving or feeling depressed, as well as how to praise in order to defeat the Enemy. You can use these praise helps over and over again as you move ahead in your praise journey.

To get the most out of your praise time, you'll need:

Intentionality. It's easy to begin the praise challenge with a skeptical heart. I understand that. But don't allow yourself to stay in that skepticism. Ask God to uproot any doubt in you, and trust the Holy Spirit to give you childlike faith for this adventure. As you progress through the challenge, you may experience God's presence in a fresh way. Tell the Lord in advance that you are ready to experience as much of Him as possible.

As you begin to be more intentional about praise, you will find that you hear God's voice more clearly. His voice might be a deep prompting in your spirit, or it might be His words in your mind calling you to some action. When you hear God speak to you in prayer, don't second-guess or question whether you imagined His voice. Instead, trust by faith that you *did* hear His voice and then respond in obedience and faith.

Praise music that prompts you to worship. Music has been a significant part of helping me quiet my heart, tune out the rest of the world, and sink into the presence of the Almighty. On page 199 is a list of praise songs I encourage you to listen to during this challenge. If you download the songs ahead of time, you won't need to interrupt your praise time. If you find that the songs I've chosen don't appeal to

you, that's fine. Just download praise music that helps you focus on the presence of God. (Of course, you can also listen to the songs at YouTube.com.)

As you listen, allow the songs to prompt your praise. You may want to play them throughout the day to remind you to keep an attitude of praise. Do what works best for you—simply use the music to aid you in your worship.

Flexibility. There are no rules for this challenge. You can praise God any time of day. I like to praise God early in the morning while it's still dark. I get down on my knees and put on music that takes me into God's presence. My husband, on the other hand, worships best outside after the sun is up. He will often take a praise walk. As he walks, he exalts the Lord. I know women who praise God during their kids' naptime and others who praise Him at night after everyone else is in bed. I want you to find a time that works best for you. And if you miss a day, no worries! This is not meant to be a legalistic practice. Just pick up where you left off the day before.

Please feel free to use the prayers as prompts but realize that you don't have to pray exactly as I've suggested. I encourage you to develop your own prayers. My desire is for the Spirit of God to lead you in this journey of praise.

A journal. At the end of each day of praise, there are some questions for you to respond to in a praise journal. Reflecting on these questions and writing down your answers will give you insight into what you are learning and enable you to record changes you see in yourself or changes that you may need to make. Some of the journal questions ask you to imagine positive changes that you might experience in a given area if you choose to praise.

God can use our imaginations to help us dream, create, and experience His presence in deeper ways. Dreaming builds and sustains hope in our lives. So don't be afraid to use your imagination. Your journal will become a record of your praise journey, which will help you remember all you experienced of God during the thirty days.

To use your Bible. Most of the scriptures have been written out for you in *The 30-Day Praise Challenge,* so even if you don't have a Bible, you can still take the challenge. But you might want your own Bible to underline and date specific passages that speak to your heart.

If you take this challenge, you *will* change. You will re-fall in love with Jesus. You will experience more joy and peace, less insecurity and envy, more boldness and courage,

and less fear and anxiety. Your faith will grow and the fruit of the Spirit will be more evident in your life. You will find that the chains that once bound you are broken, and you will experience more freedom than you ever dreamed possible!

Are you ready to fall deeper in love with Jesus? Let's get started!

Part Two

30 days of praise

Day 1

Oh, the depths of the riches of the wisdom
and knowledge of God!
How unsearchable his judgments,
and his paths beyond tracing out!
"Who has known the mind of the Lord?
Or who has been his counselor?"
Romans 11:33–34

The Invitation

My child, every day you are faced with countless decisions.
Many times you are unsure about what to do. I am the source of
all wisdom, and I know the plans I have for you, plans so that
you can prosper and thrive. Even when you don't understand
My ways, I am working behind the scenes to accomplish what's
best for you. My wisdom has no limits and My judgments are
always perfect. I have never needed a counselor and have never

*had to ask for another's opinion because all wisdom begins and
ends with Me. Today, worship and praise Me for My wisdom.
Every time you face a perplexing decision, praise Me that I can
show you what to do. As you faithfully praise Me, I will show
you which way to go. I love to generously share My wisdom with
those who praise me.* (Rom. 11:33–34; Jer. 29:11; Ps. 111:10;
James 1:5)

God is the source of all wisdom, and He can provide the
wisdom you need for every decision you face. Today, whenever you are presented with a challenge, praise God that you
can trust Him to give you His wisdom in each circumstance.
Every time you feel an uncertain angst in your soul, praise
God immediately that He will give you discernment for that
moment.

> If any of you lacks wisdom, he should ask
> God, who gives generously to all without
> finding fault, and it will be given to you.
> (James 1:5)

Listen

Listen to "God I Look to You" performed by Bethel Live, featuring Jenn Johnson, and "Sovereign Hands" performed by Hillsong United. As you listen, praise God that He will set the vision for your life and give you wisdom, moment by moment.

Pray

Lord Jesus, I praise You for being the God of all wisdom. All the treasures of wisdom and knowledge are found in You. I exalt You because Your understanding is beyond anything I can fathom. You created the world with perfect insight. Scripture tells me there are no limits to Your knowledge and that You have never needed a counselor. I praise You that although I don't have wisdom in _____ [name a specific area], *You do. You promise me that if I lack wisdom, I only need to ask, and You will give me wisdom. As I move through my day I praise You in advance for the wisdom You will plant in my mind moment by moment.* (Col. 2:3; Jer. 10:12; Rom. 11:33–34; James 1:5)

Journal

In what specific area(s) of your life are you longing for wisdom? Write out your thoughts in your journal, and then write a prayer of praise affirming your faith that God will give you the wisdom that you need.

Day 2

The LORD is the strength of his people,
a fortress of salvation for his anointed one.
Psalm 28:8

The Invitation

My beloved, I know you are tired. My strength is the perfect match for your weakness. I never grow fatigued or weary; I never lack the energy to accomplish My purposes. Praise Me for My unlimited strength. When you are weak and you praise Me, you give Me the opportunity to showcase My power. So don't be discouraged by your weaknesses; instead, praise Me that I promise to sustain and help you. I will hold you up in the moments when you feel you cannot continue. As you praise Me, My Spirit will pour strength into your soul and you will feel renewed energy rising. (Ps. 28:8; Isa. 40:28–29; 2 Cor. 12:9; Isa. 41:10)

Today, praise God for His immeasurable strength and awesome power. Praise Him that He promises to renew the strength of those who spend time in His presence and that He will give you enough strength for the coming days. Whenever you feel low in energy, immediately praise God that His power is perfected in your weakness.

> O my Strength, to you I sing praises, for you, O God, are my refuge, the God who shows me unfailing love. (Ps. 59:17 NLT)

Listen

Listen to "Hosanna (Praise Is Rising)" performed by Paul Baloche, "Please Be My Strength" performed by Gungor, and "Stronger" performed by Mandisa. Listen for His voice as you worship. Ask the Holy Spirit to show you how to create the space for more rest in your life.

Pray

I praise You, Lord, because You are my refuge and strength even during times of stress. You arm me with power when tasks feel impossible and when life feels challenging. I praise You that when I feel exhausted, You invite me to rest in You, reassuring me that You are not demanding or harsh in Your expectations for me. You promise all those who hope in You that You will renew their strength, helping them to soar on wings like eagles. Those who put their hope in You will run and not grow weary; they will walk and not faint. Thank You that when I feel weak, I can move out of the way and trust Your strength. I praise You this day that You will provide the strength I need to be who You have called me to be. (Ps. 46:10; 2 Sam. 22:2–3; Matt. 11:28; Isa. 40:31)

Journal

Write about a time when you felt extremely weak and then experienced God's strength. What do you feel God is saying to you today?

Day 3

For you created my inmost being;
you knit me together in my mother's womb.
I praise you because I am fearfully
and wonderfully made;
your works are wonderful,
I know that full well.
Psalm 139:13–14

The Invitation

You are My one-of-a-kind masterpiece! I designed you with intention. I deliberately crafted every part of your body, soul, and spirit for My glory. I know there are times when you feel frustrated with your weaknesses and limitations. But you are fearfully and wonderfully made in My image. You are a reflection of My beauty. Everything I make is good, including you. When you praise and thank Me for how I designed you, My

Spirit quiets the voices of self-doubt. I knit you together in your mother's womb. Praise Me that I chose your eye color, hair color, body build, and intellect before the foundation of the world.

Others may tell you that you must look a certain way or attain a certain level of achievement to be worthwhile. Don't listen to them. Instead, thank Me that I am continually perfecting the work I started in you. Rather than tear yourself down, exalt Me for the beauty I am exhibiting through your life. As you praise Me, I will help you let go of the anxiety you feel over your limitations. (Eph.2:10; Phil. 1:6; Ps. 139:13–14)

God is not disappointed in the way you turned out. On the contrary, He delights over you! He is continuing to change you and empower you to become the person He created you to be. Dare to praise Him today for the way He designed you. Whether you're having a good body day or a bad body day, praise and worship Him that you are fearfully and wonderfully made. Praise Him for your intellectual capacities and for His ongoing work in your life. Praise Him that He is able to bring beauty out of any

mess in your life, even those messes created by your own mistakes.

> For everything God created is good.
> (1 Tim. 4:4)

Listen

Listen to "Beautiful Things" performed by Gungor and "For Your Splendor" performed by Christy Nockels.

Pray

My Father, thank You that I have been made in Your image and bear a striking resemblance to You. I praise You, because You carefully and creatively knit me together in my mother's womb. I praise You that I am fearfully and wonderfully made! You created me in perfect wisdom. You designed me to reflect Your beauty in a world that is often not very beautiful. Thank You for shining through my eyes, speaking through my voice, and loving through my heart. I praise You that You are shaping me into the image of Your Son, Jesus Christ. "The Son is

the image of the invisible God, the firstborn over all creation."
There is no one I would rather look like than Jesus! Thank You
for continuing Your work, even when I complain. I praise You
that I was created to do good works that You prepared for me to
do long before I was even born. Please renew the image of Jesus
Christ in me today. I praise You and worship You, my Creator!
(Ps. 139:13–14; Ps. 104:24; Eph. 2:10; Col. 1:15)

Journal

Has it been difficult for you to say, "I am fearfully and wonderfully made"? Why? How have you seen God use your
weaknesses for good? How has He used your strengths to
demonstrate His love?

Day 4

"I am the LORD, who exercises kindness,
justice and righteousness on earth."
Jeremiah 9:24

The Invitation

Injustice is a part of the fallen world. When life feels unfair,
you are tempted to question My kindness. Satan, the Enemy
of your soul, fills your mind with doubts. Child, My sense of
justice is different from yours. Dare to praise Me for being
good, even when I allow circumstances to occur in your life
and in the lives of those you love that feel unfair. My every
intention toward you is good. I continually offer you kindness
as an expression of My nature. Celebrate My loving-kindness
by thanking Me for the gifts I shower on you every day. I
reign with perfect justice. There will come a day when I will
bring good out of every evil. When you worship Me, My Spirit

nurtures your faith. Test Me in this; praise Me for My justice and goodness, then watch and see how your trust in Me grows. I have your best interests at heart. Come, praise Me and feel renewed hope rising in your soul. (Ps. 118:1; Ps. 33:5; Ps. 34:8; Ps. 107:1)

Today, praise God for being just and kind. Before you turn on your praise music, spend a few moments making a list of all the ways you have experienced God's kindness in the last week. For example, you might have received a call from a headhunter just a few days after being told that your job was being terminated. Or maybe your husband brought you flowers or gave you a compliment when you were feeling like he takes you for granted. Perhaps just when you felt you couldn't handle the challenge of having a child with special needs, you experienced an unexpected breakthrough. You can trust His kindness. Praise Him that even when life feels unfair, His intentions toward you are good.

> For the LORD is righteous, he loves justice;
> upright men will see his face. (Ps. 11:7)

Listen

Listen to "Forever Reign" performed by Hillsong Live and "I Lift My Hands (Let Faith Arise)" performed by Chris Tomlin. Close your eyes and allow the music to prompt your praise.

Pray

Lord, You are worthy of all of my praise. You reign in absolute justice and kindness. Your name is good, Your heart is good, Your actions are good; everything about You shouts goodness. Yet these circumstances, _____ [name specific circumstances here], *feel unfair. I praise You that Your every intention toward me is good. Thank You that I can trust You to be just. You promise to redeem and use even the bad things that have happened in my life for my good and for Your glory. Even what others have meant for evil, You are able to turn around for my good. Lord, I know that someday You will right every wrong and bring justice. Thank You for promising to complete the good work You have started in me. Draw me deeper into knowing and trusting Your justice and goodness. You are my*

God, and I will give You thanks. Let me live to praise You!
(Ps. 119:68; Rom. 8:28; Gen. 50:20; Phil. 2:13; Ps. 118:28;
Ps. 119:175)

Journal

In a world of suffering, it is sometimes difficult to trust
God's justice and kindness. In what ways have you experienced God's goodness during challenging or painful times?
How might your life look differently if you trusted in God's
goodness right now?

Day 5

The Invitation

My child, I am the Lord who does not change. People and circum-stances in your life continually change, creating undercurrents of anxiety. When anxiety threatens to overwhelm you, come to Me and praise Me that I am holding you ever so tightly. When the waves of life roll around you, cling to Me as the One who never changes. I am Jesus Christ, the same yesterday, today, and forever. Praise Me continually, especially during tumultuous times. When you dare to praise Me, I will strengthen your confidence in Me as your rock. I am your refuge and strength, a continual help, even during seasons of transition. I am your security. My presence goes with you through every changing season. Do not fear tomorrow; I am already there. I lovingly call you to new adventures. Change

in your life doesn't happen by chance. Nothing can thwart My plans for you, plans for good and not evil. In the midst of this changing world, I am constant and never change. (Heb. 13:8, 15; Ps. 46:1, 7; Job 42:2; Jer. 29:11)

Think through the changes or possible changes you are facing right now. While many things in life are uncertain, God is steadfast. He never changes. His love never changes, His goodness never changes, His faithfulness never changes, and His grace never changes. He is the one and only constant you can trust. Declare, "I praise You, God, that You never change, and I trust You with my future." As you faithfully proclaim your praise, the truth of God's unchanging nature will be your anchor.

Jesus Christ is the same yesterday and today and forever. (Heb. 13:8)

Listen

Listen to "Your Love Never Fails" performed by Chris McClarney and "10,000 Reasons (Bless the Lord)" performed

by Matt Redman. As you listen, praise God for His steadfast nature and for all the tangible ways you have experienced His consistent nature even during times of transition.

Pray

Lord Jesus, I praise You for staying the same yesterday, today, and forever. Sometimes my life feels so unsteady. In those times, I feel out of control. Holy One, thank You for holding me tight in the crashing waves of change, even when I feel as though I am drowning. I praise You for being steady and sovereign. You work all things, even the changes to come in my future, for my good because I am Your beloved child. Thank You that the transitions I am experiencing now are preparing me for the changes to come in my future. I don't have to feel afraid or anxious, because Your love never changes. You are the one constant in my life that I can always trust. I praise You for promising to go before me, preparing the way and guiding me in paths of righteousness. I extol You, Lord. Fix my eyes on You. You are able to lead me through the transitions of life. I bow before You in worship and long to say with the psalmist David, "I have trusted in the LORD without wavering." (Heb. 13:8; Ps. 23:3–4; Ps. 25:15; Ps. 26:1)

Journal

What life changes have you experienced lately? How might continuing to intentionally praise God quiet the voices of anxiety and give you more courage in the face of uncertainty? Today, as you praised God for His unchanging nature, what changes in attitude did you experience?

Day 6

I am the Alpha and Omega,
the First and the Last,
the Beginning and the End.
Revelation 22:13

The Invitation

My child, I understand how hard it is for you to wait. You long for Me to move more quickly and to answer your prayers immediately. When you feel irritated and annoyed because things are not moving fast enough for you, take time to praise Me. Praise will help quiet the apprehension you feel. Be still in My presence, and wait patiently for Me to act. I am fully aware of all of your longings and desires. Don't take matters into your own hands. I am the Alpha and the Omega. I will move on your behalf at precisely the right moment in time. Thank Me that I am using delay to shape and change you.

Often the longer you wait for something, the more deeply you appreciate it. Delay helps prune impulsivity from your life. Declare your trust in My timing. Choose to believe that I am on time in your life, your spouse's life, your child's life, and your friends' lives. As you exalt Me, I will strengthen you to wait with grace. (Ps. 37:7, Ps. 38:9; Rev. 22:13; Ps. 90:12)

Begin your praise time today by making a list of all the things you are waiting for. If you're physically able, get down on your knees and move one by one through your list, praising God that His timing in each of those circumstances is perfect. Praise Him that He is the Lord of all time and that He is working on your behalf, even when you cannot see Him. Praise Him that He will use the delays you are facing to shape you into the likeness of His Son, Jesus Christ.

Wait for the LORD; be strong and take heart
and wait for the LORD. (Ps. 27:14)

Listen

Listen to "The First and the Last" performed by Hillsong United and "Waiting Here for You" performed by Christy Nockels. Praise Him that waiting in His presence builds your faith.

Pray

Lord Jesus, I exalt You because You are the Alpha and Omega, the Beginning and the End. You see the past, the present, and the future all at the same time. A thousand years is like nothing to You. Before time began, You were God. Even though I am tired of waiting for these things, _____ [name specific things and circumstances], *I trust You. Throughout history You have never been late. I choose to believe and thank You for working to accomplish what is best for me. I am confident that as I exalt You, I will see the goodness of the Lord. Thank You for promising to grant me the desires of my heart as I learn to enjoy and delight in You. Thank You for inviting me to be persistent in prayer. I set my hope on You.* (Rev. 22:13; Ps. 90:2; Ps. 90:4; Ps. 37:4; Luke 11:9)

Journal

What things or circumstances are you waiting and longing for? How have delays impacted your faith in God's goodness? How have delays worked in your favor?

Day 7

Praise him all his heavenly hosts,
Praise him, sun and moon,
praise him, all you shining stars.
Praise him, you highest heavens
and you waters above the skies.
Let them praise the name of the LORD,
for he commanded and they were created.
Psalm 148:2–5

The Invitation

I designed you with a need for beauty. Refresh yourself today in the beauty of My creation. The earth is Mine, and everything in it—the world and all who live in it—were created for My glory. Praise Me for the majesty of the mountains, the quiet gurgling of a brook, the chirping of a songbird, and the thunderous roar of the ocean. Drink in the magnificence of My glory reflected all

around you. Every star and planet in the galaxy is held in place by My almighty hand. The moon marks off the seasons and the sun knows exactly when to rise and set. I paint every breathtaking sunrise and every glorious sunset. I orchestrate the thunder and the lightning and drench the earth with showers.

The sea and everything in it sings My praise. Every creature on earth participates in a symphony of worship to Me, the Lord and King. Come join in the chorus of praise as it crescendos around the world. Raise your voice! Sing the song of praise that I composed for you to sing. Honor and majesty surround Me; strength and beauty are in My sanctuary. (Ps. 24:1; Ps. 89:5, 11; Ps. 145:10; Ps. 148:2–5; Ps. 96:6)

If possible, spend your praise time outside today. Allow the beauty and magnificence of nature to prompt your praise. Use your senses as you worship; see, feel, touch, and smell God's glory all around you. You were designed with a need for beauty. God met that need in His creation. Thank Him for the splendor of His artwork all around you. Take your time; don't rush. Observe the detail God gave to His design for the tiniest bug, the most intricate

plant, and the most exquisite bird. Find refreshment in His life-giving beauty.

> Let the heavens rejoice, let the earth be
> glad; let the sea resound and all that is in
> it; let the fields be jubilant, and everything
> in them. Then all the trees of the forest will
> sing for joy; they will sing before the LORD
> for he comes. (Ps. 96:11–13)

Listen

Listen to "Creation's King" performed by Paul Baloche and "The Earth Is Yours" performed by Gungor. As you listen, imagine God, the Grand Conductor, directing all of creation in a symphony of praise.

Pray

Holy One, Mighty Creator of all the earth, thank You for the massive chorus rising from all creation exalting Your glory. All of creation mirrors Your beauty. Thank You for creating such a

beautiful world for me to live in and enjoy. Praise You for all the colors that make my world so much brighter. I praise You, Lord, that each leaf, each flower, every bird, and every living creature has been designed intricately to reflect Your glory. Thank You for designing such beauty. When life feels unbeautiful, I can walk outside and see beauty all around me! I praise You for Your glory and the sheer splendor of all of Your creation. (Ps. 19:1; Ps. 150)

Journal

How does the beauty of God's creation speak to your soul? How does it meet your need for beauty? How did taking your praise time outside and observing God's creation affect you emotionally?

Day 8

I have loved you with an everlasting love;
I have drawn you with loving-kindness.
Jeremiah 31:3

The Invitation

Remember that this world is broken. Rejection is inevitable.
People will disappoint you and hurt you. Only My love is perfect
and everlasting. When you feel bruised by someone's rejection
of you, allow My love and acceptance to envelop you. You are
My beloved bride, whom I have pursued with loving-kindness.
Don't run from My love. Instead, praise and thank Me that My
love can meet your deepest needs. Don't bristle at My advances.
Instead, exalt Me and allow Me to soften your heart. I long to
hold you close, where you can hear Me singing over you. Let
Me put a new song in your heart, the song of My love for you. I
have engraved you on the palms of My hands. No matter what

rejection you have faced, My love will never fail. If your friends hurt you, I will be the friend that sticks closer than a sibling. If your mother and father abandon you, I will be a loving Abba Father to you. If your significant other breaks up with you or your spouse leaves you, I will be your comfort and strength. I will never leave you or forsake you. I have betrothed you to Me forever. Even if you pull away from Me, I will continue to pursue you. Praise and thank Me that nothing can separate you from My love. (Jer. 31:3; Zeph. 3:17; Prov. 18:24; Ps. 27:10; Hosea 2:19; Rom. 8:38–39)

Worship Jesus as the lover of your soul. He alone can fill the deepest longings of your heart. Others may reject you, but Jesus never will. In your praise time today, praise God for His love, using the alphabet as a grid. Here is a start:

> *Lord, I praise You because Your love is Awesome.*
> *I praise You because Your love is Boundless.*
> *I praise You because Your love is Compassionate.*

The LORD your God is with you, he is mighty to save. He will take great delight in

you, he will quiet you with his love, he will
rejoice over you with singing. (Zeph. 3:17)

Listen

Download and listen to "How He Loves" performed by
David Crowder Band and "My Soul Sings" performed by
Delirious? As you praise God for how deeply He loves you,
use your imagination to picture Him holding you close to
His heart. Imagine God's eyes as being filled with love for
you. Even if you can't feel His love or have trouble believing
He loves you, praise Him by faith that He does.

Pray

*Thank You, Lord Jesus, for loving me so completely. Only Your
love can truly satisfy the deepest cravings of my soul. I praise
and thank You that even when I experience rejection or disappointment, Your love remains strong. It never fails. I praise You
that as my roots sink deeply into Your love, Your Holy Spirit
will strengthen me with understanding so that I will know how
wide and long and high and deep Your love for me is. As I am*

more and more satisfied by Your love, I will be filled with Your power. I praise You for being able to do in my life more than anything I could ask or imagine! Your love is not conditional on how I behave; instead, You lavish me with Your love, pursuing me relentlessly. Thank You that I never have to wonder what You're thinking about me or worry that You might reject me. Instead, my heart is at rest, knowing that You love me eternally. Thank You for promising to satisfy me each new morning with Your love. (Eph. 3:18–20; 1 John 3:1, 19; Ps. 90:14)

Journal

In what ways have you tangibly experienced the love of God? As you spent time praising God for His love today, what feelings did you experience?

Day 9

I am the resurrection and the life.
He who believes in me will live,
even though he dies;
and whoever lives and believes
in me will never die.
John 11:25–26

The Invitation

I am the resurrection and the life. Allow Me to take your broken
dreams and replace them with new dreams. I am hope alive in
you! When you feel discouraged, praise Me that I am the Hope
Giver. I am able to breathe new life into your soul. When you
feel sad or depressed, look to Me as the One who brings beauty
out of the ashes. Bring Me your praise even when you don't
feel like it. I am working behind the scenes to bring about My
will for your life. When you worship Me, even though you are

walking through trials, it makes My heart sing, and I pour out blessing on your life. I know at times it feels like I am not listening to the desires of your heart. Trust Me, My child. I am listening, and if it is best for you, I will give you what you ask. Praise Me by faith that My plans for your life are far beyond what you can imagine. Watch and see what I will do! (John 11:25; Isa. 61:1–3; James 1:12; Heb. 13:15)

Think about any disappointments you have faced recently. Thank God that He will reshape each dismaying circumstance in your life so that—in the end—it can benefit you. Praise Him for each of the following truths:

- "You intended to harm me, but God intended it for good" (Gen. 50:20).
- "And we know that in all things God works for the good of those who love him, who have been called according to his purpose" (Rom. 8:28).
- "These [trials] have come so that your faith—of greater weight than gold … may be proved genuine" (1 Pet. 1:7).

- "And [I] will make the Valley of Achor [Valley of Tears] a door of hope" (Hosea 2:15).

Listen

Listen to "Desert Song" performed by Hillsong United, "Song of Hope (Heaven Come Down)" performed by Robbie Seay Band, "You Never Let Go" performed by Matt Redman, and "Alive" performed by Natalie Grant. Focus on Jesus as the Hope Giver. Praise Him that He can restore hope, even if your dreams have died.

Pray

Lord Jesus, I praise You for being the Hope Giver. You are the resurrection and the life. How I exalt You that out of death, You bring life; out of disappointment, You bring hope. I praise You that even in these difficult circumstances _____ [name your specific circumstances], *You promise to work for my good. Thank You for being the living hope dwelling inside me, continually present and continually pouring hope into*

my soul. I praise You that when my dreams die, You give new dreams, new life. Thank You that my hope comes from You. (John 11:25; Rom. 8:28; 1 Peter 1:3–4; Ps. 62:5)

Journal

In what areas of your life could you use more hope? As you think about each of these situations, what do you think Jesus is saying to you?

Day 10

I am the LORD, your God,
who takes hold of your right hand
and says to you, Do not fear;
I will help you.
Isaiah 41:13

The Invitation

Don't let fear hold you captive. Be strong and courageous. I will
be with you no matter what you face. I am holding you in My
strong and almighty hands. Praise Me, and as you lift up My
name, courage and peace will rise up in your heart. The chains of
worry and fear will be broken. I am the One who turned the sea
into dry land so that My children could pass through on foot. Sing
and praise My name. Singing and making music lifts your spirits;
praising My name lifts your focus. As you exalt Me, you will find
refuge in Me. I will hide you under the shelter of My wings. My

presence will comfort you, and you will sense Me near you. I will strengthen and help you as you face this day. No matter what difficulties you encounter, My love and faithfulness will surround you. So turn your panic into praise today, My child. (Gal. 5:1; Josh. 1:9; Ps. 66:6; Ps. 46:1; Ps. 90:1; Isa. 41:10; Phil. 4:13)

There is great power and authority in Jesus's name, and it is ours for the asking. Before you turn on the music and begin your praise time today, write down your fears. Then use His various names to praise Jesus. Make it personal by putting the word *my* in front of each name. For example: "Lord, I praise You for being my Prince of Peace." I've listed some of Jesus's names below to get you started. There is a more complete list of the names of Jesus Christ on page 154 in the "Taking It Further" section of this book. Throughout your day, whenever anxious thoughts come into your mind, exalt and claim the name of Jesus Christ over your fear. Praise your way out of panic!

My Advocate—1 John 2:1
The Author and Perfecter of My Faith—Hebrews 12:2
My Bridegroom—Matthew 9:15
My Counselor—Isaiah 9:6

My Deliverer—Romans 11:26

My Doctor/Healer—Luke 5:30–31

My Good Shepherd—John 10:11

My God—John 20:27–28

My Immanuel (God with Us!)—Matthew 1:23

My Prince of Peace—Isaiah 9:6

My Redeemer—Isaiah 59:20

> Have I not commanded you? Be strong and courageous. Do not be terrified; do not be discouraged, for the LORD your God will be with you wherever you go. (Josh. 1:9)

Listen

Listen to "Whom Shall I Fear? (God of Angel Armies)" performed by Chris Tomlin, "I Will Lift My Eyes" performed by Bebo Norman, and "Your Great Name" performed by Natalie Grant. As you listen, worship the Lord by agreeing with the words to each song. Praise Him by faith that you can lay down every fear at the feet of the One who is more than able to calm every anxiety.

Pray

God, You are worthy of all of my praise. How I thank You that because You are my light and salvation, I don't have to fear! I praise You for promising to be my refuge and strength. Even if the waters roar and foam or if the earth shakes and trembles, You promise to hold me. If tornadoes or fires ravish our land, Your grip never loosens. God, there are moments when I feel fearful of _____ [name your fears]. *Thank You that I can declare with the psalmist, "In God I trust; I will not be afraid" (56:11). Thank You for loving my loved ones even more than I do. I exalt You, Lord, as the only One worthy of all of my praise and all of my trust. Be exalted, O God.* (Ps. 27:1; Ps. 46:1, 4–5; Ps. 56:11; Ps. 57:11)

Journal

What did you experience today as you praised God for being your refuge? Imagine Jesus sitting in the room with you. What would He say to you to build your trust in Him?

Day 11

And I will ask the Father,
and he will give you another Counselor
to be with you forever—the Spirit of truth.
The world cannot accept him,
because it neither sees him nor knows him.
But you know him, for he lives
with you and will be in you.
John 14:16–17

The Invitation

I know there are many moments when you feel inadequate.
Voices of self-doubt pummel your mind and leave you para-
lyzed. Reject those voices. I have no doubts about you! I sent
My Spirit to live and dwell in you. Praise Me for that gift. I
have not left you alone in this world; you have a 24/7 compan-
ion. My Holy Spirit empowers you to do what I have called

you to do. When you feel sad, He will comfort you. When you feel confused, He will counsel you. When you feel rebellious, He will convict you. When you feel inadequate, He will equip you. Don't throw away your confidence by allowing the voices of self-doubt to control your thinking. Instead, thank Me that confidence is yours for the asking. It is an assurance the world can't mimic. Only My Spirit can infuse you with the strength to live life with poise and dignity. Celebrate this gift today. (John 14:16–17; Heb. 10:35; John 16:7; 2 Cor. 5:5–6)

Thank God today for the gift of His Spirit. Praise God that His Spirit:

- Counsels you when you don't know what to do. (John 14:16)
- Leads you into all truth. (John 16:13)
- Convicts you when you sin. (John 16:8)
- Encourages you. (Acts 9:31)
- Gives you new life in Christ. (Rom. 8:11)
- Brings you reassurance. (Rom. 8:16)
- Helps you in your weakness. (Rom. 8:26)
- Helps you pray. (Rom. 8:26)

- Empowers you. (Rom. 15:13)
- Cleanses you. (Rom. 15:16)
- Comforts you. (2 Cor. 1:3)
- Gives you confidence. (2 Cor. 5:5–6)
- Assures you of your adoption into God's family. (Gal. 4:6–7)
- Gives you wisdom and revelation. (Eph. 1:17)
- Strengthens and renews you. (Eph. 3:16)

The practice of spiritual breathing can be used to help us remember that we have the Holy Spirit in us. Take a moment right now to do this spiritual exercise. First, exhale while visualizing the stress going out of your body, and then, as you inhale, visualize yourself taking in the breath of the Holy Spirit. Practice this type of breathing all day. In this way, you will be able to remind yourself that the Holy Spirit is ever-present within you, empowering and enabling you to do all you are called to do.

But you will receive power when the Holy Spirit comes on you; and you will be my

witnesses in Jerusalem, and in all Judea and Samaria, and to the ends of the earth. (Acts 1:8)

Listen

Listen to "Rain Down" performed by Jesus Culture, featuring Melissa Howe. Praise Jesus for sending His Spirit, and thank Him in advance that He is more than willing to rain down new confidence into your life. Also listen to "Where the Spirit of the Lord Is" performed by Chris Tomlin.

Pray

Lord Jesus, I praise You for sending Your Spirit. I thank You that I don't have to live my Christian life by my own strength. Thank You that the Spirit is always with me and that He empowers me moment by moment to be the person God designed me to be. It's not by my own power or strength that I accomplish anything. It is by the power of Your Spirit. Thank You that I can live by faith and not by sight, and that I can choose confidence. I praise You that I don't have to "try harder"

to conjure up the fruit of Your Spirit. As I yield to You, Your fruit will grow in my life. Your Word promises me that if I live by Your Spirit, allowing You to live through me, I will not give in to temptation to gratify my own desires. I can live a holy life just by allowing Your Spirit to live through me. Thank You that Your Spirit is transforming me moment by moment into the image of Jesus Christ. (Gal. 5:22; Zech. 4:6; John 15:1–2; 2 Cor. 5:7; 2 Cor. 3:18; Gal. 4:5–7)

Journal

Go back through the list of ways the Holy Spirit helps and empowers us. For which of these are you most thankful? Why?

Day 12

Ah, Sovereign LORD,
you have made the heavens and the earth
by your great power and outstretched arm.
Nothing is too hard for you.

Jeremiah 32:17

The Invitation

I am never shocked, surprised, or caught off guard. I know there are moments in your life when circumstances feel impossible, when you cannot see any solutions to the challenges you are facing. Trust Me in the midst of your difficult moments. Seize them as opportunities to praise Me for My sovereign power. As you thank Me in advance for the solutions I hold, I will enlarge your heart to hold greater faith. At first, focusing on My sovereignty may feel scary, but as you grow more comfortable in your times of praise, it will become a source of strength and comfort.

Recognize how small you are in comparison to Me. This is a form of worship. As you bow before Me, your ability to trust Me will grow. Watch and see what I will do. Nothing is too difficult for Me. Did you catch that? Nothing, absolutely nothing, is too difficult for Me. (Jer. 32:27; Ps. 22:3; Prov. 3:5; Luke 1:37)

Think about your life right now. Are there circumstances that, from a human perspective, seem impossible? Today, focus your praise on God's sovereignty. Proclaim by faith, "God, You are sovereign. I praise You for Your power. Nothing is too hard for You. Though I may not understand Your plans, I will choose to praise You anyway."

> Though the fig tree does not bud and there
> are no grapes on the vines, though the olive
> crop fails and the fields produce no food,
> though there are no sheep in the pen, and
> no cattle in the stalls, yet I will rejoice in the
> Lord, I will be joyful in God my Savior.
> The Sovereign Lord is my strength; he makes
> my feet like the feet of a deer, he enables me
> to go on the heights. (Hab. 3:17–19)

Listen

Listen to "Mighty to Save" and "Hosanna," both performed by Hillsong United, and "Our God" performed by Chris Tomlin. Let the music prompt your praise.

Pray

O Lord, You are the great and awesome God. I praise You by faith for Your sovereign power over _____ [name specific circumstances in your life that feel impossible]. *By faith I praise You, because nothing, absolutely nothing, is too difficult for You. I praise You that I don't need to worry about my life, what I will wear, or what I will eat. I don't need to worry or become anxious over my financial situation, my relationships, my health, or my career. I praise You because You are the Almighty God, and nothing is impossible for You.* (Dan. 9:4, Matt. 6:25, Luke 1:37)

Journal

What impossible situations are you facing today? What did God say to you during your praise time today?

Day 13

Therefore, there is now no condemnation
for those who are in Christ Jesus.

Romans 8:1

The Invitation

My child, you are often weighed down by guilt and shame. I
don't condemn you and neither should you condemn yourself.
Through My abundant grace, you are forgiven because of the
work of My Son on Calvary. All your sins—past, present, and
future—have been forgiven. You are totally okay with Me.
Shame no longer has to haunt you. You are already clean. I
have clothed you in My righteous robe and crowned you with
blessing and beauty. When you are tempted to return to your
old clothes of shame, put on garments of praise instead. As you
worship Me, I will enable you to wear your righteous robe with
confidence. Others will try to manipulate you and make you

feel guilty; don't let them. Listen to My voice alone, and lift your voice in praise. If you exalt Me and look up, your face will no longer be clouded with shame; instead, it will glisten with radiant joy. (Rom. 8:1; Rom. 5:17; John 15:3; Rom. 3:21; Isa. 61:1–3; Ps. 34:5)

If you're physically able, get down on your knees for your praise time today. If you are not physically able to get down on your knees, bow your head and imagine someday bowing down in heaven. When you listen to the praise music, use headphones so you won't be easily distracted. Focus your praise on God's grace and forgiveness. Lay down every burden of guilt, shame, regret, and self-punishment. Imagine yourself clothed in Christ's righteous robe. You look as good to God the Father as His Son, Jesus Christ, does. Celebrate the forgiveness that is yours in Jesus Christ.

> God made him who had no sin to be sin for us, so that in him we might become the righteousness of God. (2 Cor. 5:21)

Listen

Listen to "Like an Avalanche" performed by Hillsong United, "Jesus Paid It All" performed by Kristian Stanfill, "Rescue" performed by Desperation Band, and "My Deliverer" performed by Mandisa,. As you listen, let go of any feelings of shame and allow yourself to relax and rest in God's amazing grace.

Pray

Lord Jesus, I praise You that I am totally right with You! Thank You that I don't have to beat myself up or engage in any form of self-condemnation. All of my sins have been completely atoned for by Your blood. I praise You for having removed my sins far away from me. Your Word tells me You have moved them as far as the east is from the west. You offer me continual compassion and mercy. Thank You that I am clothed in Your righteous robe and no longer have to worry about measuring up. In You, I am good enough. Oh, Lord Jesus, that makes me want to celebrate. I cannot thank You enough. What a gift Your grace is in my life! You are my righteousness, my holiness, and my redemption. (Rom. 3:25; Ps. 103:11–13; Rom. 11:30)

Journal

In what areas of life have you struggled with feeling guilty or ashamed? How do you think praising God might help you let go of shame?

Day 14

Then Jesus declared,
"I am the bread of life.
He who comes to me will never go hungry,
and he who believes in me
will never be thirsty."
John 6:35

The Invitation

You are hungry for so many things: love, affirmation, friend-
ship, success. My child, I am the only One who can meet
your needs completely. I am the Bread of Life and living
water. Yet you often run to other things to satisfy the crav-
ings of your soul. Those other things can become addictions.
Instead of trying to anesthetize the ache in your soul, come
and praise Me. I created you with an ache that only I can
fill. Taste and see that I am good. I fill the hungry and satisfy

the thirsty with good things. Exalt Me! I give you food to nourish and sustain your body and other gifts to delight your soul. But I never meant for you to become obsessed with My gifts. I want to be your obsession. All you are longing for is found in Me. As you praise Me, the cycle of addiction is broken. Delight yourself in Me, and you will find that I can satisfy your cravings. Those who set their appetite on Me will be blessed. (John 6:35; John 4:10; Ps. 34:8; Ps. 107:9; 1 Tim. 6:15 PH; Matt. 5:6)

God is able to meet your deepest longings. One way to praise Him is by agreeing with Him that you need Him more than anything else in your life. Over the next few days, in order to increase your appetite for God, try fasting from some of what you run to for comfort (chocolate cake, coffee, shopping, Facebook, alcohol, etc.). **Please note:** *If you struggle with an addiction to dieting, do not fast from food.*

He has filled the hungry with good things.
(Luke 1:53)

Listen

Listen to "We Are Hungry / I Will Not Be Silent" performed by Jesus Culture and "My Delight Is in You" performed by Christy Nockels. As you listen, express any hunger you are experiencing (hunger for love, affirmation, success, physical touch, or any other hunger) and then praise Jesus by faith that He is able to satisfy every longing of your heart and heal any addiction.

Pray

Lord Jesus, I praise You for being the Bread of Life and the living water. Thank You for quenching my thirst and satiating my hunger. Thank You for being more than able to heal my addictions: _____ [if you have an addiction(s), name it here—this could include overeating, compulsive dieting, shopping, alcohol, coffee, prescription drugs, or other things]. *I praise You that the ache You placed within my heart can only be filled by You. Thank You, Holy Spirit, for enabling me to be disciplined and balanced so that I can enjoy the Father's gifts without becoming obsessed with*

them. I know there are times when I run to _____
[name your addiction(s) here once again] *for comfort, because
I am lonely or bored. I praise You, Holy One, that You are healing my addictions with Your love. Thank You that Your love can
bring comfort and fill the deepest longings of my heart. I will
sing of Your love forever!* (John 6:35; Ps. 107:9; Ps. 63:5; Gal.
5:22; Ps. 63:4)

Journal

What do you turn to when you are lonely, bored, or in
pain? Think back to your childhood. What were some of
the messages you received about these things when you were
growing up? As you praised Jesus for being your Bread of
Life, what did He say to you about some of the longings or
addictions you have?

Day 15

The one Jesus loved.
John 20:2

The Invitation

You have significance simply because I love you. You are My beloved child. That is your identity. Don't measure your value in terms of how successful you are or what roles you play. You are valuable because I have declared you precious and honored. When life feels mundane and you are caught up in laundry, work, or cooking, it's easy to doubt your importance in My kingdom. Nothing could be further from the truth. When feelings of insignificance torment you, come and praise Me. As you worship Me, your identity becomes more firmly rooted in Me, rather than in who you know or what you do. Thank Me for the price I paid for you. You are worth everything to Me. When you praise Me, you are more

able to let go of worries about your worth and efforts to try to prove yourself. Always remember that you are a royal priest or priestess with a divine calling in My kingdom. It doesn't get any better than that! (1 John 3:1; Isa. 43:4; Eph. 1:4; 1 Cor. 6:20; 1 Peter 2:9)

Focus your praise time on the truth that you have value and worth as God's beloved child. Praise God that He calls you precious and honored. Because of Jesus Christ, your significance is ensured for all eternity. Praise Him that you have a divine calling as a royal priest or priestess.

> You are precious and honored in my sight,
> and … I love you. (Isa. 43:4)

Listen

Listen to "All the Poor and Powerless" performed by All Sons & Daughters. As you listen, praise Jesus that He has a special place in His heart for the poor and powerless, the bloody and bruised, the messy and marginalized.

Pray

Lord Jesus, thank You that my identity and worth is firmly rooted in You. My job doesn't define me, my relationships don't define me, and my various roles don't define me. I praise You for declaring me holy and dearly loved. You paid the highest price for my soul. How I thank You that I have value and significance in You. I am Your masterpiece, and You have gifted me uniquely for the roles You desire for me to play in Your kingdom. Thank You that I don't need to compare my gifts to the gifts of others in order to feel special. In Your kingdom, I am a royal priest/ priestess. I praise You that I am a coheir with Christ and have inherited every blessing through Him. (Col. 3:12; 1 Cor. 6:12; Eph. 2:10; Isa. 43:4; Rom. 8:17)

Journal

Think through your different roles (child, friend, spouse, parent, teacher, musician, and so on). Why might it be harmful for you to define yourself in terms of these roles? How would your life be different if you defined yourself as "the one Jesus loves"? What did you experience today in your time of praise?

Day 16

I have called you friends,
for everything that I learned from my Father
I have made known to you.
John 15:15

The Invitation

I have invited you to be My intimate friend. When you feel
lonely and long for companionship, come and praise Me. I am
continually pursuing you, and it delights Me when you respond
to My love with thanksgiving. Nothing gives Me greater joy than
spending time with you. Before I created the world, I chose you to
be My close friend. I sent My Holy Spirit as a seal of My commit-
ment to our relationship. In your world, friendships go through
changing seasons, and feelings of closeness ebb and flow. I know
there are times when even those closest to you feel distant or too
busy. This is not so with Me. I always have time for you and will

be forever faithful. When you praise Me, you are more able to hear how My heart longs to spend time with you. Relax with Me; let go of worries that you aren't good enough. Enjoy our friendship today! (John 15:15; John 14:15–20; Prov. 18:24)

As humans, we long for close friends, and we can have no better friend than the friend we have in Jesus. Focus your praise today on the deep friendship He offers you. Jesus will never leave you or ditch you. He wants to be your confidante for all eternity. He longs for you to share the deepest places of your heart with Him. When you spend time in His presence, you are more able to hear His heart.

> Greater love has no one than this, that one
> lay down his life for his friends. You are my
> friends. (John 15:13–14)

Listen

Listen to "Friend of God" performed by Israel & New Breed and "Jesus, Friend of Sinners" performed by Casting Crowns

Pray

Lord Jesus, thank You for inviting me to be Your friend. I will exalt You forever, because You laid down Your life for me. I can't even fathom that kind of love. I thank You for being the greatest friend I will ever have. I don't have to hide anything from You because You know me completely, and yet You still persist in pursuing my friendship. You understand when I feel lonely or left out. You understand when I feel insecure or embarrassed. Thank You for Your unconditional acceptance. I am so grateful that You promise never to leave me or forsake me. Thank You for always being available and never too busy to be with me. I praise You that the moments when I feel lonely are moments when I can lean into Your friendship more deeply. I worship You because even when I can't feel it, Your presence is always with me. (John 15:13–15; Heb. 13:5; Ps. 63:8; Ps. 139:7)

Journal

Think about your friendships. Are there times when you feel lonely or that you aren't connecting well with others? Have there been times in your relationship with Jesus when

He has met your deepest longings for a close friendship? If so, write about those times. If not, spend some time praying and reflecting on how you might develop this kind of a relationship with Him. What kinds of things could you do to make Jesus your closest friend?

Day 17

And he will be called
Wonderful Counselor, Mighty God,
Everlasting Father, Prince of Peace.
Isaiah 9:6

The Invitation

Crown Me as your Prince of Peace. I continually offer you the
gift of serenity, even in the midst of chaos. Praise Me, and I
will quiet your heart. My peace is not based on perfect circum-
stances. It is a peace that comes from living in My presence.
When you worry about what might happen, you sabotage your
tranquility. So don't let your mind go to worry. Discipline your
thoughts. Reign them in. The moment you begin to worry, praise
Me instead. My child, you have a choice about whether you
allow My peace to rule in your heart. Thank Me that I lovingly
reign over every circumstance in your life. As you praise Me,

My Spirit strengthens your heart to trust Me more. This is the best antidote to anxiety. Worship Me as the Lord of peace, and I will envelop you with supernatural calm. (Isa. 9:6; Matt. 6:34; Col. 3:15; 2 Thess. 3:16)

Today, focus your praise on Jesus as the Prince of Peace. It's easy to worry and feel anxious, isn't it? When we choose to praise God, the Holy Spirit calms our anxious hearts and gives us the ability to trust God more fully. Today, don't allow your mind to entertain what-ifs. Every time an anxious thought threatens to sabotage your peace, immediately start to praise God.

> Do not be anxious about anything, but in everything, by prayer and petition, with thanksgiving, present your requests to God. And the peace of God, which transcends all understanding, will guard your hearts and your minds in Christ Jesus. (Phil. 4:6–7)

Listen

Listen to "Came to My Rescue" performed by Hillsong United and "Praise You in This Storm" performed by Casting Crowns. As you listen, praise God that He comes to your rescue and offers you peace even in the storms of life.

Pray

Lord Jesus, I worship You as my Prince of Peace. Thank You that I can trust You with my life. Your Word tells me I don't have to worry about what I'll eat or what I'll wear. You promise that even when bad things happen I can allow peace to rule in my mind, because You love me and will work things out for good. I also don't have to worry about my loved ones _____ *[name each one], because each one is held in Your loving hands. Lord, worry doesn't accomplish anything, so teach me to praise You by faith. Thank You that I can turn every concern over to You, because You care so deeply for me. I bow before You, Lord Jesus. I lay down every worry at Your feet. I place every care on You, because You are strong enough and loving enough to carry my burdens. Hallelujah!*

You are the Lord God Almighty, and You reign over every situation I feel concerned about. I praise You that You reign over

_____ [name every person you are worried about and every situation you feel anxious about]. *I praise You that I can trust You. You are the King of Kings and Lord of Lords. Thank You for being my Prince of Peace.* (Matt. 6:25–27; Col. 3:15; 1 Peter 5:7; Ps. 55:22; Rev. 19:6, 16)

Journal

Spend some time journaling about each of the situations and people you feel anxious about. Then write a prayer of praise that you can place all these worries in the hands of Jesus, trusting that He will take care of each situation and person.

Day 18

Do not judge,
and you will not be judged.
Do not condemn,
and you will not be condemned.
Forgive, and you will be forgiven.
Luke 6:37

The Invitation

Praise Me for the people who drive you crazy and are difficult to love. Thank Me for their annoying habits and irritating idiosyncrasies. I can use these people to mold and shape you into My image. Thank Me that I am able to meet your needs even when others let you down. Praise Me that I am able to transform their lives as well as yours. Just as My Son died for you, My child, He died for them. When you judge and condemn them, your attitude breaks My heart. I love the very

ones you condemn. Praise Me for the good things I am teaching you through your most difficult relationships. Thank Me for the opportunity to offer grace to those who offend you and forgiveness to those who hurt you. You become more like Me every time you offer mercy instead of judgment. When you dare to praise Me for the difficult people in your life, I receive honor and glory, and you receive blessing. As you look into My face and worship Me, My love shines through you. (Matt. 7:1; Rom. 8:28; Matt. 6:14; 1 Peter 3:9)

Today, praise God for the difficult people in your life and how He is using them to shape you. I know this will be hard, but if you will do this, the Holy Spirit will soften your heart and help you forgive these people. Forgiveness is not something natural. It is a supernatural work of the Spirit in our lives. Praise Him by faith that He will empower you to forgive.

> Do not repay evil with evil or insult with insult, but with blessing, because to this you were called so that you may inherit a blessing. (1 Peter 3:9)

Listen

Listen to "Losing" performed by Tenth Avenue North and "Oh Great Merciful God" performed by Ben and Noelle.

Pray

Lord Jesus, I thank You for the difficult people in my life. Thank You for _____ *[name specific people]. I praise You that although they irritate me, misunderstand me, or spread rumors about me, You are using them to refine my faith and to teach me about forgiveness. I know that as I thank You for them, You will set me free from judging them and will empower me to forgive them. Thank You that even when I feel angry with them, You empower me to refrain from pouring out my anger. God, it feels impossible to love those who have hurt me deeply, but I praise You that nothing is impossible with You. I praise You that as I struggle to love these people, You promise to be my refuge. If at any point I feel overwhelmed, I can hide in You.* (1 Peter 1:6–7; Ps. 37:8; Luke 1:37; Ps. 73:28; Ps. 17:8)

Journal

What did God say to you during your praise time today with regard to the difficult people in your life?

Day 19

I will be a Father to you,
and you will be my sons and daughters,
says the Lord Almighty.
2 Corinthians 6:18

The Invitation

I am your Abba. Your name is engraved on the palm of My hand. You are My precious and dearly loved child. I love you beyond anything you can imagine! Before time began, I chose the very family into which you were born. I know that My decisions are sometimes difficult for you to understand, but trust Me. I can turn the messiest life story into the most beautiful of stories. As you were growing up, I was holding you close to My heart. Even in your darkest moments, I never left your side. Human parents fail. Even the best earthly parents are not perfect and can leave emotional scars. If you allow Me to do so, I can heal

your wounds. Fractured hearts are made whole in My presence. When you praise Me as your loving Abba, you unleash My healing presence. I will give you a quieted soul like a child who is completely comfortable with her mother. Praise opens your heart to experience My love and nurturing more completely! (1 John 3:1; Ps. 27:10; Ps. 131:2)

Focus your praise today on God as your perfect, loving parent. Scripture teaches us that He loves us beyond the most nurturing mother. If you suffered abuse as a child, know I am praying for you as I write this. I understand and have been there as well. But as I learned to praise God every day, He began to heal those wounds. I'm confident that He will do the same for you as you bring Him your praise and thanksgiving.

> Never again will they hunger; never again will they thirst. The sun will not beat upon them, nor any scorching heat. For the Lamb at the center of the throne will be their shepherd; he will lead them to springs of living water. And God will wipe away every tear from their eyes. (Rev. 7:16–17)

Listen

Listen to "Broken Hallelujah" performed by Mandisa and "Hold Me Together" performed by Ben and Noelle. As you listen, praise God that He was with you in your childhood. If tears come, allow them to flow. Sometimes our worship is best expressed in weeping.

Pray

My Father, You are the One who hears every cry of my heart and bends down to listen. I praise You for tenderly loving me as a mother loves her infant. I thank You for the family into which I was born. Thank You that although I experienced _____ _____ [name hardships here: verbal abuse, neglect, harsh punishment, sexual abuse, spiritual abuse, forms of legalism, etc.], *You were always with me. You never left. Thank You for promising to wipe away every tear. You promise to heal, redeem, and restore all the broken places of my heart. Thank You. I praise You, Abba, that You are able to heal any abandonment, depression, perfectionism, or other emotional issues linked to my childhood. Thank You*

for making all things—even difficulties in childhood—work together for my good. (Ps. 86:1 NLV; Isaiah 49:15; Isaiah 66:13; Isaiah 61:1–3; Romans 8:28)

Journal

Please note: *Today's journal exercise will require more time than usual. You may want to postpone it until you have adequate time.*

Take some extended time today and journal about your childhood. It can be helpful to create a time line from birth to age twenty. List both the good things you experienced and the hard things. How has your childhood impacted who you are today? How has God redeemed and healed the difficult memories? Finish by writing a prayer of praise to God for being your Abba and for redeeming any pain you experienced in childhood.

Day 20

Come with me
by yourselves to a quiet place
and get some rest.
Mark 6:31

The Invitation

Time pressure and deadlines pull you in many directions, and the adrenaline rush of a busy life can be addicting. Your mind needs rest and renewal. Come and worship Me in a quiet place, and there you will find refreshment for your spirit, soul, and body. Allow Me to show you a healthier pace for your life. Praise Me for establishing the boundaries of twenty-four-hour days. Your body cannot handle going nonstop. When you praise Me, you find renewal in the shadow of My wings. People, projects, and promotions are not as important as your time with Me. As you lift your focus off your deadlines and onto My face, I will

help you prioritize your tasks, and you will feel less stress. The best prescription for reducing tension is time spent worshipping Me. There, in that sacred sanctuary, I will soothe your soul. (Ps. 74:17; Ps. 91:1; Jer. 31:25; Matt. 11:28)

Today, during your praise time, don't put pressure on yourself to think of things to praise God for. Instead, let the praise music simply quiet and refresh your soul. Part of worship is allowing yourself to rest in God's presence. If you have a job outside the home, you may be facing deadlines that feel insurmountable. If you are at home with toddlers and small children, you may feel pulled in a thousand directions. When your to-do list comes to mind, purposefully release it into the Lord's hands. Allow yourself to receive the rest and refreshment that comes from worshiping Him.

Be still, and know that I am God. (Ps. 46:10)

Listen

Listen to "Meet with Me" performed by Ten Shekel Shirt, "I Love Your Presence" performed by Bethel Live and featuring

Jenn Johnson, and "The More I Seek You" performed by Kari Jobe.

Pray

Lord, at times it feels as though there are not enough hours in the day. I bow before You as the creator of time. Thank You for the boundary of time. I praise You because You lived and worked on this earth and confined Yourself to a twenty-four-hour day. Because of that, You understand the time crunches I am facing. Thank You for modeling an unhurried rhythm of life even though those around You wanted You to meet their needs. I lay at Your feet every demand, deadline, and difficulty I am facing. Some of the deadlines I am up against feel impossible, but "with Your help I can advance against a troop and with [You] I can scale a wall." I thank You that You will bless me and help me succeed at the things You have called me to do. I praise You that You will help me to order my day according to Your wisdom and that Your favor will rest on the work of my hands. Thank You for what You will accomplish through me this day. (Mark 1:32–38; Ps. 18:29; Ps. 20:4; Ps. 90:12, 17)

Journal

In which areas of life are you feeling most productive? The least productive? What did you sense the Lord saying to you during your praise time today?

Day 21

I have told you these things,
so that in me you may have peace.
In this world you will have trouble.
But take heart!
I have overcome the world.
John 16:33

The Invitation

The world feels dark at times. The news is filled with reports of terrorism, neighborhood violence, natural catastrophes, and a failing economy. My child, in this world you will have trouble. When adversity strikes and it feels as though evil is winning, praise Me that I have overcome the world. Satan hates it when you praise Me. He flees at the sound of My great name. So use My name wisely. Shout My name, sing My name, and declare the power of My name over your life. When you praise the name of Jesus, the Enemy is

defeated, and your faith is strengthened. I have won the victory over evil and have declared you victorious as well. You overcome evil by declaring the word of your testimony. Your testimony, My child, is simply the story of how your life changed when you placed your trust in Me. You also overcome evil by proclaiming the power that is in the blood of the Lamb. Salvation and glory and power belong to Me and Me alone. As you praise Me, I will strengthen you to persevere, even in the face of evil. (John 16:33; John 14:1; Phil. 2:9–11; Rev. 12:11; Rev. 19:1)

Today focus on Jesus Christ as the victor over evil. Here are some helpful passages from Revelation to meditate on in your praise time: Revelation 5:9–10, 12–13; 7:10–12; 11:17; and 19:1, 6–8.

But thanks be to God! He gives us the victory
through our Lord Jesus Christ. (1 Cor. 15:57)

Listen

Listen to "Overcome" performed by Jeremy Camp and "God of This City" performed by Chris Tomlin. As you praise and

worship today, allow renewed faith that Jesus Christ does indeed reign rise up in your heart. He will be the everlasting victor over evil.

Pray

Lord Jesus, I praise You, because You are the Lord God Almighty. You are the One who is and was and is to come. Worthy are You, Lamb of God, because You were slain to receive power and wealth and wisdom and strength and honor and glory and praise! You have overcome the evil one by Your death and resurrection. Evil holds no power over me because I belong to You. I am so grateful for the victory that You won, not only for me but for all of creation. I praise You, Lord Jesus, that when You return, there will never again be hunger, terrorism, violence, or evil of any kind. You will wipe away every tear, and forever You will sit on Your throne and reign. Thank You for empowering me to persevere in hope and righteousness until You come again. How I praise You that someday every knee will bow before You and every tongue will confess that You are Lord. I exalt You, Lord Jesus, for You deserve all the honor and glory. (Rev. 11:17; Rev. 2:26; Phil. 2:10–11)

Journal

Think through the news reports you have heard over the last week. What feelings did those news reports stir up in you? Write about those feelings in your journal. Then finish by writing out a prayer of praise that Jesus is the victor and that someday He will overcome all evil.

Day 22

And my God will meet all your needs
according to his glorious
riches in Christ Jesus.
To our God and Father be
glory for ever and ever.
Amen.
Philippians 4:19–20

The Invitation

I am God, and I abundantly provide for your needs. When the economy is failing and job loss statistics rise, many grow fearful. My child, don't give in to the temptation to doubt My ability to give you what you need. Instead praise Me for being the God Who Provides. Whether you are doing well financially or struggling to pay the bills, whether you have a job or are unemployed, train yourself to give Me thanks in all things.

Thank Me for small gifts as well as big gifts. I love it when My children say, "Thank You." Gratitude opens the door to greater blessing.

Don't set your hope on wealth. It is uncertain and rises and falls with the stock market. Instead, praise Me. Watch and see how I provide for all your needs. I provided manna in the wilderness and water in the desert for My children. I provided the lamb for Abraham on mount Moriah. This was a beautiful foreshadowing of what I would do later in history by providing My own Son, Jesus Christ, as the ultimate sacrifice for all that you need. Trust Me, My child. Everything you have needed, I have provided. (Mal. 3:10; Matt. 6:33; Psalm 11:4–5; Heb. 13:15; Isa. 43:20; Gen. 22:8; 2 Cor. 12:9; Phil. 4:11–12)

God is the God Who Provides. Praise Him that your financial situation or job situation is not catching Him off guard. Thank Him that He has promised to provide for your needs. If you don't struggle financially, thank and praise God for His blessings. Thank Him that He will provide in the future for every need, even those you are not aware of at this time.

The eyes of all look to you, and you give them their food at the proper time. You open your hand and satisfy the desires of every living thing. (Ps. 145:15–16)

Listen

Listen to "Blessed Be Your Name" performed by Matt Redman.

Pray

I exalt You, God; You are my King. Sometimes fear grips my heart as I look around and see what's happening in the economy in our country and around the world. Thank You that I can trust You to provide for my needs. You are the God of abundance who consistently provides. Thank You that stock-market crashes, job losses, and financial disasters can't separate me from Your love. I praise You, because You grant peace during times of financial upheaval, and You promise to satisfy me with food that comes directly from Your hand. I extol You, Lord, because none of my needs catch You off guard. Thank You for teaching

me how to be content, no matter what my circumstances. I am so grateful that whether I have a little or a lot, You provide opportunities for me to trust You. Thank You that You are the Lord of my finances, and that as I place You first in my giving, saving, and spending, You will pour out more blessing than I can imagine. (Ps. 145:1; Phil. 4:19; Rom. 8:36–38; Ps. 147:14; Phil. 4:11; Matt. 6:33)

Journal

Think through your financial situation. How might praising God consistently help you move toward contentment and freedom from worry about finances? Did God speak to you about your finances during your praise time today? If so, what did He say?

Day 23

Therefore, I urge you, brothers,
in view of God's mercy,
to offer your bodies as living sacrifices,
holy and pleasing to God—
which is your spiritual act of worship.
Do not conform any longer
to the pattern of this world,
but be transformed by the
renewing of your mind.
Romans 12:1–2

The Invitation

My child, all worship begins with open hands and bowed knees. I desire absolute supremacy in your life. The things you cling to most tightly become idols that you worship instead of worshipping Me. Open your hands, and let go. I know it

can feel terrifying for you to surrender. But when you place your life, and the lives of those you love, completely in My hands, I am able to accomplish My perfect will through you. You have not been placed here on the earth to live your own life and seek your own fulfillment. You are here to glorify Me, to have My life lived through you. The only way for this to happen is for you to join Me in My crucifixion. Praise Me that as you die to your selfish desires, I am reborn in you and the power of My resurrection becomes evident in your life. Then, and only then, can you be the person I have called you to be. Only then can I give all of Myself to you. In the end, that is your greatest desire. (Rev. 19:10; Col. 1:18; Gal. 2:20; Heb. 11:17–19)

As you worship today, get down on your knees if you can. What is the hardest thing for you to surrender? As you listen to the praise music listed in today's Listen section, imagine God inviting you to place in His hands your spouse or your desire for a spouse, your children or your desire for children, your career or your desire for a career, your friends, your home, and your health. Then when you are ready, open your hands to symbolically surrender. Place

everything in the Lord's hands and acknowledge that He alone is worthy of all your praise.

> I have been crucified with Christ and I no
> longer live, but Christ lives in me. (Gal. 2:20)

Listen

Listen to "Arms Open Wide" performed by Hillsong United and "At the Cross" and "I Surrender," both performed by Hillsong Live.

Pray

Lord Jesus, I bow before You. You are the holy and exalted One, and the only One who is worthy of all my praise. I surrender my longings, my spouse, my children, my parents, my friendships, my finances, my dreams, and my home. Take my entire life. I give You my body, my health, my emotions, my gifts and abilities, and my strengths and weaknesses. Nothing that I may be tempted to hold on to compares to You. I worship and praise You above all else. Thank You for inviting me to place all that

in Your hands when I follow You. Thank You for promising to use me for Your glory, and that when I surrender everything to You, I will find true life in the end. I praise You for promising that I will receive a hundred times more than anything I could ever give up for Your name. I worship You, Lord Jesus. (Matt. 10:37–38; Matt. 19:29)

Journal

What are you most terrified to surrender to God? How might praising God fill you with enough courage to open your hands and let go?

Day 24

I am the LORD, who heals you.
Exodus 15:26

The Invitation

When you are suffering, whether physically, emotionally, or spiritually, call on Me for healing. I am the Lord who heals you. Too often, My child, you hesitate to ask Me for healing for fear that you will be disappointed. But this doesn't protect you; it only prevents you from experiencing all that I desire to give you. Instead, praise Me for My healing power. Healing may come in this lifetime, or I may call you to heaven for your final and complete healing. Either way, I want you to trust Me. I am filled with compassion for you, and My presence will always be with you. Exalt Me as your Messiah who rises with healing in His wings. As you praise Me, I will draw you deeper into My healing power; memories, emotions, and

bodies are all healed in My presence. Even though you do not always understand My decisions about healing, will you dare to praise Me anyway? Within the scope of eternity, weeping only lasts for a short time, and joy comes in the morning. Someday there will be an end to all physical and emotional suffering. (Ex. 15:26; Mark 10:51; Luke 7:22; Mal. 4:2; Ps. 30:5)

In your worship time today, focus on Jesus's healing power. Too often we hesitate to ask Him for the very healing He desires to bring us. Praise Him that He longs to heal your memories, emotions, addictions, and body. Praise Him for His healing power in the lives of those you love.

By his wounds you have been healed.
(1 Peter 2:24)

Listen

Listen to "Healing" performed by Ben and Noelle and "Healer" performed by Kari Jobe.

Pray

Holy Healer, I praise You for Your healing. Thank You that I am made whole in Your presence and that You desire to heal my body, soul, and spirit. I lay before You these needs of healing _____ [name any physical ailments, emotional pain, painful memories, addictions, or compulsions], *and I praise You for the healing You will bring. Thank You that I can call on the elders in my church and other mentors in my life to pray on my behalf for healing. How thankful I am that I can trust You, even though I don't always understand Your ways. I praise You that as I worship You, You promise to turn my valley of weeping into a place of abundant blessing. Thank You that You are a God who restores health and heals wounds. As You heal me, You will bring opportunities for me to share the healing work You have accomplished in my life for Your glory. How I praise You!* (Mal. 4:2; James 5:16; Ps. 84:5–6; Jer. 30:17; Ps. 107:15, 20)

Journal

In what areas of life have you experienced God's healing presence? Write a prayer of praise for the healing He has already brought to your life.

Day 25

And we know that in all things
God works for the good of
those who love him,
who have been called according
to his purpose.
For those God foreknew he also
predestined to be conformed to
the likeness of his Son.
Romans 8:28–29

The Invitation

I take even your mistakes and failures and turn them around for
good so that you might become more like My Son, Jesus Christ.
When you fail, confess your sin, but don't wallow in shame.
Instead, praise Me that I forgive and use that failure for good in
your life. I am well aware of your frailty and am mindful of how

easily you make mistakes. I can use your weaknesses to humble you so that you are more open to My grace and mercy. Thank Me that sin cannot be your master, because you died to sin and now live for Me. I am the sovereign ruler of your life. Your faults can lead you to deeper dependence on Me. I am not looking for perfection but for perseverance in becoming conformed to the image of My Son. Praise Me that you don't have to live according to some rulebook; instead, you can enjoy a life enveloped in grace. (Rom. 8:28–29; Heb. 12:10; 1 John 1:9; Rom. 6:14; Ps. 103:14)

Praise God today for the way He has used even your weaknesses for His glory. Thank Him that even your failures are a part of the "all things" that He promises to use for good in your life. As you move throughout the rest of your day, any time you fail or make a mistake, immediately praise God that He is able to take the mistake and turn it around for good in your life.

> But thanks be to God, who always leads us in triumphal procession in Christ and through us spreads everywhere the fragrance of the knowledge of him. (2 Cor. 2:14)

Listen

Listen to "Amazing Grace (My Chains Are Gone)" performed by Chris Tomlin and "We Will Run" performed by Gungor.

Pray

God, it's so easy for me to become frustrated with myself. I long for Your perfection. I exalt You, because You invite me to share in Your holiness. Thank You for hearing my cry for mercy. You restore me and cleanse me. God, You are amazing! Even my failures and mistakes _____ [name any failures and mistakes that come to your mind] *are included in the "all things" that You work out for my good. How I praise You for never giving up on me, no matter how many times I fail. You are compassionate and understanding. You know each one of my weaknesses. Lord Jesus, thank You for being my Savior, for granting me repentance, and for teaching me Your truth. I am astounded that all of my limitations are not only covered by Your grace but also used for Your glory. What a blessing! Even when I wander from You, You come looking for me. You pursue*

me continually. Oh Lord, I am so grateful that You are so faith-ful. (Rom. 8:28–29; Ps 6:9; 2 Tim. 2:25–26; 2 Tim. 2:13)

Journal

In what areas of your life have you seen God take a failure of yours, turn it around for your good, and then use it for His glory? Describe what God did in each of these areas.

Day 26

The Invitation

Come, My beloved child, worship Me as the God who bends down to listen. Praise Me that I am always attentive to your voice. Even before you can verbalize the words, I know your longings. I am present in your every need, so don't be afraid to ask Me for the desires of your heart. As a loving Father, I love to ask you, "What do you want Me to do for you?" When you thank Me in advance for the answer I will give to your prayers, you demonstrate that you have faith that I will meet your needs. I invite you to come into My presence with

boldness, believing that I can do all that you have asked me to do. When you choose to delight yourself in Me, I shape your will so that My desires for your life become your desires for your life. I am honored when you ask Me and then thank Me with confidence. Seek My presence, and you will find Me. (Ps. 86:1 NLV; 1 Peter 3:12; Mark 10:51; Heb. 4:16; Ps. 37:4; Matt. 7:7)

Today, praise God that He is always attentive to your voice and that you can come boldly into His throne room at any time. He invites you to ask big! Think through the different requests that have been on your heart over the last few weeks. Make a list if it helps you focus. Then, go back through your list one by one and praise God for the answer He will give for each request. Thank Him that He is moving in each of the situations you listed and that His heart is delighted that you came to Him for help.

> For the eyes of the Lord are on the righteous and his ears are attentive to their prayer. (1 Peter 3:12)

Listen

Listen to "Hear Us from Heaven" performed by Jared Anderson.

Pray

I love You, Father, because You invite me to come boldly into Your presence at any time and to bring my requests to You. I exalt You because You love the sound of my voice. How I praise You for bending down to listen and for delighting in answering my prayers. Thank You for hearing every cry of my heart, whether the issue is big or small. You invite me to pray without ceasing and to pray continually. Thank You for never rushing me when I am talking with You. Instead, You invite me to pour out every detail of my heart, and You lovingly and attentively listen. You promise that if I ask, it will be given to me, and that if I seek, I will find You. I exalt You, Lord Jesus, because You have invited me to use the authority of Your name when I lay my requests before God, the Father. You intercede for me before the Father. Holy Spirit, I praise You because sometimes I don't even know how to pray about a situation, but You translate my

requests to the Father. I am so thankful because You literally groan for the concerns I have on my heart. How amazing it is to realize that each member of the Trinity—Father, Son, and Holy Spirit—is helping me in my prayer life. Thank You that I don't have to try harder to pray eloquently; I only need to show up and talk with You. (Heb. 4:6; Ps. 86:1 NLV; Matt. 7:7; 1 Peter 3:12; 1 Thess. 5:17; Heb. 7:25; Rom. 8:26–27)

Journal

Imagine that Jesus is sitting in the room with you. He looks you tenderly in the eye and gently asks, "What would you like Me to do for you?" How would you answer?

Day 27

Trust in the LORD with all your heart
and lean not on your own understanding;
in all your ways acknowledge him,
and he will make your paths straight.
Proverbs 3:5–6

The Invitation

Trust Me by yielding control to Me. Worship Me by allowing
Me to direct your paths. My child, you try so hard to control
your world and often give in to compulsive planning in an
effort to anticipate every scenario. This is exhausting. You have
many plans, but My purposes will prevail. When unexpected
changes come into your day, praise Me that I am in sovereign
control of your world. Your offering of thanksgiving allows Me
to shape and mold you into a more flexible person, someone
who lives in complete dependence on Me. Open your heart

and allow Me to lead you today. I will guide you, but only as you yield control to Me. Those who praise Me give up control and have no fear of bad news; their heart is steadfastly trusting in Me. Their heart is secure, because as they worship Me, their trust in Me grows. (Prov. 3:5–6; Prov. 19:21; Ps. 23:3; Ps. 112:7–8)

God is the Blessed Controller of all things. Nothing in your day will catch Him off guard. Throughout today practice saying, "Lord, I trust You." Thank Him in advance for every unexpected circumstance and every interruption that will occur. As you do these things, the Holy Spirit will strengthen your heart to trust God more fully.

> Your attitude should be the same as that of Christ Jesus: Who, being in very nature God, did not consider equality with God something to be grasped, but made himself nothing, taking the very nature of a servant, being made in human likeness. (Phil. 2:5–7)

Listen

Listen to "Trust" performed by Sixpence None the Richer and "You Hold My World" performed by Israel Houghton. As you enter God's presence, open your hands as a symbolic act of allowing Him to control your whole day.

Pray

Lord, I bow before You as the Blessed Controller of all things. I confess that I often struggle with wanting to be in charge of the details in my life. I feel so much more secure when the day goes as I have planned, but I realize You want to shape me into a more flexible display of Your glory. I praise You that I can trust You with every unexpected circumstance, every unforeseen interruption, and every plan that goes awry. Thank You that through the power of Your Holy Spirit I can open my hands and offer you a continual sacrifice of praise. I am so grateful that I don't have to be in charge of my life; I can simply trust You and follow as You lead me through each day.

I praise You that as I yield more and more of my life to the authority of Your Holy Spirit, I will be less tempted to try to

control my own world. Thank You that I don't have to strive for control, but instead, I can let go and allow Your Spirit to produce Your fruit in my life. I am so grateful that if I abide in You, I can accept every interruption or unexpected event as passing through Your loving, almighty hands. Lord, I praise You for Your unseen purposes in my life. (1 Tim. 6:15 PH; Heb. 13:15; Ps. 23:3; Gal. 5:16, 22; John 15:5)

Journal

Spend a few minutes reflecting. Are you a planner? Do you ever struggle with control issues? How flexible are you when your plans suddenly change? How do you handle interruptions? What does it look like for you to let go and yield all control to God?

Day 28

Am I now trying to win the
approval of men, or of God?
Or am I trying to please men?
If I were still trying to please men,
I would not be a servant of Christ.
Galatians 1:10

The Invitation

My child, come and praise Me for the freedom that is yours in
Me. I have called you to live without the burden of keeping
others happy. Don't worry so much about what others think.
If you let their expectations drive you, you will live in bondage
to them. Their opinions become like chains, keeping you from
experiencing My love. The way to break free from bondage is to
worship Me alone. My child, I bought your freedom with My
blood. Live to please Me alone. I came to give you life, abundant

and free. Only as you praise Me will I give you a single focus and the ability to hear My voice above the cacophony of other voices in your life. (Prov. 29:25; Eph. 5:8–10; 1 Thess. 5:18; John 10:10; Jer. 32:39)

As you enter the presence of the Lord today, lay aside the expectations of other people. Focus your praise on the freedom you have in Christ. Thank God that His expectations for you are simple and uncomplicated. As you spend time praising Him, the shackles of worrying about others' opinions will fall off.

> It is for freedom that Christ has set us free.
> Stand firm, then, and do not let yourselves
> be burdened again by the yoke of slavery.
> (Gal. 5:1)

Listen

Listen to "In Christ Alone" performed by Travis Cottrell and "Exalted Alone" by Shannon Wexelberg.

Pray

Lord Jesus, I am so thankful that You are at work in my life and that You will continue to be so until I reach heaven. As I yield to Your power, You are able to set me free from old patterns of people pleasing. Thank You that You are able to set my heart at rest and untangle the knots in my stomach when I can't keep everyone happy. I praise You that even when others are disappointed in me, You are still completely pleased with me. I can feel secure in Your acceptance. When I let others down, it gives You the opportunity to work in their lives for Your glory. Thank You for the Holy Spirit who lives inside me and who can alert me when I am falling into old patterns that will once again place me in bondage to others. I praise You that You will help me discern what is best for my life as I learn to live my life for Your applause alone. (Phil. 1:6; 2 Tim. 1:14; Phil. 1:9–11)

Journal

Think of a time when you've disappointed others. How did God use that in their lives and in yours? How might praising God heal your need to keep everyone happy?

Day 29

You were slain,
and with your blood you
purchased men for God
from every tribe and language
and people and nation.
Revelation 5:9

The Invitation

Exalt and honor Me, Jesus Christ, the Lamb of God. I am at work not only in your life but also around the world. In every nation, tribal group, and tiny cluster of people, I am inviting men and women into My love and grace. Join the crescendo of praise that is circling the globe. As My children learn to praise Me, revival will sweep the nations. My glory will be displayed all around the earth. I have anointed you to be part of this great revival and to bring My message of salvation to the ends of the

earth. Exalt Me as the God who has a heart for every people group. I died for the sins of the whole world. As you exalt Me, I will enlarge your heart to embrace what I am doing globally. You will find yourself loving and interceding for people from all over the world. My desire is for all to come to repentance so that no one would die without hearing of My love. Worship Me as the answer to the world's problems. Praise Me that I have gifted you uniquely to join Me in speaking My message of grace to the world. Praise Me that someday you will gather with people from every corner of the world to worship before the Lamb. (Rev. 5:9; Matt. 5:14–15; Acts 13:47; 1 John 2:2)

In your praise time today, focus on what God is doing around the globe. Lay out a map of the world and praise God for what He is doing in different countries. For instance, praise Him for revivals breaking out in countries such as Poland, Ethiopia, India, Mozambique, Korea, and China. Then spend time praising God that He invites you to join Him in telling others of His grace.

Be exalted, O God, above the heavens, and
let your glory be over all the earth. (Ps. 108:5)

Listen

Listen to "He Reigns" performed by Newsboys and "Hope of the World" performed by Hillsong Live.

Pray

Lord Jesus, precious Lamb of God, I praise and exalt You for dying for all people. You are the God of all nations. You love all people groups and don't reject any who embrace Your grace. Your plan is so amazing; I can't begin to praise You enough. Your Spirit is moving in so many different areas of the world. It's incredible! How I praise You that revival is springing up in so many nations, especially as Your people learn the power that is unleashed through praising You. Lord, this is such an exciting time to be alive. I realize You have me here at this time in history to be used to bring glory to Your name. Lay specific nations on my heart so that I may pray for them and have the opportunity to be a small part of what You are doing around the world. Lord, as I continue to praise You, bring my spirit into perfect union with Yours so that I will view people as You do. Be exalted, Almighty God, and let Your glory be

experienced all over the earth. (John 3:16; Ps. 106:2; Esther 4:14; Ps. 108:5)

Journal

Rate yourself on a scale of one to ten (one being almost nothing, ten being very informed) about how informed you are as far as what God is doing around the world. Is God drawing you to pray for any particular area of world? Which area or countries? How might praising God enlarge your heart for people groups around the world?

Day 30

You need to persevere so that
when you have done the will of God,
you will receive what he has promised.
Hebrews 10:36

The Invitation

My child, I know there are days when you feel like quitting.
Faithfulness in living a life of praise is difficult. The world is
a negative place filled with people who gripe and complain.
When you prioritize thanksgiving, you stand out from the
crowd, and I am honored. In seasons of great pressure, it's easy
to believe that I am not on your side and that I am not really
changing your life. This is not the truth. Rejoice that the chal-
lenges you face are producing perseverance in you. Continue
on the path where I have called you. There will be times of
great pressure in the days ahead when you will need to know

My presence more deeply. Remember, praise unlocks the door to experiencing My presence. Faithfulness in worship will pay off as you continue. Gradually, you will find yourself being transformed into a more positive, hopeful, and confident person. As you continue to praise Me, I will bring your heart into a deeper understanding of My love.

My child, don't quit too soon. If you persist in giving Me praise, you will receive the blessings I have promised, and you will find that your endurance in other areas of life will grow. Now that you have learned to have intentional times of praise, learn to have an attitude of worship 24/7. Live your life with a continual awareness of My presence. Push back against the demands of your day to prioritize continually offering Me a sacrifice of praise. (Heb. 10:36; Rom. 5:3; James 1:12; Heb. 13:15)

Throughout your time today praise God in faith for empowering you to persevere in making praise a priority in your life. Often when we praise God there is a breakthrough in what appears to be a hopeless situation. So unless God has specifically called you to quit in some area, praise your way to perseverance.

Therefore, since we are surrounded by such a great cloud of witnesses, let us throw off everything that hinders and the sin that so easily entangles. And let us run with perseverance the race marked out for us. (Heb. 12:1)

Listen

Listen to "Running" performed by Hillsong Live and "At Your Name (Yahweh, Yahweh)" by Phil Wickham.

Pray

Lord Jesus, You are worthy to receive glory and honor and power because You are faithful to everything the Father has called you to do, even death on the cross. I thank You that when I feel like giving up _____ [name the areas of life where you are feeling like giving up], *I can draw from Your faithfulness, and You will strengthen me to persevere. I praise You that even at this moment, there is a crowd of Your faithful followers in heaven cheering me on to the finish line. Thank You*

that if I fix my eyes on You, Lord Jesus, I can run the rest of my life's race with perseverance. You are the One who called me, and You promise to pour out Your faithfulness through me. Now that I have learned to be intentional in praise, I long to have my worship life grow so that I have a heart of praise all day long. How can I say thank You for being so good to me? By Your grace, I will persevere in keeping my vows to You so that You will be exalted and glorified in my life. I worship You, Lord Jesus. (Rev. 4:11; Heb. 12:1–2; 1 Thess. 5:24; Ps. 113:2; Ps. 116:13–14)

Journal

Identify areas of your life where you feel tempted to quit or give up (your marriage, finances and getting out of debt, disciplining children, job responsibilities, praying for the salvation of a loved one, relationships, commitments you've made to the Lord, prioritizing time with God, or any other area where you have felt God's calling). How has this journey through the thirty days of praise helped you to persevere in that area? What is the most significant change you have experienced during the 30-day praise challenge?

Part Three

taking it further

praising God through His names

Now that you have completed the 30-day praise challenge, my prayer for you is that you will want to continue the practice of praise. Our ultimate goal as believers is to glorify God and enjoy His presence. Living a life of praise is one of the most important elements of fulfilling that goal.

You will notice that this final section encourages you to use Scripture in your praise. When we combine Scripture and praise, it unleashes a power in our lives that is unstoppable!

Since I began praising God through His names and through what those names mean to me, my faith has been deepened and strengthened. During my times of praise, The following list of names is in front of me, and I use

them to focus my praise. I have listed names for God the Father, God the Son, and God the Spirit. Notice that each person of the Trinity—Father, Son, and Holy Spirit—possesses the name Holy One. This understanding is especially important because we live in an age where some are questioning the concepts of the Trinity and the deity of Christ. Father, Son, and Spirit are all equally God.

God the Father

Abba—Mark 14:36

Consuming Fire—Hebrews 12:28–29

Creator—Isaiah 40:28

Deliverer—Psalm 70:5; Psalm 144:2

Everlasting God—Isaiah 40:28

Father—Isaiah 64:8

Father to the Fatherless—Psalm 68:5

Fortress—Jeremiah 16:19; Psalm 144:2

God Almighty—Genesis 17:1

God Most High—Genesis 14:18–19

God My Savior—Psalm 18:46; Habakkuk 3:17–18

God My Stronghold—Psalm 144:2

God of All Comfort—2 Corinthians 1:3

God of Glory—Psalm 29:3

God of Peace—Hebrews 13:20–21

God Who Sees Me—Genesis 16:13

Guide—Psalm 48:14

Hiding Place—Psalm 32:7

Holy One—Isaiah 43:15

Husband—Jeremiah 31:31–32

I Am—Exodus 3:14

Jehovah-jireh (the Lord Will Provide)—Genesis 22:14

Judge—Psalm 75:7

King—1 Samuel 12:12

Light—Psalm 27:1

Lord Who Heals—Exodus 15:26

Redeemer—Isaiah 54:8

Refuge—Deuteronomy 33:27

Rock—1 Samuel 2:2

Shepherd—Psalm 23:1

Shield—Psalm 18:2

Spring of Living Water—Jeremiah 2:13

Strength—Exodus 15:2

God the Son–Jesus Christ

Advocate—1 John 2:1

Alpha and Omega—Revelation 1:8; 22:13

Author of Life—Acts 3:15

Blessed Controller of All Things—1 Timothy 6:15 (PH)

Branch—Zechariah 3:8

Bread of Life—John 6:35

Bridegroom—Luke 5:34–35

Christ, the Son of the Living God—Matthew 16:16

Creator—Colossians 1:16

Cornerstone—Ephesians 2:20; 1 Peter 2:6

Counselor—Isaiah 9:6

Deliverer—Romans 11:26

Desired of All Nations—Haggai 2:7

Everlasting Father—Isaiah 9:6

Eternal Life—1 John 5:20

Faithful Witness—Revelation 1:5

Firstborn from the Dead—Revelation 1:5

God of Peace—1 Thessalonians 5:23

God, Forever Praised—Romans 9:5

Head over Everything—Ephesians 1:22

Heir of All Things—Hebrews 1:2

High Priest—Hebrews 4:14

Holy One—Luke 4:34; Acts 3:14; Revelation 3:7

Horn of Salvation—Luke 1:69

I Am—John 8:58

Image of God—2 Corinthians 4:4

Immanuel—Isaiah 7:14; Matthew 1:23

Jesus—Matthew 1:21; 1 Thessalonians 1:10

King of Israel—John 1:49

King of Kings—Revelation 19:16

Lamb of God—John 1:29, 36

Life—John 14:6

Light of the World—John 8:12

Lion of the Tribe of Judah—Revelation 5:5

Living Stone—1 Peter 2:4

Lord God Almighty—Revelation 15:3

Lord of All—Acts 10:36

Man of Sorrows—Isaiah 53:3

Mediator—1 Timothy 2:5; Hebrews 12:24

Messiah—John 1:41

Mighty God—Isaiah 9:6

Morning Star—2 Peter 1:19; Revelation 22:16

Nazarene—Matthew 2:23

One and Only—John 1:14, 18; 3:16

Passover Lamb—1 Corinthians 5:7

Physician—Luke 4:23

Priest—Hebrews 5:6

Prince of Peace—Isaiah 9:6

Redeemer—Job 19:25; Isaiah 59:20

Righteous One—1 John 2:1

Rising Sun—Luke 1:78

Savior—Luke 2:11

Son of God—Matthew 27:54

True Vine—John 15:1

Truth—John 14:6

Way—John 14:6

Word—John 1:1

God the Holy Spirit

Breath of the Almighty—Job 33:4

Counselor—John 14:16

Eternal Spirit—Hebrews 9:14

Helper—John 14:16 (NASB)

Holy One—1 John 2:20
Holy Spirit—Acts 20:28
Holy Spirit of God—Ephesians 4:29–30
Power of the Most High—Luke 1:35
Spirit of Christ—Romans 8:9
Spirit of Faith—2 Corinthians 4:13
Spirit of God—Matthew 3:16–17
Spirit of Life—Romans 8:2
Spirit of the Lord—Judges 6:34
Spirit of Sonship—Romans 8:15
Spirit of Truth—John 14:16–17

Here is an example of a prayer of praise using the names of the triune God:

Holy One, I praise You because You are the triune God: Father, Son, and Holy Spirit. I exalt You, Father, because You are my Abba, the One who tenderly loves me as a daddy would love his little child. Lord Jesus, I praise You because You are not only the Son of God but God Himself. I exalt You as my advocate before the Father. How I praise You for constantly pleading my case before Him. I praise You, Jesus, that You are the Bread of

Life, able to meet the deepest longings of my heart. I praise You for loving me completely and for being my eternal bridegroom. Holy Spirit, I praise You for being my Helper and my Counselor. Thank You for being the power of God living in me! I exalt You as the Spirit of truth who is able and willing to lead me into all truth. I exalt You, triune God, and declare that I have placed my faith and trust in You. You alone are worthy of all my praise.

praising God using the Psalms

When I want to praise God but lack words, I borrow some from Scripture. I often use five or six verses from the Psalms in my praise time.

One way to praise God is to write some psalms on index cards and take a walk, praying the verses back to God. Or, while listening to music, use the verses as your language of praise. You might pray something like this using the psalms:

Lord, I will give thanks today because of Your righteousness. I will sing praises to Your name. I will praise You with all my heart. Holy Spirit, bring my will into perfect union with Yours so that I can praise God with a whole heart. I will be glad and rejoice in You; I will sing praise to Your name, O Most High. Lord, Your

name is majestic and Your glory is above all the heavens. When I think of Your names, so many come to mind. Each one teaches me more about Your nature. Thank You for revealing Yourself to me and for allowing me to know You better through Your names. I praise You for Your unfailing love! I praise You that I can trust Your love and don't have to worry that You will ever stop loving me or pursuing me. God, You have been so good to me, I could never find enough words to describe Your goodness. (Pss. 7:17; 9:1–2; 8:1–2; 13:5–6)

How I praise You for being my Rock, Fortress, and Deliverer. I praise You that I can find refuge in You and that I don't have to be afraid. When life feels as though it is too difficult, I can take refuge in the shelter of Your wings. You promise to shield me from the Enemy. I praise You, Lord, that You are my Rock and that You live! (Pss. 18:1–3, 46, 49)

Here are some prominent passages of praise found in the Psalms to get you started:

Psalm 7:17—"I will give thanks to the
Lord because of his righteousness and

will sing praise to the name of the LORD Most High."

Psalm 8:1–2—"O LORD, our Lord, how majestic is your name in all the earth! You have set your glory above the heavens. From the lips of children and infants you have ordained praise."

Psalm 9:1–2—"I will praise you, O LORD, with all my heart; I will tell of all your wonders. I will be glad and rejoice in you; I will sing praise to your name, O Most High."

Psalm 9:11, 14—"Sing praises to the LORD, enthroned in Zion; proclaim among the nations what he has done ... that I may declare your praises."

Psalm 13:5–6—"But I trust in your unfailing love; my heart rejoices in your salvation. I will sing to the LORD for he has been good to me."

Psalm 16:7–8—"I will praise the LORD, who counsels me; even at night my heart

instructs me. I have set the LORD always before me. Because he is at my right hand, I will not be shaken."

Psalm 18:1–3—"I love you, O LORD, my strength. The LORD is my rock, my fortress and my deliverer; my God is my rock, in whom I take refuge. He is my shield and the horn of my salvation, my stronghold. I call to the LORD, who is worthy of praise, and I am saved from my enemies."

Psalm 18:46, 49—"The LORD lives! Praise be to my Rock! Exalted be God my Savior! … Therefore I will praise you among the nations, O LORD; I will sing praises to your name."

Psalm 19:1—"The heavens declare the glory of God; the skies proclaim the work of his hands."

Psalm 21:13—"Be exalted, O LORD, in your strength; we will sing and praise your might."

Psalm 22:3—"Yet you are enthroned as the Holy One; you are the praise of Israel."

Psalm 22:22–23, 25—"I will declare your name to my brothers; in the congregation I will praise you. You who fear the LORD, praise him! All you descendants of Jacob, honor him! Revere him, all you descendants of Israel! … From you comes my praise in the great assembly."

Psalm 28:6–8—"Praise be to the LORD, for he has heard my cry for mercy. The LORD is my strength and my shield; my heart trusts in him, and I am helped. My heart leaps for joy and I will give thanks to him in song. The LORD is the strength of his people, a fortress of salvation for his anointed one."

Psalm 29:1–2—"Ascribe to the LORD, O mighty ones, ascribe to the LORD glory and strength. Ascribe to the LORD the glory due his name; worship the LORD in the splendor of his holiness."

Psalm 30:4—"Sing to the LORD, you saints of his; praise his holy name."

Psalm 30:11–12—"You turned my wailing into dancing; you removed my sackcloth and clothed me with joy, that my heart may sing to you and not be silent. O LORD my God, I will give you thanks forever."

Psalm 31:21—"Praise be to the LORD for he showed his wonderful love to me."

Psalm 32:11—"Rejoice in the LORD and be glad, you righteous; sing, all you who are upright in heart!"

Psalm 33:1–3—"Sing joyfully to the LORD, you righteous; it is fitting for the upright to praise him. Praise the LORD with the harp; make music to him on the ten-stringed lyre. Sing to him a new song; play skillfully, and shout for joy."

Psalm 34:1–3—"I will extol the LORD at all times; his praise will always be on my lips. My soul will boast in the LORD; let the afflicted hear and rejoice. Glorify the LORD with me; let us exalt his name together."

Psalm 35:10, 18, 28—"My whole being will exclaim, 'Who is like you, O LORD?' … I will give you thanks in the great assembly; among throngs of people I will praise you.… My tongue will speak of your righteousness and of your praises all day long."

Psalm 40:3—"He put a new song in my mouth, a hymn of praise to our God."

Psalm 41:13—"Praise be to the LORD, the God of Israel, from everlasting to everlasting."

Psalm 42:5–6—"Put your hope in God, for I will yet praise him, my Savior and my God."

Psalm 43:4—"Then will I go to the altar of God, to God, my joy and my delight. I will praise you with the harp, O God, my God."

Psalm 44:7–8—"But you give us victory over our enemies, you put our adversaries to shame. In God we make our boast all day long, and we will praise your name forever."

Psalm 45:17—"Therefore the nations will praise you for ever and ever."

Psalm 47:2, 6—"How awesome is the LORD Most High, the great King over all the earth! … Sing praises to God, sing praises; sing praises to our King, sing praises. For God is the King of all the earth, sing to him a psalm of praise."

Psalm 48:1, 10—"Great is the LORD, and most worthy of praise, in the city of our God, his holy mountain…. Like your name, O God, your praise reaches to the ends of the earth."

Psalm 51:15—"O Lord, open my lips, and my mouth will declare your praise."

Psalm 52:9—"I will praise you forever for what you have done; in your name will I hope, for your name is good. I will praise you in the presence of your saints."

Psalm 54:6—"I will praise your name, O LORD, for it is good."

Psalm 57:9–10—"I will praise you, O LORD, among the nations; I will sing of you among the peoples. For great is your love,

reaching to the heavens; your faithfulness reaches to the skies."

Psalm 59:17—"O my Strength, I sing praise to you; you, O God, are my fortress, my loving God."

Psalm 61:8—"Then will I ever sing praise to your name."

Psalm 63:4–5—"I will praise you as long as I live, and in your name I will lift up my hands. My soul will be satisfied as with the richest of foods; with singing lips my mouth will praise you."

Psalm 64:10—"Let the righteous rejoice in the Lord and take refuge in him; let all the upright in heart praise him!"

Psalm 65:1—"Praise awaits you, O God, in Zion; to you our vows will be fulfilled."

Psalm 66:1–4—"Shout with joy to God, all the earth! Sing the glory of his name; offer him glory and praise! Say to God, 'How awesome are your deeds! So great is your power that your enemies cringe before

you. All the earth bows down to you; they sing praise to you, they sing praise to your name.'"

Psalm 66:8—"Praise our God, O peoples, let the sound of his praise be heard."

Psalm 67:3—"May the peoples praise you, O God; may all the peoples praise you."

Psalm 68:4—"Sing to God, sing praise to his name, extol him who rides on the clouds—his name is the LORD."

Psalm 68:19—"Praise be to the LORD, to God our Savior, who daily bears our burdens."

Psalm 68:26, 34–36—"Praise God in the great congregation; praise the LORD in the assembly of Israel.... Proclaim the power of God, whose majesty is over Israel, whose power is in the skies. You are awesome, O God, in your sanctuary; the God of Israel gives power and strength to his people. Praise be to God!"

Psalm 69:30—"I will praise God's name in song and glorify him with thanksgiving."

Psalm 71:6, 8—"I will ever praise you.... My mouth is filled with your praise, declaring your splendor all day long."

Psalm 71:22–23—"I will praise you with the harp for your faithfulness, O my God; I will sing praise to you with the lyre, O Holy One of Israel. My lips will shout for joy when I sing praise to you—I, whom you have redeemed."

Psalm 72:18–19—"Praise be to the LORD God, the God of Israel, who alone does marvelous deeds. Praise be to his glorious name forever; may the whole earth be filled with his glory."

Psalm 75:1—"We give thanks to you, O God, we give thanks for your Name is near; men tell of your wonderful deeds."

Psalm 75:9—"As for me, I will declare this forever; I will sing praise to the God of Jacob."

Psalm 86:12—"I will praise you, O Lord my God, with all my heart; I will glorify your name forever."

Psalm 89:1—"I will sing of the LORD's great love forever; with my mouth I will make your faithfulness known through all generations. I will declare that your love stands firm forever, that you established your faithfulness in heaven itself."

Psalm 92:1–2—"It is good to praise the LORD and make music to your name, O Most High, to proclaim your love in the morning and your faithfulness at night."

Psalm 95:1–2, 6—"Come, let us sing for joy to the LORD; let us shout aloud to the Rock of our salvation. Let us come before him with thanksgiving and extol him with music and song.… Come, let us bow down in worship, let us kneel before the LORD our Maker."

Psalm 96:1–4—"Sing to the LORD a new song; sing to the LORD, all the earth. Sing to the LORD, praise his name; proclaim his salvation day after day. Declare his glory among the nations, his marvelous deeds

among all peoples. For great is the LORD and most worthy of praise."

Psalm 97:12—"Rejoice in the LORD, you who are righteous, and praise his holy name."

Psalm 100:4—"Enter his gates with thanksgiving and his courts with praise; give thanks to him and praise his name."

Psalm 103:1–2—"Praise the LORD, O my soul; all my inmost being, praise his holy name. Praise the LORD, O my soul, and forget not all his benefits."

Psalm 103:20–22—"Praise the LORD, you his angels, you mighty ones who do his bidding, who obey his word. Praise the LORD, all his heavenly hosts, you his servants who do his will. Praise the LORD, all his works everywhere in his domain. Praise the LORD, O my soul."

Psalm 104:1—"Praise the LORD, O my soul. O LORD my God, you are very great; you are clothed with splendor and majesty."

Psalm 104:33, 35—"I will sing to the LORD all my life; I will sing praise to my God as long as I live.... Praise the LORD, O my soul. Praise the LORD."

Psalm 105:1–3—"Give thanks to the LORD, call on his name; make known among the nations what he has done. Sing to him, sing praise to him; tell of all his wonderful acts. Glory in his holy name; let the hearts of those who seek the LORD rejoice."

Psalm 106:1–2—"Praise the LORD. Give thanks to the LORD, for he is good; his love endures forever. Who can proclaim the mighty acts of the LORD or fully declare his praise?"

Psalm 107:1, 32—"Give thanks to the LORD, for he is good; his love endures forever.... Let them exalt him in the assembly of the people and praise him in the council of the elders."

Psalm 108:3–5—"I will praise you, O LORD, among the nations; I will sing of you among

the peoples. For great is your love, higher than the heavens; your faithfulness reaches to the skies. Be exalted, O God, above the heavens, and let your glory be over all the earth."

Psalm 109:30—"With my mouth I will greatly extol the LORD; in the great throng I will praise him."

Psalm 111:1–3—"Praise the LORD. I will extol the LORD with all my heart in the council of the upright and in the assembly. Great are the works of the LORD; they are pondered by all who delight in them. Glorious and majestic are his deeds."

Psalm 112:1—"Praise the LORD."

Psalm 113:1–3—"Praise the LORD. Praise, O servants of the LORD, praise the name of the LORD. Let the name of the LORD be praised, both now and forevermore. From the rising of the sun to the place where it sets the name of the LORD is to be praised."

Psalm 117—"Praise the LORD, all you nations; extol him, all you peoples. For great is his love toward us, and the faithfulness of the LORD endures forever. Praise the LORD."

Psalm 119:108—"Accept, O LORD, the willing praise of my mouth."

Psalm 119:164—"Seven times a day I praise you for your righteous laws."

Psalm 119:175—"Let me live that I may praise you."

Psalm 134:1–2—"Praise the LORD, all you servants of the LORD who minister by night in the house of the LORD. Lift up your hands in the sanctuary and praise the LORD."

Psalm 135:1, 3—"Praise the LORD. Praise the name of the LORD; praise him, you servants of the LORD.... Praise the LORD, for the LORD is good; sing praise to his name, for that is pleasant."

Psalm 135:19–21—"O house of Israel, praise the LORD; O house of Aaron,

praise the LORD; O house of Levi, praise the LORD; you who fear him, praise the LORD. Praise be to the LORD from Zion, to him who dwells in Jerusalem. Praise the LORD."

Psalm 138:1–2—"I will praise you, O LORD, with all my heart; before the 'gods' I will sing your praise. I will bow down toward your holy temple and will praise your name for your love and faithfulness."

Psalm 144:1—"Praise be to the LORD, my Rock, who trains my hands for war, my fingers for battle."

Psalm 145:1–3—"I will exalt you, my God the King; I will praise your name for ever and ever. Every day I will praise you and extol your name for ever and ever. Great is the LORD and most worthy of praise; his greatness no one can fathom."

Psalm 145:10, 21—"All you have made will praise you, O LORD; your saints will extol you.… My mouth will speak in praise

of the LORD. Let every creature praise his holy name for ever and ever."

Psalm 146:1–2, 10—"Praise the LORD. Praise the LORD, O my soul. I will praise the LORD all my life; I will sing praise to my God as long as I live.... The LORD reigns forever, your God, O Zion, for all generations. Praise the LORD."

Psalm 147:1—"Praise the LORD. How good it is to sing praises to our God, how pleasant and fitting to praise him!"

Psalm 148:1–2, 13—"Praise the LORD. Praise the LORD from the heavens, praise him in the heights above. Praise him, all his angels, praise him all his heavenly hosts.... Let them praise the name of the LORD, for his name alone is exalted; his splendor is above the earth and the heavens."

Psalm 149:1, 3, 6—"Praise the LORD. Sing to the LORD a new song, his praise in the assembly of the saints.... Let them praise

his name with dancing.... May the praise of God be in their mouths."

Psalm 150—"Praise the LORD. Praise God in his sanctuary; praise him in his mighty heavens. Praise him for his acts of power; praise him for his surpassing greatness. Praise him with the sounding of the trumpet, praise him with the harp and lyre, praise him with tambourine and dancing, praise him with the strings and flute, praise him with the clash of cymbals, praise him with resounding cymbals. Let everything that has breath praise the LORD. Praise the LORD."

praising God from the book of Revelation

Someday we will all praise God for all eternity. It's difficult to wrap our minds around that thought. I like to think of my time of praise here on earth as my dress rehearsal. It helps me remember that in heaven it is completely natural to praise God. To remind myself of this, I use some of the prayers of praise found in Revelation in my praise time. Here are some that I have found particularly helpful:

> Revelation 4:8, 11—"Holy, holy, holy, is that Lord God Almighty, who was, and is, and is to come.... You are worthy, our Lord and God, to receive glory and honor and power, for you created all things, and

by your will they were created and have their being."

Revelation 5:9–10, 12–13—"You are worthy to take the scroll and to open its seals, because you were slain, and with your blood you purchased men for God from every tribe and language and people and nation. You have made them to be a kingdom and priests to serve our God, and they will reign on the earth.... Worthy is the Lamb, who was slain, to receive power and wealth and wisdom and strength and honor and glory and praise!... To him who sits on the throne and to the Lamb be praise and honor and glory and power, for ever and ever!"

Revelation 7:10, 12—"Salvation belongs to our God, who sits on the throne, and to the Lamb.... Praise and glory and wisdom and thanks and honor and power and strength be to our God for ever and ever. Amen!"

Revelation 11:16–17—"We give thanks to you, Lord God Almighty, who is and who was, because you have taken your great power and have begun to reign."

Revelation 15:3–4—"Great and marvelous are your deeds, Lord God Almighty. Just and true are your ways, King of the ages. Who will not fear you, O Lord, and bring glory to your name? For you alone are holy. All nations will come and worship before you, for your righteous acts have been revealed."

praising God to defeat the Enemy

When we become serious about praising God, Satan gets ticked. Often he will attack when we least expect it. He may attack our minds, our bodies, or our spirits. It is important that we are aware of his antics but also that we have a plan to deal with him. God's Word instructs us to "Be self-controlled and alert. Your enemy the devil prowls around like a roaring lion looking for someone to devour. Resist him, standing firm in the faith" (1 Peter 5:8–9).

Praise combined with the power of Scripture is the most effective method I know for bolstering my faith and defeating Satan. When we praise God, Satan flees. We see this principle illustrated in 2 Chronicles 20. Enemies surrounded King Jehoshaphat and the army of Judah on every side. The

situation looked hopeless, but Jehoshaphat came up with a bizarre battle plan. He instructed the choir to march out in front of the army and to sing praises to the Lord for the splendor of His holiness. As the choir followed the king's instructions, singing, "Give thanks to the LORD, for His love endures forever" (2 Chronicles 20:21), the Lord sent ambushes against the enemies and they were annihilated. The only weapons lifted by the Judeans were the weapons of praise and Scripture.

There are times in my life when problems seem to surround me on every side, and I feel overwhelmed, discouraged, fearful, or anxious. When those feelings come, I know that Satan is close, so I have learned it's best to have a plan. Here is my plan: Purposefully praise God, and use Scripture in my praise. When I do that, Satan flees.

Let me show you how this works, and then give you some passages of Scripture to use for specific attacks from the enemy. In the space below, you may want to add scriptures that have been particularly meaningful to you.

_____

_____

_____

_____

_____

_____

_____

_____

_____

_____

_____

When I believe Satan might be attacking me, I immediately begin praying a prayer similar to this:

Lord Jesus, I exalt You as the King of Kings and Lord of Lords. I praise You that You have overcome the evil one and that by Your death and resurrection, Satan has been hurled down. Thank You for reigning in my life and that my days are in Your hands. I trust You because You promise to deliver me from evil. Thank You that I don't have to fear the evil one because You have already defeated him. Because of Your blood I stand as a victor over every evil plan of his to attack me.

I praise You that all power, authority, and honor belong to You and that someday every knee will bow. All the nations will come and worship You alone. (Rev. 19:16; Rev. 12:10; Ps. 31:15; Rev. 15:4)

Some of my favorite passages of Scripture to use to defeat the Enemy are listed below.

when Satan is attacking me with fear:

Psalm 27:1—"The LORD is my light and my salvation—whom shall I fear?"

Psalm 46:1–3—"God is our refuge and strength, an everpresent help in trouble. Therefore we will not fear, though the earth give way and the mountains fall into the heart of the sea, though its waters roar and foam and the mountains quake with their surging."

Psalm 91:1–2, 4–5—"He who dwells in the shelter of the Most High will rest under the shadow of the Almighty. I will say of the

LORD, 'He is my refuge and my fortress, my God, in whom I trust.' ... He will cover you with his feathers, and under his wings you will find refuge; his faithfulness will be your shield and rampart. You will not fear the terror of night, nor the arrow that flies by day."

Philippians 2:9–11—"Therefore God exalted him to the highest place and gave to him the name that is above every name, that at the name of Jesus every knee should bow, in heaven and on earth and under the earth, and every tongue confess that Jesus Christ is Lord, to the glory of God the Father."

when Satan is attacking me with self-doubt:

John 15:5—"I am the vine; you are the branches. If a man remains in me and I in him, he will bear much fruit."

Philippians 4:13—"I can do everything through him who gives me strength."

Hebrews 10:35–36—"So do not throw away your confidence; it will be richly rewarded. You need to persevere so that when you have done the will of God, you will receive what he has promised."

when Satan is attacking me with feelings of being overwhelmed:

Psalm 45:4—"In your majesty ride forth victoriously in behalf of truth, humility and righteousness; let your right hand display awesome deeds."

1 John 2:14, 20—"The word of God lives in you, and you have overcome the evil one.... But you have an anointing from the Holy One, and all of you know the truth."

Revelation 12:11—"They overcame him by the blood of the Lamb and by the word of their testimony."

when Satan is attacking me with feelings of guilt or shame:

John 15:3—"You are already clean because of the word I have spoken to you."

Colossians 1:22—"But now he has reconciled you by Christ's physical body through death to present you holy in his sight, without blemish and free from accusation."

Revelation 5:12–13—"Worthy is the Lamb, who was slain, to receive power and wealth and strength and honor and glory and praise!… To him who sits on the throne and to the Lamb be praise and honor and glory and power, forever and ever!"

when Satan is attacking me with disparaging thoughts about my body:

Psalm 139:13–14—"For you created my inmost being; you knit me together in my mother's womb. I praise you because

I am fearfully and wonderfully made; your works are wonderful, I know that full well."

when Satan is attacking me with thoughts of despair:

John 11:25—"I am the resurrection and the life."

1 Peter 1:3–5—"Praise be to the God and Father of our Lord Jesus Christ! In his great mercy he has given us new birth into a living hope through the resurrection of Jesus Christ from the dead, and into an inheritance that can never perish, spoil or fade—kept in heaven for you, who through faith are shielded by God's power."

praising God through a
declaration of faith

There are times, especially when fighting doubt, when it can be extremely helpful to praise God by declaring our faith out loud. One of the most basic declarations of faith is called the Apostles' Creed. If you grew up worshipping in a liturgical church or are presently attending one, you will be familiar with the words. Many congregations recite this out loud as a part of their worship celebration. I believe the Apostles' Creed can even play a role in our private worship. You can use it as a model to write your own declaration of faith or you might want to use the creed itself as your declaration. Read the declaration out loud several times slowly, then listen to "Manifesto" performed by The City Harmonic. As you listen, allow

the words of the creed to be the words of your heart as you declare your faith.

The Apostles' Creed

I believe in God, the Father Almighty,
maker of heaven and earth:

And in Jesus Christ, His only Son, our Lord,
who was conceived by the Holy Spirit,
born of the virgin Mary,
suffered under Pontius Pilate,
was crucified, died, and was buried.
He descended into hell.
On the third day He rose again from the
dead.
He ascended into heaven
and sits at the right hand of God the
Father Almighty;
from thence He will come to judge the
quick and the dead.

I believe in the Holy Spirit,
    the holy Christian church,
    the communion of saints,
    the forgiveness of sins,
    the resurrection of the body,
    and the life everlasting.
    Amen.

praising God when you are grieving or feeling depressed

Each of us will experience loss or pain at some point in our lives. During those times, it is normal to experience sadness and even depression. Praising God builds a shield around our hearts and minds so that we don't sink into despair.

Several years ago I experienced many losses and felt overwhelmed and discouraged. During those months I made a commitment to continue my habit of praising God every morning. Some mornings while I listened to worship music, I knelt and cried. As I offered God my tears and my trust, some of my sadness was released and my faith was rekindled. Like Job, I was able to say, "The LORD gave and the LORD has taken away; may the name of the LORD be praised" (Job 1:21). As

I knelt in worship each morning, God's presence came close and I felt comforted in my sorrow.

Here are some tips for praising God during times of grieving, sadness, or discouragement:

Look back. Praising God for how He's been faithful in the past can give you hope that He will continue to be faithful in the present and in the future.

Let your tears flow. Praising God doesn't always come from a happy heart. It's okay and even good to allow yourself to cry during times of grief. Sometimes weeping is our worship.

Develop a set of "emergency verses." During times of grief, it is comforting to praise God using Scripture that is familiar and special to you personally. Some of my favorites are Psalm 34, Psalm 46, Psalm 91, and John 15.

Take a worship walk. Walking releases endorphins, and worship strengthens your faith. Combined, you'll find your spirits lifted.

Keep a Thankful List. I learned this during a particularly rough season in my life. Each night before I went to bed, I recorded three to five things that had happened that day for which I felt thankful. After praising God for each one, I was able to fall asleep feeling encouraged.

Letter from the Author

Dear Friend,

I hope you have enjoyed the 30-day praise challenge and that you'll continue in your journey of praise. Praise never grows old or boring. I know, because I've now been praising God intentionally for over twelve years. My praise times have deepened and developed into the most precious times I experience with God. Praise renews and sustains me each day.

My prayer for you has been that you have experienced a spiritual revival in your soul and that you will continue to praise God every day. It's possible that you've experienced not only changes in your attitude, but also freedom from addictive behaviors or destructive patterns of thought. There might even have been a couple of miracles along the way. If you feel

comfortable sharing your experiences, I'd love to hear from you! When we share our stories of life transformation, we encourage one another to continue praising God. You can contact me at www.beckyharling.com to learn more about my ministry and what God is doing in my life.

list of praise songs
to download

Please note, the songs are listed in the order in which they appear in the book. This way you can download all the songs at once and develop a master playlist for your praise times.

Day	Song Title	Performed By
1	"God I Look to You"	Bethel Live, ft. Jenn Johnson
1	"Sovereign Hands"	Mia Feldes/ Hillsong United
2	"Hosanna (Praise Is Rising)"	Paul Baloche
2	"Please Be My Strength"	Gungor
2	"Stronger"	Mandisa
3	"Beautiful Things"	Gungor
3	"For Your Splendor"	Christy Nockels
4	"Forever Reign"	Hillsong Live
4	"I Lift My Hands (Let Faith Arise)"	Chris Tomlin
5	"Your Love Never Fails"	Chris McClarney
5	"10,000 Reasons (Bless the Lord)"	Matt Redman
6	"The First and the Last"	Hillsong United
6	"Waiting Here for You"	Christy Nockels
7	"Creation's King"	Paul Baloche
7	"The Earth Is Yours"	Gungor

Day	Song Title	Performed By
8	"How He Loves"	David Crowder Band
8	"My Soul Sings"	Delirious?
9	"Desert Song"	Hillsong United
9	"Song of Hope (Heaven Come Down)"	Robbie Seay Band
9	"You Never Let Go"	Matt Redman
9	"Alive"	Natalie Grant
10	"Whom Shall I Fear? (God of Angel Armies)"	Chris Tomlin
10	"I Will Lift My Eyes"	Bebo Norman
10	"Your Great Name"	Natalie Grant
11	"Rain Down"	Jesus Culture, ft. Melissa Howe
11	"Where the Spirit of the Lord Is"	Chris Tomlin
12	"Mighty to Save"	Hillsong United
12	"Hosanna"	Hillsong United
12	"Our God"	Chris Tomlin
13	"Like an Avalanche"	Hillsong United
13	"Jesus Paid It All"	Kristian Stanfill
13	"Rescue"	Desperation Band
13	"My Deliverer"	Mandisa
14	"We Are Hungry / I Will Not Be Silent"	Jesus Culture
14	"My Delight Is in You"	Christy Nockels
15	"All the Poor and Powerless"	All Sons & Daughters
16	"Friend of God"	Israel & New Breed
16	"Jesus, Friend of Sinners"	Casting Crowns
17	"Came to My Rescue"	Hillsong United

Day	Song Title	Performed By
17	"Praise You in This Storm"	Casting Crowns
18	"Losing"	Tenth Avenue North
18	"Oh Great Merciful God"	Ben and Noelle
19	"Broken Hallelujah"	Mandisa
19	"Hold Me Together"	Ben and Noelle
20	"Meet With Me"	Ten Shekel Shirt
20	"I Love Your Presence"	Bethel Live, ft. Jenn Johnson
20	"The More I Seek You"	Kari Jobe
21	"Overcome"	Jeremy Camp
21	"God of This City"	Chris Tomlin
22	"Blessed Be Your Name"	Matt Redman
23	"Arms Open Wide"	Hillsong United
23	"At the Cross"	Hillsong Live
24	"I Surrender"	Hillsong Live
24	"Healing"	Ben and Noelle
24	"Healer"	Kari Jobe
25	"Amazing Grace (My Chains Are Gone)"	Chris Tomlin
25	"We Will Run"	Gungor
26	"Hear Us from Heaven"	Jared Anderson
27	"Trust"	Sixpence None the Richer
27	"You Hold My World"	Israel Houghton
28	"In Christ Alone"	Travis Cottrell
28	"Exalted Alone"	Shannon Wexelberg
29	"He Reigns"	Newsboys
29	"Hope of the World"	Hillsong Live

Day	Song Title	Performed By
30	"Running"	Hillsong Live
30	"At Your Name (Yahweh, Yahweh)"	Phil Wickham
Part Three:	"Manifesto"	The City Harmonic

acknowledgments

Special thanks to …

My husband, Steve. Thank you for being not only my husband but also my encourager and friend. Thank you for giving me your heart for the world. You have a larger global heart than anyone I know. You bring so much adventure and fun to our marriage. I love you, babe.

My kids:

Bethany, I couldn't have done this book without you. Thanks for running the field test for *The 30-Day Praise Challenge* and for helping me with editing, content, and song choices. You brought so much wisdom to this book. I love your compassionate and tender heart and the way you praise God even in the midst of difficult circumstances. I love you and am so thankful for your partnership in ministry.

Josiah, I love the godly man you are. God is using your leadership skills in remarkable ways, not only in the States but also in many other countries. I'm so proud of you. Thanks for believing in this project. I love you, Josiah.

Stefanie, I love your passion for God, your heart for justice, and your sense of humor. Thanks for all your encouragement and insight as I wrote this book and for participating in the field test. You bring so much joy to my life. I love you, Stef.

Kerith, I love your heart for worship and praise. God is using your shepherding skills and leadership skills in such a powerful way. It's so much fun to watch you become the woman God designed you to be. Never stop singing and leading others into His presence. Thanks for your help with the song choices for this book and for being a part of the field test. I love you, Keri Joy.

My sons-in-law and daughter-in-law:

Chris, I love your gentle servant's heart. Even though you are such a strong leader, you are always willing to serve. You model the heart of Jesus so well! Thanks for being such a great husband to Bethany and a wonderful father to Tyler. I love you, Chris.

Dave, I love your heart of mercy and your love for the Word of God. You consistently have a heart for the poor and wounded. Thank you for being a great husband to Stef and a wonderful father to Charlie and Selah. I love you, Dave.

Zach, I love the joy you bring to our family. Your energy, positive spirit, and heart for God bring such life to our family. I love how intentional you are in your walk with God. Thanks for being such a great husband to Keri. I love you, Zach.

Shaina, I love your sweet and gentle heart. I see so much of the fruit of the Spirit in your life. Thank you for being part of the field test, for giving your valuable insight, and for being an amazing wife to JJ and a wonderful mom to Joshua. I love you, Shaini.

My grandchildren, Charlie, Tyler, Joshua, and Selah. You make this Mimi's heart sing! My prayer for each of you is that you continue to grow up to love and praise Jesus Christ. I love you all so much—you can't even imagine.

My amazing editor Liz Heaney. Wow! What would I do without you? It is such a privilege to work with you. I have learned so much from you and count myself as blessed because you are in my life. Thank you.

Linda Dillow. How can I ever thank you enough for initially giving me the praise challenge? Little did you know in that moment how much my life would change! I love you.

All the women who participated in the field test. There are too many of you to name, but God used each of you to shape this project and I will be forever grateful.

Justin Bullis, my worship pastor. Thanks so much for all your help with the music for this book. Justin, God is using you mightily as you lead people into His presence.

Kathy Worland. Wow, Kathy, God brought you into our lives at exactly the right moment. Thanks for helping Steve and me stay organized!

Linda Evans Shepherd and all my AWSA sisters. You have prayed me through this project and cheered me on along the way. I love each of you.

Jarred Butler. Thanks so much, Jarred, for all your help with my website. You are awesome!

Terry Behimer. Thank you for believing in this project and for encouraging me to make it a reality.

John Blase and all the others at David C Cook. It is a privilege to be published by you. Thank you for having a heart for this book.

acknowledgments

All the musicians and worship leaders who are mentioned in this book. As I get down on my knees early in the morning, each of you has led me into the presence of God through your music. Thank you!

*Study questions for small-group use are available
for download at www.beckyharling.com.*

Songs of Restoration

with Kari Jobe, Don Moen and more

Healer features renowned worship artists offering 15 songs of healing, hope, and restoration. From **Kari Jobe's** *Healer* to **Don Moen's** *Rescue* to **Laura Story's** *Mighty To Save*, these powerful songs create the perfect setting to help listeners know the heart of God and experience His faithfulness in times of need.

Available now at **IntegrityMusicDirect.com**

"The positive power of praise has seldom been as joyfully explored as in Becky Harling's *The 30-Day Praise Challenge*. Take up Harling's challenge and set out on a journey into the joy of praise."

Dr. Mark Rutland, former
president of Oral Roberts University
and author of *ReLaunch*

"If you crave a deeper encounter with God, *The 30-Day Praise Challenge* is the guide you need to the life-changing power of praise."

Poppy Smith, international speaker, spiritual life
coach, and author of the Golden Scroll Award
Winner *Why Can't He Be More Like Me?*

"This powerful challenge has the ability to renew, restore, and revive every weary place."

Dr. Saundra Dalton-Smith,
author of *Set Free to Live Free*

"I was challenged, I was moved, and I was nudged to begin praising God. *The 30-Day Praise Challenge* shines with

What people are saying about …

The 30-Day Praise Challenge

"If you long to rise out of the ashes of dashed hopes or discouraging circumstances with a spirit of renewed hope, fresh faith, and enduring joy, read *The 30-Day Praise Challenge*. This could be the most important book you read this year!"

Carol Kent, speaker and author of *When I Lay My Isaac Down* and *Between a Rock and a Grace Place*

"If you hunger for more of God, Becky's book will show you how to use praise, prayer, Scripture, and worship to 'dwell in the shelter of the Most High.' It just might change your life!"

Dr. Juli Slattery, psychologist, author, and cofounder of Authentic Intimacy

"What my heart aches for everyone to know is what Becky reveals beautifully in this book: praising God changes everything. Take this journey into the throne room of God."

Lisa Williams, former host of the K-LOVE Morning Show